epistemic obligations

epistemic obligations

Truth, Individualism, and the Limits of Belief

Bruce R. Reichenbach

BAYLOR UNIVERSITY PRESS

Cover Design by Natalya Balnova

Library of Congress Cataloging-in-Publication Data

Reichenbach, Bruce R.
Epistemic obligations : truth, individualism, and the limits of belief / Bruce R. Reichenbach.
284 p. cm.
Includes bibliographical references (p. 263) and index.
ISBN 978-1-60258-623-9 (hardcover : alk. paper)
1. Responsibility. 2. Belief and doubt. 3. Epistemics. I. Title.
BJ1451.R45 2012
121'.6--dc23

2012007965

Printed in the United States of America on acid-free paper with a minimum of 30% post-comsumer waste recycled content.

To my teachers, mentors, and colleagues

Stuart Hackett, Arthur Holmes, Henry Veatch,
Alvin Plantinga, William Alston, Larry Crockett,
and Melville Stewart

whose influence as Christian philosophers helped shape
the ways I think and sharpened my philosophical ideas.

Contents

Preface

The other day I attended the reading of a paper with colleagues from another department. The prediscussion turned to the question framed by my writing project: do we have a right to believe whatever we want? Without blinking an eye, one colleague replied that of course we have the right to believe whatever we wanted—so long as we do not hurt anyone else. The response was not unlike that given by many of my students when I posed the same question in class, and it accorded with the prevalent do-no-harm utilitarian ethic that predominates in popular culture.

When I followed up her response with the question whether we had any obligations to believe the truth, she immediately responded that there was no truth. Her response piqued my curiosity. How, I wondered, did she grade her multiple-choice tests? If a student put down an answer and she marked it wrong, could not the student object to her evaluation on the grounds that there is no truth? The student, she replied, was under obligation to put down the correct answer in the context of the test. Whatever my colleague determined was correct was the answer to be placed on the test, regardless of the fact that there was no true answer (since there is no truth). Perhaps, I mused to myself, the pedagogical paradigm that lay behind such an approach to tests invoked the ancient Athenian principle that might makes right; the answer the teacher determines to be correct is correct because the teacher possesses the power of assigning the grade.

But still, I asked her, if the student had the right to believe whatever the student wanted so long as it did not harm anyone, giving the answer the student believed to be correct hardly could be conceived as harming anyone (although it might offend the teacher since it might fail to correspond to her own beliefs about how the question should be answered). The right to believe is a warrant, and her admission that one had the right to believe whatever one wanted provided the warrant to believe that the answer given was not only correct but acceptable (and acceptable even if incorrect). I could see no grounds on which she could deduct points from the student, regardless of the answer given, so long as the student either believed the answer itself or believed it to be correct. Even the context could not justify her action, since her view of truth would not even allow it to be true that the student's answers did or did not correspond with her own.

It would be a mistake to think that I convinced my colleague (though from the outset I never entertained such an illusion); from her perspective her position on the right to believe was correct. But it highlighted the relevance and seriousness of the question that I had pondered for several years. It is the question that William Clifford raised in a short but poignant piece over a century ago, a question about what have come to be called epistemic obligations: do we have the right to believe whatever we want, or rather, do we have certain obligations with regard to what we believe—either that the proposition itself be true or that we be able to justify our belief?

Although I have found few educators who have thought much about epistemic obligations, the very task and structure of education presupposes that we take a position on the issue of whether we have such obligations. Educators not only act as if there are truths; they maintain the firm belief that students, like educators, also ought to pursue truths, and that being in academic classes, taking copious notes on what is said, reporting on and understanding the texts, and researching are important means to enabling students to fulfill these obligations. Otherwise, examinations, assessment of papers and assorted assignments, laboratory reports, and research projects would have little significance beyond expressing the authors' opinions; they could not be graded or assessed, even for such elementary features as grammar and spelling. Discussion, too, would become an exercise in intellectual gymnastics. Even if we don't pursue true beliefs directly, we do so indirectly by encouraging the formation of intellectual virtues that aim at developing the proper epistemic habits of critical thinking, careful examination of evidence, open-mindedness, and analysis of reasoning, thereby fostering the proper motivation to understand and know—to attain wisdom.

Fortunately, some recent philosophers have thought seriously and deeply about epistemic obligations. I stand on their shoulders in writing this book. That is not to say that my positions will agree with theirs. As would be expected among any group of philosophers, no uniformity of views exists on the subject, though it is fair to say that one can find a general consensus among many. I will argue for views that run contrary to this consensus—views about a deontological basis for epistemic obligations, about the ground for these obligations, about the extent of our control over our beliefs, and about the nature of believing itself. The views I propound ultimately accord with my contention that education encourages, if not demands that, students and teachers not only seek truth and the justifications that might be given for beliefs held and advanced, but in doing so develop the appropriate epistemic virtues. And not only education, but every discipline and every endeavor, depends—yes, even thrives—on presupposing that we have epistemic obligations. I leave it to the reader to judge how successful I am in advancing and defending this important cause.

1

The Challenge of Epistemic Obligations

"I have a right to believe whatever I want." An academic year never goes by without at least one of my students or peers uttering this phrase or something equivalent to it, such as "I am entitled to my beliefs." In part, the phrase reflects and is an extension of our individualist culture, where persons view themselves as having a right to do their "own thing," to be their "own person," or to form their own beliefs without anyone telling them what to believe. The phrase usually is uttered in a context where speakers assume that it is wrong for people to judge them or others with respect to what they are thinking, writing, or saying. This book concerns this seemingly innocuous phrase. Ultimately I want to question whether it is really true that we have such a right. But answering the question is more difficult than might first appear. The phrase raises philosophical issues that are substantive, complex, and greatly disputed in the literature. The issues drive to the core of human epistemology and merit serious and extended consideration. The task of this book is to conduct this careful exploration.

Before I proceed to undertake the requisite serious philosophical analyses, I first will make more precise what I am interested in with respect to this common phrase. I will then introduce four cases (three actual and one partly hypothetical) about which one might invoke this phrase. These case studies reveal that the issue is neither merely abstract nor artificially constructed but indeed is live and relevant for contemporary society and thought.

THE RIGHT TO BELIEVE WHAT WE WANT

To have a right is to have the basis for making a claim. Having a right to go to the orchestra concert tonight means that the person has a basis for making a claim for entry to tonight's performance venue. In such a case the right is established by means of the possession of some token of entry the person justly has acquired in some way (e.g., by purchase). Persons also may have rights by virtue of other things: by being born in a particular country (the right of citizenship), by accomplishing some feat (the right to the trophy), by signing a contract (the right to be paid for services rendered), by being in need (the right to adequate health care), or even by doing nothing at all (the right to privacy). That a right is the basis for making a claim is what makes rights such a powerful notion. If one *actually* has the right to *x*, the answer to the question whether the person is justified in claiming *x* is already provided. One might question whether someone actually or legitimately has a particular right (is the concert ticket a forgery; is the person really a natural-born citizen?) or whether there really is a right of a certain sort (the right of privacy and to adequate health care are the subjects of much strident debate); but if the person's right to *x* is granted, that person's claim regarding *x* cannot be legitimately denied. There might be some extenuating circumstances, such as, for example, a conflict between rights, but the right is not denied, only mitigated or accommodated in some way.

"Rights" appear in diverse contexts. One might consider rights from a legal perspective: the employee has the right to park here because she purchased the required parking permit. Legal rights invoke laws or contracts between persons.

Our concern with whether one has a right to believe whatever one wants is not understood as a legal right, for at least in our current Western context the legal system cannot legislate belief. Legal rights apply not to our beliefs but to our actions, so that despite what we believe, we may or may not have a right to act in a certain way, depending on the laws enacted or the contracts made.[1] Neither is the issue we are interested in about free speech, namely, the legal right to say whatever we want. It may be the case that when people say that they have a right to believe whatever they want, they really are thinking about free speech: the right to say whatever they want. But if this is what they really mean, it would clearly be a mistake. With regard to free speech we don't have the right to say whatever we want. Libel, perjury, and falsely crying "Fire!" in a crowded theater are examples of not legally protected speech. We may have a right to responsible free speech, but not to untrammeled free speech per se. And as soon as one qualifies "free speech" with "responsible," questions about what constitutes responsible speech arise. Where lies the border between personal criticism and personal attack, as in advertisements broadcast during political campaigns, and libel? What constitutes racist hate speech for which one can be prosecuted and speech that might be constitutionally protected? These are socially and personally important but not easy questions to answer.

But this book is not about freedom of speech. It does not consider the issue whether we have the right to say or write what we want and what circumstances condition that right. Rather, this book is concerned with the epistemic right to *believe* whatever we want. I will argue that we do not have unlimited epistemic rights, that we do not have a right to believe whatever we want. Our right to believe is circumscribed by our epistemic obligations. By our having *epistemic obligations* I mean that we have an obligation to minimize, if not eliminate, our false beliefs and maximize contextually significant true beliefs. That is, we have an obligation to hold contextually significant true beliefs and eschew false beliefs. How epistemic obligations are parsed more precisely and how they connect with an obligation to hold justified beliefs will be the topic of chapters 2 and 4.

BELIEFS FOLLOWED BY ACTIONS

In 2008 eleven-year-old Kara Neumann died from undiagnosed and untreated juvenile diabetes. For her healing her parents relied on prayer rather than on taking her to a health care professional for treatment. By the time her aunt, living in another state, intervened by telephoning the authorities and Kara was taken to the hospital, it was too late. Kara was pronounced dead on her arrival.[2]

Her parents, Leilani and Dale, follow a religious group, Unleavened Bread Ministries, that maintains that stories in the Bible about Jesus healing individuals provide guidance for contemporary Christian faith and practice. The group's website contains the writings of its leader, David Eells, who affirms that

> we are not commanded in scripture to send people to the doctor but to meet their needs through prayer and faith. As anyone here in the ministry will tell you, we are not against doctors for those who have their faith there and never condemn or restrict them in any way. But we know that the best one to trust in for healing is Jesus Christ.[3]

Members of this group believe that healing comes by faith and prayer.

At her husband's trial, Leilani Neumann reiterated this view: "We are not against the [doctors]. The [doctors'] practice we consider not biblical." In response to the question whether she believed that sickness is caused by sin, she "explained that God doesn't want people to harbor disobedience and unforgiveness inside themselves and that there is a spiritual root cause to sickness."[4] Dale compared his experience with that of Job, who lost his ten children to the activity of the Adversary. "If I in a moment of crises [*sic*] and a moment of time I went to anyone else but the Lord, it would not have been favorable to God. It would have been idolatry and sin because it is disobedience." He said that the family had prayed that evening for Kara's healing. "It could have been flu, it could have been fever, but whatever it was, she was very sleepy. It needed attention so we prayed for our faith."[5]

Since parents have primary responsibility for the health and well-being of their children, it is prima facie clear that the Neumanns had significant, if not complete, responsibility for the death of their daughter. From the reports that indicate that they were caring parents we can assume that they had the best intentions for their daughter. At Dale's trial Leilani said, "I'm a mother and I love my children. If I sensed I needed to watch her closer, I would have."[6] Yet despite these good intentions, their failure to act had fatal consequences that provided the grounds for the State of Wisconsin legally to indict the Neumanns on the charge of second-degree reckless homicide. Our common moral sense tells us that since they failed in their moral obligations toward Kara, they are morally accountable for the suffering and death that resulted from their actions and inactions. To what degree they are legally blameworthy is another matter; subsequent legal proceedings found both parents guilty of second-degree reckless homicide.

Granted that the Neumanns are morally and legally accountable for what they did or did not do, and that their religious beliefs about the means to healing apparently led to their actions of praying for Kara's healing and their inaction of not taking her to a health care provider when she was seriously ill, we want to press further and ask whether they also should be held accountable for their *beliefs* about the relation of God to sickness and healing by prayer, and specifically how these beliefs connect to their daughter's sickness and death. Their court statements indicate that they believe that faith in God alone brings healing. Thus, we might ask, do Kara's parents have epistemic obligations regarding the beliefs they hold, in this case, about God, sickness, and healing? If so, what specifically is the content of those obligations in this case, and further, what is the basis for these obligations? If not, if they have the right to believe whatever they want, does this affect our assessment of their responsibility for their actions, especially because we may reasonably believe that their actions followed consistently from their beliefs?

Since their belief about the connection between prayer and divine healing was confirmed for them by their past experiences, we can conclude that they did not believe in faith healing irrationally or on a whim. On the witness stand Dale told the jurors that "10 years of back pain disappeared after he listened to the Holy Spirit in 2005 or early 2006. The Holy Spirit told him to destroy some books and figurines he had, and Dale said once he did that, the pain went away. That was a spiritual cause of a physical ailment. . . . Dale also told jurors that he has seen 'cancers fall off in meetings,' women who couldn't have children, have children after being healed by God, and women healed of breast cancer. 'I've seen physical healings in meetings I have attended and been part of.' "[7] Since the parents observed that prayer apparently worked to bring about healing in the past, both to themselves and to others, their experience provided experiential justification for them for their belief that through prayer God would heal in Kara's case as well. It is possible to say that from their perspective they had a justified belief, evidenced by previous experience, about what was sufficient to bring about Kara's healing, although in this case their belief that God would heal proved not to be true.[8]

In filing their plea of not guilty, the Neumanns insisted, through their attorney, that they had the constitutional right to practice their religion. But what exactly this right consists of is unclear. Does the right encompass both belief and practice, belief but not necessarily practice, or neither? According to Marathon County Circuit Judge Vincent Howard, our rights extend to belief but not necessarily to practice. "The free exercise clause of the First Amendment protects religious belief, but not necessarily conduct." Although individuals possess the (legal) right to believe what they want, they do not necessarily have the (legal) right to act on those beliefs. And though the judge clearly was speaking from a legal point of view, one might suggest that much the same thing might be said from a moral point of view.

To have the right to believe what one wants but not to be able to act on those beliefs renders beliefs to which we may have a right inoperative in those cases where action is constricted. But what advantage or purpose is there to belief holders to have a right to believe something—or anything they want—if they have no right, legal or moral, to act on the belief, since beliefs are what inform our actions? We act out of or from our beliefs. The right to free belief may allow us to cultivate our own private life, but at the cost of divorcing it from our public existence. Perhaps restraints that are placed on our actions should be echoed in some manner on our beliefs, so that just as we lack the right to do what we want when, for example, it causes harm to others, we lack the right to believe anything we want if those beliefs are injurious to others. That is, perhaps we, like the Neumanns, not only have moral obligations but also have epistemic obligations. Epistemic obligations connect with truth; the beliefs we have should be true. But what does this mean? Are we to believe everything that is true? Or only certain truths? Or merely avoid false beliefs? Further, do our beliefs have to be justified? Be both true and justified? Or must our beliefs possess some other set of properties or characteristics to satisfy the epistemic obligation? Clearly, the question of epistemic obligations is important and needs to be addressed if we are to provide an answer to the question of the kind of epistemic responsibility and resulting accountability that, if not we, the State of Wisconsin expected in this case.

The Neumann case is difficult because it is quite possible that beliefs held by the Neumanns—that God heals, and that in this particular case God chose not to heal Kara—are true. To show this belief is true or false is difficult, if not impossible. When one is working with an agent, natural laws do not determine what actions the agent might take. Science cannot tell us whether God heals or has healed. Based on their past personal experiences of alleged divine healing, where they witnessed their own or others' healings by prayer, they may argue that they possess a justified belief that genuine healing comes from God. Thus, it is possible that they did, in one form or another, prima facie meet their epistemic obligations regarding justification, though the belief with respect to Kara led to actions that eventuated in her death. Of course, one might hold that the Neumanns lacked adequate evidence for this belief about God in general and Kara in particular and that the decline in Kara's health signaled that other actions should be taken. One might hold this on the grounds that God does not exist, that God does not heal, or that even if God exists and heals, God would want us to use the best medical practices. These beliefs, however, were not part of the paradigm used by the Neumanns in evaluating actions to be taken. Whether they should have been part of the paradigm is an aspect of the debate regarding what one is justified in believing given the evidence available.

What is problematic is that the application of their belief led to their daughter's death. Thus, one might also suggest that Kara's death bears out that the Neumanns' belief about God and healing was unjustified. But one must be careful not to introduce future results into the determination of justification of a belief at a given time. That is, one cannot determine whether or not their belief was justified based on the outcome alone, for the belief preceded Kara's death, and that is the belief one is assessing. The fact that Kara died does not show that their placing faith in God's healing powers at that time was irrational or unjustified. The rationality of their belief has to be established on the basis of the evidence available for divine healing at the time the Neumanns made their decisions.

FALSE BELIEFS FOLLOWED BY ACTIONS

Other cases where we might assess epistemic obligations are less ambiguous. In August 1955, a fourteen-year-old boy named Emmett Till, visiting from Chicago, was challenged by his friends to make good on his boast that he dated white girls. He approached Carolyn Bryant, a young mother tending a store in Sumner, Mississippi, and asked her for a date. This ill-conceived and untimely proposition led eventually to his being forcibly kidnapped from his uncle's home, savagely pistol-whipped, and shot by J. W. Milam and his half-brother Roy Bryant. Till's body, tied to a cotton gin fan with barbed wire, was retrieved later from the Tallahatchie River. Although both Milam and Bryant were summarily acquitted by the jury, they later confessed to the killing in a *Look* magazine story. Milam told the author, William Huie,

> Well, what else could we do? He was hopeless. I'm no bully; I never hurt a nigger in my life. I like niggers—in their place—I know how to work 'em. But I just decided it was time a few people got put on notice. As long as I live and can do anything about it, niggers are gonna stay in their place. Niggers ain't gonna vote where I live. If they did, they'd control the government. They ain't gonna go to school with my kids. And when a nigger gets close to mentioning sex with a white woman, he's tired o' livin'. I'm likely to kill him. Me and my folks fought for this country, and we got some rights. I stood there in that shed and listened to that nigger throw that poison at me, and I just made up my mind. "Chicago boy," I said, "I'm tired of 'em sending your kind down here to stir up trouble. Goddam you, I'm going to make an example of you—just so everybody can know how me and my folks stand."[9]

Whereas one might provide a reasonable account (from a particular theistic perspective) for the Neumanns' beliefs about faith healing, it is more difficult to provide a reasonable justification for Milam's racist litany. Yet unfortunately, the set of beliefs expressed by Milam led to Emmett Till's savage death. Again, our purview is not the immoral actions of beating and killing that Milam and Bryant perpetrated but rather the beliefs Milam held. Does Milam have a right to his racist beliefs, or rather has he violated his epistemic obligations regarding the truth, a failure that led to moral if not legal culpability? None of us, I presume, would find epistemic value in what Milam believed. If we had the opportunity, we would want to educate Milam, expose him to the truth about people different from him, and find ways to bring him to understand and believe the truth that all human beings, regardless of skin color or social status, deserve respect. We might use information, evidence, persuasion, exposure to sensitivity training, and perhaps other means to help him to change his mind. And for this, undoubtedly, we would be praised. But why ought we to do this? The answer clearly involves the concept of epistemic obligations: Milam is obligated to believe the truth—in this case, to hold true beliefs about people different from himself. But why is he so obligated? One might argue that his obligation is based on the fact that from his false beliefs came a morally repugnant action. His epistemic failure contributed significantly to his moral failure.

If Milam has epistemic obligations with regard to his beliefs, what actions are others justified in taking with regard to him in respect to holding his beliefs? The law helps spell out what actions people are justified in taking when others violate their legal obligations, and though the illegal actions Milam perpetrated were not justly adjudicated (in that the jury found him innocent), the laws still remain clear about what should happen to those who are guilty and consequently convicted of the kind of actions in which Milam admittedly engaged. Moreover, not only do laws address actions perpetrated, but some laws specifically address actions that are accompanied by the failure to meet epistemic obligations. As we have already noted, laws dealing with hate crimes address both epistemic and legal obligations jointly. In crimes that fall under the jurisdiction of such laws, what are punished are both the crime and the belief (here, hatred against others based on racial or sexual preferences) that led to the crime. The charge changes and the penalty is increased when the jury determines that the crime committed was motivated by discriminatory hate beliefs about the victim. In these cases not only is the action deemed relevant to determining guilt, but the beliefs are seen as contributors to the kind of crime committed.

BELIEFS WITHOUT ACTIONS

In 2009 Pope Benedict XVI rehabilitated four bishops who had been excommunicated because of their views on the liberalizing reforms enacted by Vatican II. The four, members of the conservative-thinking Society of St. Pius X, particularly opposed absolving contemporary Jews of the responsibility for the crucifixion of Jesus. When it was reported that one of the reinstated bishops, Richard Williamson, was what is termed a Holocaust denier, the pope's action prompted an immediate outcry from various quarters, including from Jewish groups and the head of the German government, Chancellor Angela Merkel. Williamson's statements indicated that he believed that Jewish deaths did not exceed three hundred thousand and that "there were no gas chambers."[10]

Pope Benedict promptly responded to the uproar and ordered Williamson to recant his views on the Holocaust. He must, the pope ordered, "absolutely, unequivocally and publicly distance himself from his positions on the Shoah." Unless he recanted, Williamson would not be allowed to resume his duties as a bishop in the Roman Catholic Church.

The papal order, important as it is for internal and external relations within and outside the Catholic Church, raises some very interesting and important philosophical questions for epistemic obligations. Suppose, for example, that Williamson responded that the pope had no right to tell him what he could or could not believe, that Williamson had an epistemic right to believe whatever he wanted. What then would follow philosophically?

It is clear that the pope, given his churchly relations as the superior to Williamson, has the authority to restrict Williamson's religious actions vis-à-vis the Church. Whether or not he could serve as a bishop is properly within the pope's jurisdiction. But the pope did not restrict Williamson's actions so much as his beliefs. According to the pope, if Williamson chose to believe certain things about the Holocaust, he could not serve as a Catholic bishop. This case differs from the case of Kara Neumann and Emmett Till in that there are no immoral actions stemming from Williamson's beliefs, according to which we can say that Williamson failed in his moral accountability. He neither participated in the Holocaust nor abetted it in any way. Nor is he encouraging others to participate in genocidal activities. So here we have an instance of pure epistemic obligations that have not led to immoral actions. Hence, our interest in this case lies in the question whether, as the pope seems to think, Williamson has epistemic obligations with respect to his beliefs, in particular about the Holocaust, or whether Williamson has the right to believe what he wants—quite apart from any actions Williamson has taken (other than expressing his viewpoint, which I take it is not immoral in and of itself).

The pope ordered Williamson to recant, that is, not to believe what he previously affirmed he believed. Of course, Williamson could simply resign his post and the pope would no longer have ecclesiastical authority over him. But that does not resolve the question of epistemic obligations, namely, whether Williamson has an obligation to believe certain things about the Holocaust. Williamson also could go public and recant his beliefs about the Holocaust.[11] He could claim that he no longer believed what he previously affirmed and by doing so satisfy the pope's demand that he distance himself from his previous position. If his recantation were not genuine, then he would be a hypocrite, believing one thing but saying another (in this instance in order to be restored to his bishopric). It is difficult to imagine that the pope would be interested in an insincere recantation (though untold numbers of such forced recantations have occurred in the history of Christendom). The pope presumably wanted a genuine change of beliefs.

But if Williamson's recantation is to be genuine, it raises the following important philosophical questions. Turning to a first set of issues, does Williamson have not only moral obligations to act rightly and have a moral character, but also the epistemic obligation to hold true beliefs? Is it appropriate to suggest that Williamson has violated his epistemic obligations by holding a false belief about Nazi activities? Was the pope then on solid grounds when, on discovering Williamson's views, he ordered Williamson to abandon them? Should Williamson protest about the pope's attempts, the pope might say it was *good* for him to believe differently or that he *ought* to undertake such efforts to change his beliefs.

First, supposing that Williamson has the obligation to believe the truth about the Holocaust, how is what is true to be determined? Is the truth to be determined by what Williamson thinks is true, by what certain special interest groups (like the Jews, the German government, the Church, the media) consider to be true, what most people hold to be true, or what everyone considers to be true? If the latter, it is unlikely that anyone fulfills his or her epistemic obligations in believing what is true, since universal agreement is impossible to obtain on significant issues. If truth is determined with respect to specific groups, the determination of what is true now caters to special interests. If a particular person determines what is true, the problem arises how to select the person or persons with whom our ideas must correspond. And if each of us is the determiner of truth, then the mere holding of beliefs one takes as true would be sufficient to satisfy our epistemic obligations, a position that is not very credible.

Second, what do Williamson's beliefs tell us about Williamson? Suppose that Williamson does believe what he professed, that the Holocaust was a relatively minor incident and that the Nazis did not use gas chambers to liquidate people. What does this belief say about Williamson's character? On the one hand, does it inform us about his moral character, that he is an immoral person? He has not done any immoral acts with regard to the Holocaust; he was not a participant in Nazi German government or society, nor is he a present persecutor of Jewish people. Or does it tell us about his moral character or virtue in that he has violated an epistemic obligation by holding a false belief, in particular, a false belief about actions that are held to be immoral? But is moral character connected to the beliefs one holds? Does holding a false belief in and of itself create or exhibit an immoral character, or must it be a false belief that leads to an immoral action? But leading to immoral actions is not the case with Williamson as it was with Milam. (Or at least we have no evidence that Williamson's public statements of his Holocaust views incited others to immoral acts, such as persecuting Jews.) Would his (and Milam's) moral character undergo substantial improvement if he held true beliefs? At the heart of these questions is the issue concerning the relation of character to beliefs, and beneath this, the deeper question whether Williamson is morally accountable for his beliefs regardless of his actions. If epistemic obligations are connected with moral obligations, then some ground might be found for such a contention. But if they are unconnected or at best contingently connected, the ground for such judgments is significantly weakened.

Perhaps moral character is connected to epistemic character through epistemic virtues. Does he, from an epistemic virtue perspective, have the obligation to develop a particular kind of epistemic character that successfully results in true beliefs? On this view we are to assess both morality and knowledge in terms of the respective personal virtues that the persons doing the acts and holding the beliefs have. To assess epistemic character, we have to assess the person's commitment to being a critical thinker, the person's epistemic motivation, and whether that motivation successfully leads to true beliefs. If it does, we can conclude that the person acts with intellectual virtue. On this account, we have moral duties of being intellectually motivated and engaging in epistemic practices that lead to truth. The motivation is to know, not necessarily to arrive at moral actions or beneficial consequences. We are obligated to hold true beliefs, but beliefs are not justified in themselves; it is persons holding them who are justified in holding the beliefs. Persons are justified in holding beliefs when they are motivated by appropriate intellectual virtues. But perhaps Williamson has been so motivated. Does the fact that he holds a false belief show that he has not properly exercised his intellectual virtues, or should we so define intellectual virtue that its employment successfully arrives at truth?

Perhaps the issue is not of morality but of rationality. Perhaps Williamson's beliefs do not tell us about his moral or epistemic character but about his rational faculties. And if so, what do they say? Do these beliefs tell us that he is irrational? Does holding a false belief, an unpopular belief, even a belief many think is false or unjustified, establish irrationality? But, he might respond, he looked at the evidence and came to the conclusions that he did. One cannot conclude automatically that someone who holds a false belief is thereby irrational. Nor can one conclude that someone who is rational will arrive at true beliefs. Rational persons may look at all the evidence available to them, consider and weigh the evidence judiciously, and still arrive at a false belief. Alternatively, does it tell us that Williamson was intellectually lazy, that he did not obtain or have the appropriate evidence and that he should have done more research before he stated his beliefs? But how do we know that someone who holds a false belief is intellectually lazy? No necessary connection exists between falsity and intellectual apathy. Further, what research should Williamson have done, and how much? Is the answer to "how much research" or "lack of appropriate evidence" determined by the conclusion one comes to—that is, if one does not come to the "right" conclusion, does that mean one has conducted inadequate research? But this approach begs the question by assuming that someone or other has the right answers and that all have to accede to these or else be deemed intellectually lazy (or irrational). Or rather, again alternatively, does the fact that he holds these beliefs inform us about his critical thinking abilities? Since the evidence for the Holocaust is so plain, like any rational person he should have come to a different conclusion based upon the evidence. The fact that he did not make the appropriate judgments shows weakness of his critical thinking faculties. But again, this presupposes a strong rationalist position, namely, that all critical thinkers will arrive at the same conclusion and that failure to do so casts aspersions on one's critical thinking abilities, acumen, or initiative. But one does not have to look far to observe legitimate belief disagreement over important issues by good critical thinkers. Professional journals, including and especially those in philosophy, provide prime examples. Indeed, it is often heralded that careful, reasoned disagreement stands as a hallmark of critical thinking, not an indication of its absence.

Third, if we have an obligation to hold true beliefs, what is the role of justification in determining what is true? As we have already seen in this and the first case, one may be justified in holding beliefs without those beliefs being true. At the same time, mere truth is not sufficient to establish justification either, for one might hold a true belief for absolutely abysmal reasons, or indeed, for no reasons at all; one might have come about holding those beliefs merely by accident. So precisely what constitutes Williamson's epistemic obligation: to hold true beliefs, to have justified beliefs, or to have both of these? This question, which we asked in the Neumann case, also applies here.

The Williamson case introduces a second set of philosophical issues as well. The demand for a genuine recantation raises the philosophical question whether Williamson can actually carry out the pope's request. To do so means that he has the power or ability to voluntarily control his beliefs. Note that the pope did not ask him to reexamine the evidence or to provide a reconsidered view in light of his perusal of the evidence. Rather, the pope asked him straightforwardly to change his beliefs. But is willfully and directly changing our beliefs in our power; is it possible to bring about or alter our beliefs directly in the manner demanded by the pope? Or is it rather that holding beliefs is something that happens to us? We come to hold a belief, not voluntarily or intentionally, but involuntarily. The evidence, among other factors, brings us or causes us to believe.

But if we have no control over our beliefs, then not only are epistemic obligations to hold contextually significant true beliefs and eschew false beliefs unwarranted, but we are unaccountable for our beliefs. In a real sense we cannot help what we believe. Beliefs are caused sometimes by features we control, also by features mostly out of our control.

Perhaps, as David Hume suggested, it is passion and emotion that root our beliefs, not reason. If this is so, then we would be hard pressed to attempt to encourage Williamson or Milam to change their respective beliefs, since they have no control over them.

Some will argue that, though we don't have direct control over our beliefs, we have indirect control through the relation of evidence to belief. By looking at the appropriate evidence and engaging our critical thinking skills, we can arrive at true beliefs. Thus, in all the above cases what is needed is for the individuals in question to attend more carefully to the evidence. This is something over which they have control, and thereby they have indirect control over their beliefs. But this radically changes the nature of epistemic obligations; the obligation is no longer to hold true beliefs but to look carefully, openly, and critically at the grounds or evidence for our beliefs. The epistemic obligation is to think critically. However, although critical thinking might get us to true beliefs, at the same time it might not.

A third set of philosophical issues concerns whether we would have grounds for attempting to get Williamson to change his beliefs. I am not asking whether we have grounds for thinking Williamson is mistaken in his beliefs. Rather, I am asking whether we would be justified in recommending he change his beliefs or in taking some action to get him to change his beliefs, on the grounds that he has violated his epistemic obligations. And if so, what steps are we justified in taking to disabuse Williamson of his beliefs? Can we demand outright change, as the pope did, perhaps with some behavioral penalties? But if we lack control over our beliefs, is this even possible for him? Can we demand that he relook at the evidence, since, as he noted, he had not reviewed the evidence on the basis of which he formed his view? And if Williamson refused, should the pope recommend stronger measures—for example, that he receive education or be provided with critical pieces of evidence that would acquaint him with the relevant facts? Would the pope be justified in engaging in some form of indoctrination to "make sure" that

Williamson held a true belief? Is there a clear causal connection between evaluation of evidence or indoctrination and true belief? The actions that should be taken regarding people holding false beliefs might hinge on whether the measures taken to control inappropriate actions can be legitimately invoked to bring about the appropriate belief. Here the question of epistemic obligations touches on matters of persuasion, education, and indoctrination, sticky topics in themselves.

In short, what does the fact that Williamson holds beliefs that many take to be false or unsupported but on which he does not act really tell us? Does he have epistemic obligations? If he does, what does he have obligations to, why does he have those obligations, and how are they to be satisfied? If not, then does it matter what he or anyone believes, and do we then lose any right or obligation to encourage people to believe certain things? If our beliefs do not matter, why engage in education or persuasion?

NEITHER BELIEFS NOR ACTIONS

Although prior to the late eighteenth century there had been periodic conflict between the Ottoman majorities and the Armenian minority, the latter had been viewed generally as a loyal *millet* (religious–ethnic community). Though their political and personal rights and freedoms were limited under the Muslim *dhimmi* system, Armenians were guaranteed the right to worship. In 1894 the Armenians in Sassoun, in the eastern province of Bitlis, were involved in a disturbance. Conflicting reports of their cause aside—whether political agitation for autonomy or Armenians defending themselves against Kurdish raiders—the events precipitated an attack by Ottoman troops and Sultan Abdul Hamid II's irregular Kurdish regiments (Hamidiye). Initial fatalities were estimated to be about eight thousand. The Ottoman government conducted an investigation that not only absolved but praised the commander, Zeki Pasha. Protests by the British, French, and Russian delegates at the outcome of the inquiry heightened the tensions and led to a climate of continued protest. The result was a series of massacres in eastern Turkey of even greater proportion. Fatality figures for Armenians vary greatly, from as low as thirty thousand to as high as three hundred thousand.

In 1908 the Committee of Union and Progress (Young Turks) overthrew the existing government of Abdul Hamid II but could not stem the decline of the Turkish Empire. By 1912 the Ottomans lost half of their empire and were militarily unsuccessful in attempting to reclaim territory lost to the Russians earlier. The losing general, Enver Pasha, blamed the defeat on the region's Armenian population, who, he claimed, sided with the Russians. The Armenians were no longer viewed as a loyal *millet* but as a rival nationality, especially since their protests for more autonomy were viewed as calls for independence. In 1915 the Turkish government disarmed, demobilized, grouped into work battalions, and then massacred Armenian solders for fear that they might form a fifth column fighting internally in the army against the Turks. Turkish repression of the Armenians spread from the elite to the general populace. Civilian property was seized, houses were burned, and people were deported from their villages and force-marched in caravans into the Mesopotamian desert to places such as Aleppo and Deir-el-Zor. On the caravan marches, which were calculated to produce death by depriving people of food and water, civilians were killed or died in large numbers. Between one and one and a half million Armenians lost their lives between 1915 and 1918, as whole areas that had been populated by them, especially in central and eastern Turkey, were now largely emptied.[12]

Consider Adalet, a young woman of Turkish descent who has lived a normal life and has never even thought about the significance, if any, of the Armenian genocide. Indeed, she never heard in her high school history class about the events in Turkey and consequently has never been faced with questions of her belief or disbelief about them. If she were asked about whether the U.S. or Turkish governments ought to acknowledge the killings as genocides, she might have no opinion. No one has required her to take any actions regarding the Armenian genocide, including affirming or denying that it occurred.

On the one hand, it does not seem that she has any *moral* obligations with respect to the genocide. Her moral character remains unaffected if she neither has any beliefs about the events nor makes any statements about events occurring in Turkey at the turn of the twentieth century. But on the other hand, does Adalet have any *epistemic* obligations to hold particular beliefs regarding events between Turks and Armenians in Turkey at the turn of the twentieth century? *Should* she believe that genocide did or did not occur in Turkey? It is true that despite her ethnic heritage, she has never been presented with the issue of a possible genocide and is ignorant of it or its issues. But if she has no obligation to believe the truth about these events, then does she have any obligation to believe the truth about things about which she currently does not know or have an interest? If she has such an obligation, what is she obligated to believe? We cannot say that she is obligated to believe everything that is true, since the number of truths she does not know or have an interest in is indefinitely large and would take an infinite number of lifetimes to ascertain. So what criteria might we use to indicate what she ought to believe?

Perhaps one might say that what she ought to believe depends on her circumstances. If she is living in Turkey, then perhaps it is important or significant for her to understand and believe truths about an important event in Turkish history. Having true beliefs about the history of one's country is good, even epistemically virtuous. If she or her parents are immigrants to Germany or America, her context or situation is different. Perhaps these events are unimportant to her insofar as she has adopted a new country and identifies with the culture or history of this new location. Such a judgment indicates that what she ought to believe is contextualized. However, perhaps true beliefs about such a significant event in history are something one should have simply as a human being, regardless of one's current cultural context. Genocides are such horrible events that all people should have true beliefs about them, if for no other reason than fostering the hope that such widespread beliefs might counter any future attempted genocides. In any case, although we might conclude that she does not have any obligation to believe truths about the Armenian genocide in particular, we might contend that she has epistemic obligations to believe true propositions about some things that she is not now believing or has not considered in the past.

In education we hold that believing—indeed, more strongly, knowing—particular things is necessary, not only to pass a test or a course, but to apply for a business or professional position, to go on to graduate school, to be qualified to hold positions in a company, to practice a trade like being a plumber or electrician, or to function adequately in human relations. In the religious community, educational community, medical community, or legal community, one is obligated to know certain things in order to be qualified to practice as a cleric, educator, physician or nurse, judge or lawyer. These professions are not unique; one could repeat this contention across the board for any occupational community. And it is irrelevant whether the participant is interested in believing these truths or does not know about them. To engage in the profession or trade, one *ought* epistemically to believe truths relevant to these professions or trades, and the function of education or training is to make students or apprentices aware of what they do not know and bring them to the true belief or knowledge of what is contextually relevant. To practice the professions or trades, the requirement to believe or know certain things is contextual. The beliefs to be held are relative to a certain context because they are necessary for successful practices of a given sort. Judges do not have to have the true beliefs relevant to the physician, and vice versa. But they both have to believe certain truths about which they might not now be cognizant.

But are beliefs of a more general nature obligatory as well? Do we, by virtue of being human beings, have obligations to believe true propositions about which we are currently ignorant or uninterested or both? If so, what are these true propositions we should believe and how are they to be determined? What beliefs should we as educators be espousing to enable our students to become liberally educated or to be responsible citizens of the community or society? Educators assume this burden of extending true beliefs but unfortunately often are not very thoughtful about what these beliefs should be. They are comfortable about inculcating certain beliefs respective to their disciplines, but educated people who are to function as citizens often must have true beliefs that go beyond a narrow disciplinary focus. Educating the whole person involves the serious and difficult question of what beliefs really matter to be successfully functioning, culturally sensitive, broadly and thoughtfully aware, knowledgeable human beings.

How does one bring about these beliefs? With moral obligations, educators and parents create rewards and punishments to bring about the correct moral behavior. Is there an analogy with epistemic obligations? Or would rewards and punishments, voluntary encouragement, or compulsion be inappropriate with respect to inculcating the desire to fulfill one's epistemic obligation, to acquire true beliefs about what one does not already know or have an interest in? What are the implications of encouraging beliefs, and what are the proper methods to be used, for example, for educating youth, parenting children, training in values, and developing religious practice, where teachers, parents, and clergy attempt to inculcate certain beliefs in their students?

Finally, as we noted above, all of this connects with the question whether we have voluntary control over our beliefs. If we lack control over our beliefs, then attempts to get people to believe will have to be of the sort where the beliefs follow necessarily from the evidence or where people are coerced. In the first, one has to wonder whether beliefs really follow necessarily from evidence, given that many people remain unconvinced even in the face of what others take as conclusive evidence. In the second, one might question whether the coerced persons really hold the beliefs forced on them and whether belief coercion can itself be morally justified when it infringes on basic human rights and freedoms.

THE IMPORTANCE OF EPISTEMIC OBLIGATIONS

The above four cases and their respective questions hint at reasons why consideration of epistemic obligations to hold contextually significant true beliefs and eschew false beliefs is important. The issues are not only of philosophical import; but as I have already indicated, they also apply in other dimensions of life. I will reflect on two areas, beginning with a topic on which I have already touched, namely, education. As an educator, I want my students not only to develop critical thinking skills but to be able to use those skills to arrive at truth. My goal is not simply the formation of opinions; people do not need education to develop opinions. Rather, I want to help students to form true beliefs, and indeed, form them based upon carefully acquiring data, testing those data to discern their reliability and relevance, drawing proper inferences from the data, assessing presuppositions and arguments, and so on. They should come to hold justified true beliefs that can undergo the scrutiny of critical thinking. But I also want them to realize that justification does not guarantee truth, and though justification is very important for coming to the truth, in the end it is truth that really matters. As students, let alone as human beings, they have an obligation to hold true beliefs and avoid false beliefs.

Mike Degenhardt identifies two different versions of epistemic obligations as applied to education.[13] One concerns epistemic obligations regarding the forming of beliefs. Here the educator is concerned with taking proactive steps to encourage proper belief-forming behavior. This involves fostering the habits of attentive curiosity and perceptive awareness, relevant evidence gathering and understanding, construction of cogent and sound logical arguments, patient perseverance in pursuit of data, and careful critical assessment. But epistemic obligations extend beyond the belief-forming (doxastic) behavior; they also concern coming to hold true beliefs. As he notes, the latter may at first seem unattractive and "hardly palatable to enthusiasts for liberal democratic values." Yet, if one looks at educational assessment tools, what educators test for is precisely the latter. We want to know what our students now know, and if knowledge is a form of belief, what they believe. Thus, in various ways the educator tests not merely for formation of doxastic habits and processes—we want to know whether our students have learned to learn and think appropriately and critically—but also for results of their application of these skills in terms of true beliefs. We would be much chagrined if as a consequence of our teaching our students turned out to be racial bigots, deprecators of science, sociological egotists, greedy and callous businesspersons, athletic cheaters, or aesthetically unappreciative, while at the same time wonderfully able to construct elaborate arguments for their views. We should be concerned about the connection of beliefs with truth. The educator will take "truth seriously. One who thinks there is no such thing as truth can hardly be virtuous in the search for it."[14] It is to the assessment of truth claims that much of our educational assessment is directed.

If, as we will discuss in chapter 3, there are epistemic virtues, and epistemic virtues are defined in terms of their successful practice, that is, the actual attaining of true beliefs, then we can say that educators direct their pedagogical practice to the formation of epistemic virtues. They attempt to assist students to become motivated to develop the requisite epistemic practices that are part of the endeavor to obtain understanding and wisdom.

If there are no epistemic obligations to hold contextually significant true beliefs and eschew false beliefs, what reason do we have for the educational profession and practice except for its contextual utility? True beliefs can be useful, but restricting such beliefs to usefulness leaves nothing more than utility—and wishful thinking—in view. What will we do with true beliefs that are not particularly useful? Should they be encouraged also? For what reason? Should they be encouraged for their possible useful future access? But we have no way of knowing which beliefs of our own or our students will prove useful in the future. And indeed, it might well be the case that false beliefs might, in certain circumstances, work as well as true beliefs.[15]

Similarly, if we have no direct control over our beliefs, then the best that educators can hope for is to find the mechanisms that cause the desired belief. But this would seem to differ from student to student, the causal process being personally conditioned. Education then comes more and more to look like manipulation rather than any kind of considered search for wisdom and truth. When we give students both direct and indirect control over beliefs, they assume responsibility for what they believe and meaningfully meet their epistemic obligations.

In short, the fundamental educational enterprise presupposes that we not only have epistemic obligations with regard to our believing the truth, but also have significant say in or control over the beliefs that we form and hold. Hence, the answers we give to the questions posed regarding the four case studies have significant implications for the educational endeavor: for educators' missions, goals, objectives, and methods.

The issue of epistemic obligations also has import for religion insofar as it impacts certain theological considerations. Many Christians and Muslims hold that divine judgment awaits us after death, when individuals are called to account not only for their actions but also for their beliefs. Christianity, for example, affirms not only the role of proper deeds (Matt 25:31-46), but the role of proper beliefs. The role of belief in obtaining salvation runs throughout the New Testament. Paul and Silas respond to the frightened jailor, "Believe in the Lord Jesus, and you will be saved—you and your household" (Acts 16:31). Listeners are told to believe in Jesus to have eternal life (John 3:15-16). Indeed, one might accurately claim that the Gospel of John is about proper belief and its role in human salvation. John identifies Jesus with the Truth, which is the proper object of belief. The early disciples were called believers (Acts 1:15, 2:44, 4:32) and only later Christians (followers of Christ).

The New Testament message appears to be an affirmation of the epistemic obligation to believe the truth. Belief in the truth brings eternal life, failure to believe the truth leads to death. Thus, the Gospel writers see Jesus as teaching the obligation to believe, not just in anything, but in himself as the Truth and in his words. Belief results not only indirectly, through critical reflection on the special events in the ministry of Jesus (Matt 11:4-6), but also directly on the basis of Jesus' testimony about who he is (John 3:11). But if belief is recommended to follow from the command to believe, the New Testament authors held not only the necessity of believing but also, perhaps uncritically, that the powers to believe are within our control.[16]

Muslims likewise place significant emphasis on belief and affirmation. The first of the five pillars or duties required of all Muslims is the *Shahadah* (the profession of faith), which affirms that God is absolute or one (there is no God but Allah) and that Mohammed is his prophet who conveys God's final word. This declaration of belief is essential to being a Muslim and to receiving the promise of an afterlife.

These are merely two examples of a myriad of cases where true belief is held to be obligatory, in some cases simply for itself because the aim of belief is truth, and in other cases for the actions or consequences that are to follow from the belief. From the common saying "You had better believe it" to the politician's request to "believe that he can bring change," belief in the truth is recommended. From the bar exam to the medical board to the practice of plumbing, true beliefs are required. It is in light of this that we need to systematically explore epistemic obligations to maximize true beliefs and minimize false beliefs, and the important presuppositions that lie behind any claim that we have these obligations.

STRUCTURE OF THE BOOK

In the course of presenting the case studies, we have posed a series of nine questions to make the ensuing discussion manageable. The first question sets the stage for the entire discussion: do we have such things as epistemic obligations? The answer to this depends in part on the second question, what are epistemic obligations? Third, do we have an epistemic obligation to believe only what we have an interest in? Fourth, what is the basis or ground for epistemic obligations? This raises the fifth question: given our epistemic fallibility, how do we know which propositions are true, and how does this connect with epistemic obligations? This leads to the sixth question: do we have control over our beliefs? Seventh, what is the nature of belief? Eighth, can we hold persons accountable for their beliefs? Finally, how do we bring about epistemic change so that persons meet their epistemic obligations? Clearly these questions are intertwined; some readers may wish to order them differently. But since nothing ultimately hinges on the particular order so long as the treatment is thorough, we will consider them as proposed.

This nexus of questions not only shows the importance of the issue of whether we have epistemic obligations, but forms the context of the discussion in the following chapters. The tacit argument in the first three cases above, if not in all four, is that we have epistemic obligations to hold contextually significant true beliefs and eschew false beliefs. The Neumanns, Milam, and Bishop Williamson not only have clear moral obligations to act rightly or virtuously, but they also have epistemic obligations to believe the relevant truths, for at least in the first two instances seriously defective actions stemmed from their beliefs, and a career hung on fulfilling such obligations in the third. And, as I have suggested, the belief that we have epistemic obligations underlies all important societal activities, including education and religion. Subsequent chapters will take up the remaining questions. In the next chapter we consider more carefully the issue of what epistemic obligations are. What might we be obligated to believe? In chapter 3 we examine what the basis or ground for epistemic obligations might be. In chapter 4 we address questions having to do with the relationship between epistemic obligations and justification. Since our knowledge claims are fallible, we need to attend to processes that help us determine the truth and ask what implications epistemic obligations have for those processes. In chapter 5 we turn to the underlying issue whether beliefs are held voluntarily. Do we have control over our beliefs, or do beliefs simply arise from our experiences of certain events or our engagement in critical thinking activities? In chapter 6 we discuss what beliefs are. Are beliefs only dispositions, or can one also give a partial account of believing as an action? Finally, in chapter 7, we raise the question of moral accountability with respect to our beliefs. If we are accountable, what is the role and nature of actions meant to facilitate belief change? By the end, we will have provided the groundwork for responding to the critical questions posed by the four important cases considered in this chapter.

2

Epistemic Obligations

Philosophical literature is not altogether clear on exactly what epistemic obligations are. Whereas moral obligations apply to persons with respect to their actions, epistemic obligations apply to persons with respect to their beliefs. Roderick Chisholm attempts to specify carefully our epistemic obligations in terms of doxastic requirements (an obligation to believe). Two of his definitions are particularly relevant.

> D2 p imposes a *doxastic requirement* =Df There is a doxastic state such that p requires one to be in that state or p requires one not to be in that state.

And in his typically careful manner, Chisholm specifies a doxastic state as

> D1 S is a *doxastic state* =Df Either S is a believing; or S is the withholding of a believing; or S is the preferring of one believing to another believing, or of a believing to a withholding, or of a withholding to a believing, or of a withholding to a withholding.[1]

But what is it that we are obligated to be believing or withholding our believing from, or what believing are we to be preferring to another? As agents, in believing we do not consciously intend to hold false beliefs, or undertake critical thinking or justificatory endeavors for our beliefs in order to arrive at falsehood.[2] Beliefs, one might say, "aim at truth."[3] Consequently, epistemic obligations have to do with connecting our beliefs with or reflecting the truth—to be in an appropriate relation to the truth. And if we are obligated to be in a particular doxastic state with regard to the truth, what is this appropriate relation?

One can find the idea of epistemic obligations in William James, and before him notably in William Clifford. In James' discussion of epistemic imperatives, he affirms the obligation to know the truth and avoid error.[4] James sees Clifford before him as stressing the primacy of avoiding error. But James counsels that we need to keep both commandments. "Believe truth! Shun error!—these . . . are two materially different laws; and by choosing between them we may end by coloring differently our whole intellectual life. We may regard the chase for truth as paramount, and the avoidance of error as secondary; or we may, on the other hand, treat the avoidance of error as more imperative, and let truth take its chance."[5] For James the appeal of truth is so great that he is willing to risk error ("being duped") in order that he may believe the truth. Risking error and believing the truth are not two sides of the same coin, but two different things. By avoiding error we are not thereby believing the truth, and by not believing the truth we are not thereby avoiding error. Further, it is not that we do one rather than the other, but that we both avoid error and believe the truth in ways that result in epistemic excellence. But exactly what is involved in doing both? What is the appropriate doxastic state with respect to true and false beliefs?

Before we answer this question, it is important to note a significant difference between Clifford and James, a point that will become more important in chapter 4. Clifford's injunction has less to do with believing the truth and avoiding error than with having sufficient evidence for one's beliefs. "Every time we let ourselves believe for unworthy reasons, we weaken our powers of self-control, of doubting, of judicially and fairly weighing evidence. . . . It is wrong always, everywhere, and for anyone, to believe anything upon insufficient evidence."[6] Clifford is an evidentialist when it comes to believing. James, on the other hand, while not rejecting evidence but affirming its role for what is amenable to evidential considerations, puts the epistemic obligation in terms of certain doxastic states of believing truth and avoiding error. In this chapter we will pursue the Jamesian quest, postponing our detailed consideration of Clifford and justification based on evidence to chapter 4.

BELIEVING WHAT IS TRUE

For the moment, let us focus on the obligation to believe what is true. The starting point in determining our epistemic obligations is that we have an obligation to believe true propositions. But this is ambiguous. One understanding would be that for any given proposition, if it is true then we are obligated to believe it.[7] This is an unlikely interpretation of epistemic obligations. Since ought implies can, we can have no such ought, for our epistemic obligations to believe all truths—an infinite number—could never be fulfilled. There are simply too many true propositions. Further, to embark on the project of believing every true proposition would be a horrendous waste of time and effort. Even if accomplished, it would have little to do with knowledge and the good life; knowledge consists of more than merely believing every conceivable true proposition.[8] Third, we could engage our epistemic obligations in a most irresponsible manner, for one could progress toward the end of believing all true propositions by believing all propositions. But this would not produce the trait of epistemic excellence, since in believing all propositions proposed to us and thereby all true proposed propositions, one would at the same time have believed an even larger number of false propositions. Finally, the mere fact that a proposition is true might not be a sufficient reason to believe it. Even if a proposition is true, there might be instances where we ought to suspend judgment about its truth if we have no reliable information about the truth of the proposition. As Richard Feldman notes, the fact that a randomly flipped coin came up heads provides no reason for someone to believe it if that person has no evidence or information that it came up heads but is simply guessing.[9]

A second possible understanding of epistemic obligations is that we have an obligation to bring it about that every belief that we hold is true. This initially sounds plausible in that it limits what is to be believed, but on some understandings of belief it may suffer from the sheer enormity of what is required. If beliefs are mere dispositions (and not active conscious states), the number of our beliefs is very large, making it impossible in any practical sense to carry out a program that would show that all of our beliefs understood as dispositions are true.

One reply to the objection that the large number of possible beliefs makes this impossible to carry out is to make a distinction, developed by Robert Audi, between (dispositional) beliefs and the disposition to believe.[10] Although we will take this up in detail in chapter 6, we might anticipate the point. Audi argues that although to have a belief is a disposition, in many cases we do not actually have the belief but rather are disposed to form the relevant belief given the appropriate cause or impetus. If this is the case, the number of beliefs, considered as dispositions, would be considerably and reasonably reduced; in the place of many of them we would have a more general disposition to believe, given a certain set of circumstances.

But this move from beliefs to a disposition to believe significantly alters the character of epistemic obligations. We no longer are obligated to believe significant truths; rather, we are obligated to form a more general disposition to believe, given a relevant set of circumstances. This move disconnects epistemic obligations from the question of truth and moves it into the arena of disposition formation: we are now obligated to form the disposition to believe, which may or may not be connected to truth considerations.[11]

Roderick Chisholm suggests a third interpretation: "We may assume that every person is subject to a purely intellectual requirement—that of trying his best to bring it about that for any proposition *h* that he considers, he accepts *h* if and only if *h* is true."[12] Although this indicates a less demanding approach, putting the obligation in terms of merely trying one's best is much too weak. Since on Chisholm's view we have no requirement to actually realize true beliefs, we could fulfill our epistemic obligations without holding a single true belief.[13] We might say that we tried our best but could not conjure up the appropriate belief, or that we tried to find conclusive evidence to support our belief but that without conclusive or sufficient evidence we ought to suspend judgment, or that we never realized the belief inducements necessary to produce the belief. We may, like the exhausted skeptic who follows Clifford's injunction to continually examine all his beliefs, at best be agnostic.[14]

We might modify our first suggestion—the obligation to believe all true propositions—to hold that we are obliged to believe only every *significant* truth.[15] If a belief is significant, we should hold it. This responds to the first two objections noted above: we are no longer required to believe every truth, and we don't have to waste our time believing trivial or insignificant truths (though believing them does not violate our epistemic obligation). However, this view remains problematic because it runs into problems parallel to the first view. For one thing, we don't have the ability or time to determine all the truths that might be significant and therefore obligatory for us to believe. Further, as above, why should we have to believe *every* significant proposition? Significance is a contextual matter. Truths regarding safety-harnesses and how to maneuver on and around the steel beams on a construction job high above the ground are important for an iron worker but irrelevant to a chef, for whom safety has to do with the cleanliness of the food preparation area and proper use of the cutlery. Since significant beliefs have to be continually contextualized, there is no reason to think we have an obligation to believe every significant proposition, but only those that are significant to our context.

While this qualification importantly moves the discussion in the right direction, merely contextualizing significant beliefs is insufficient for meeting epistemic obligations. In any given context we might inquire whether we epistemically ought to change the context in reference to which we are considering true propositions, since there might be significant propositions—about future marriage partners, career opportunities, national health insurance, government misconduct, automobile recalls, environmental carcinogens, retirement plans, the existence of God, principles of physics or logic, and so on—that we ought to hold but that are not part of or relevant to our current context. If we are only required to know the truths significant in a particular context, we may not be obligated to think about whether the context itself needs changing; to do so we would need to have a belief present in the given context about the importance of or need for changing the context and about the significance of other contexts in which we are not already participating. But if we contextualize significance, there is no reason to suppose that the current context will contain truths that require one to move to another context, so that whether or not we have beliefs requiring contextual change is a contingent matter, not stemming from obligations.

Feldman suggests a fifth interpretation of the truth involved in epistemic obligations, namely, that the obligation in question concerns not every significant truth, but must be localized with respect to particular propositions in which the person has an interest. The epistemic question concerns whether persons are obligated to believe a particular proposition, given any particular belief in which they have an interest.[16] The question is not whether the proposition is significant or not, but what are their obligations with regard to the particular proposition that they are now entertaining. Their epistemic obligation is that with respect to every proposition they seriously consider or entertain, they should attempt to believe that proposition, provided that it is true.[17] And this obligation only applies to persons' synchronic, not diachronic, beliefs—to the beliefs that they are entertaining now, not to those they might entertain in the future.[18] If there is a role for *significance* in regard to particular beliefs, it is that significance connects to what persons have an interest in.

This formulation of epistemic obligations in terms of propositions of interest helps us sharpen the matter of context, for context connects with interest. In many cases the interests of the chef will match the chef's context, for we derive our beliefs from our experiences. But this view also is problematic for reasons similar to those just given, for it applies only to propositions in which persons already have an interest, to propositions that they are considering or related to them and their context. But we have epistemic obligations to consider propositions that we are not presently considering or having an interest in. In the example of the Armenian genocide that we used in chapter 1, we might commend the U.S. ambassador to Turkey Henry Morgenthau for taking an interest in the truth of the situation involving the Armenian displacement, for it might have been the case that he (or a different ambassador) had no interest in the Armenian question and hence felt no obligation to believe the truth about or to lobby for investigation into the forced deportations and deadly persecution of the minority population.[19] From one perspective, it is possible to create the argument that as an American diplomat to Turkey he should have had an interest in what was occurring in Turkey (as in fact he did) and hence had an obligation to learn the truth—an obligation that was not only moral but epistemic. Even on the general ground of humaneness, we can reasonably argue that he should have had an interest in events that were causing mass fatalities. On the other hand, the Turkish government might well respond that since this was a matter of internal Turkish affairs, Morgenthau should not have had any interest in these events. Morgenthau was representing U.S. political interests, and the Armenian situation was not germane to American political interests. So the question becomes, what are we obligated to have interest in? We have epistemic obligations with regard to what we seriously consider or have an interest in. But we also have epistemic obligations to seriously consider events or principles—truths—other than those we are currently interested in, because they can be significant to us or of general significance to our future context, to the society in which we participate as citizens, or to humanity as a whole because we are human beings. For example, a person might not have an interest in environmental issues, the accumulating amount of CO_2 in the environment, dramatic global weather changes, unprecedented melting of the polar and glacial ice, the rapid disappearance or dislocation of endangered species, the desertification of agricultural land, deforestation, and the like, but such matters concern the well-being of humans and other earth inhabitants and thus should be matters about which the person has true beliefs. Or again, if persons never had or no longer have school-age children, they might think that having quality schools, adequate educational resources, ethnically diverse education, and effective teachers are not among their interests. Yet, since quality education is of societal importance affecting our community, we should have true beliefs about the education occurring in our community so that, for example, we can vote intelligently in the school bonding issue or for members of the school board, engage in meaningful political lobbying, or just be passive witnesses to the educational improvement of the youth in our community. In other words, epistemic obligations extend beyond merely believing or not believing the propositions that are before us and in which we already have an interest; they encompass believing significant events that involve ourselves, our community, our country, our humanity, and our world, and principles that affect our reasoning concerning these. Feldman at least helps us move significantly in the right direction.

Turning to James' admonition to shun error and hence disbelieve false propositions, much of what we have said with respect to true beliefs will also apply. It would be impossible for us to disbelieve all false propositions. Again, there are simply too many false propositions for us to disbelieve, and attempting such a project would be a horrendous waste of time. Moreover, some have contended that there are false propositions that we are warranted or even obligated to believe.[20] The evidence for a proposition that turns out to be false might be so strong that we would be acting unreasonably in not believing it. It would have been unreasonable for citizens of medieval society to believe that the earth went around the sun rather than vice versa or that earth-bound humans could travel through space to distant planets. To do so would have required them to go against all their sensory evidence and the received opinion of that day.

In short, we can agree with Audi's suggestion that we have an obligation to cultivate the disposition to form true beliefs relevant to the situations in which we find ourselves. This might be termed a doxastic rather than an epistemic obligation. Our doxastic obligations do not attach to any specific proposition, but rather attach to our doxastic practices. However, this still leaves the question of what our epistemic obligations are with respect to specific true propositions.

ANALOGY WITH MORAL OBLIGATIONS

One way to address the question of what we are obligated to believe, the question about our appropriate relation to the truth, is to invoke the analogy of epistemic obligations with moral obligations; this analogy can provide direction for discerning the nature of epistemic obligations regarding truth and falsity. We delineate moral obligations in terms of acts we should not do (prohibited) and acts that we should do (required).

As we have moral prohibitions about what we should not do, we can also have epistemic *prohibitions* about what we should not believe. Epistemic prohibitions are like ethical prohibitions in that they are universalizable.[21] They can be understood in two ways. On the one hand, we simply should not believe any propositions that are false. That is, none of our beliefs should be false. This follows from the fact that our believing is directed to truth; we do not intend for ourselves to believe false propositions.[22] The determining condition here is the truth or falsity of the belief. We may argue that Milam and Williamson and possibly the Neumanns, as discussed in chapter 1, fail in their epistemic obligation in this regard. On the other hand, we can understand epistemic prohibitions in terms of justification of our beliefs, where the obligations are relative to the agent's own knowledge, evidence, or context. Understood in this sense, we ought not to hold a belief for which we possess adequate evidence for its falsity or, more weakly, where we do not possess adequate evidence for its truth. Regarding the evidence we possess, we might not know that the proposition is true but rather have good evidence or reason to believe that the proposition is false and hence that we should not believe it. In this case we have an obligation not to believe what we think is false—although it happens that the proposition is true. Here epistemic obligations have less to do with falsity per se than with the evidence or reasons we have for the proposition's falsity or truth. The justificatory account is the weaker of the two options for two reasons: first, although the prohibition is universal, the application depends upon the agent's knowledge. Whereas the injunction not to hold false beliefs applies regardless of the knowledge possessed by the individual agent, the justificatory formulation is individualized according to the knowledge of the agent, for whether the agent should not believe depends upon what justificatory account is available to the agent. Second, it is weaker because on the justificatory view we might be justified in holding false beliefs, something prohibited under the strict injunction not to hold false beliefs. We might not have good or even any evidence that something is not the case even though it is not. Or we might have evidence that something is the case though in fact it is not. In such situations, we might argue that, as rational critical thinkers, we should go with the evidence available to us even though (unknown to us) the belief is false. So any adequate account of epistemic obligations needs to determine whether the obligations should be understood as a strict injunction not to hold false beliefs or as applying to the justification we might have for the belief. We will return to this in chapter 4.

Epistemic *requirements* are analogous to moral requirements in that just as we should fulfill what is morally required of us in a given context or situation, epistemically we should maximize the contextually significant truths we believe. Not holding beliefs about what is contextually significantly true or actually disbelieving contextually significant truths means that we have failed in our obligations and puts us in a position of possible condemnation.[23] The determination of the context or contexts for any given person is challenging. With regard to moral obligations, cases arise where we are obligated to act outside of our immediate and current context. For example, my immediate context has nothing to do with the devastating floods ravaging Pakistan and the millions of displaced persons suffering there. Minnesota is a long way from Pakistan; although I have acquaintances in Pakistan, I do not currently know anyone affected by the floods; no direct appeals have been made to me for contributions to flood relief. However, moral obligations invoking the principle of beneficence might demand of me that I expand my current context to consider the needs of other sufferers and take proactive steps to contribute some of my wealth to help alleviate the suffering. My present context can be widened to create a broadly human context wherein obligations to assist are morally compelling. Similarly, we can be obligated to believe truths outside of our immediate context. As we noted previously, there might be significant truths, related to contexts that are not immediately relevant to what we currently believe, that we should believe on the grounds that they might be relevantly significant to our personal, societal, human, and environmental well-being in noncurrent contexts. If we are going to hold to requiring belief in significant truths, the requirement has to include obligatory beliefs that both are immediately contextual and extend beyond our understanding of our immediate context. These beliefs connect in a broad sense to contexts related to our being human, to our being knowers and doers involved in complex living, and to our being participants in social relationships of varying intimacy, citizens in a particular community or larger society, and members of earth's environment. They concern our functioning as persons with diverse social relations, vocations, occupations, friendships, and social responsibilities in a society whose interests and needs are diverse and to whose contexts of justification we have access. They also connect with the values that not only we hold but that we ought to hold, for these values help to determine significance. Although the facts of the case might not tell us what our obligations are in that case, they do help determine which values have relevance in any given context. And the understanding and assessment of those values are necessary to determine significance. The beliefs include not merely beliefs about particular events and things, but beliefs about true principles or theories that affect or color our interpretations of particular events.

In effect, our situation can be analyzed in terms of our participating in multiple contexts (daughter, sibling, wife, physician, church volunteer, resident of *a*). It can be progressively broadened conceptually from specific or particular contexts—chef or iron worker—through citizen to human being. And present contexts can be broadened temporally to incorporate future contexts. What lends this last contextual broadening its ambiguity is our contemporary ignorance of what these future contexts are or might be. The ambiguity manifests itself in the practical problem faced by many university students who are at a loss as to what academic courses to take because they do not know what they might be doing in five years. There are contextually significant truths about that future occupation and its requisite skills and knowledge they need to know, but they do not know what those truths might be, other than that the truths might differ from their present interests. As we already noted, this does not differ from the situation we encounter with morally obligatory acts. There are innumerable morally obligatory actions of which we currently have no cognizance. What will be required of us in the future or in other contexts we really don't know at present. We know that we are obliged to do the right action and to achieve the good, but how these are realized depends on the particular facts in some particular context. Moral judgments of obligation are situational in that what is required depends on the empirical facts of the particular case; the particular set of facts invokes the relevant goods to be achieved, duties to be performed, and principles to be followed. For example, even though one is morally obligated to tell the truth, what truths this telling involves and how those truths are to be told depend on the context. When applying for a job, persons are obligated to respond truthfully to the interviewer's questions. They are forbidden to lie, but they are not under obligation to share all their personal information with the interviewer. Or again, if someone asks for advice, what is shared should be done truthfully, but the sharing should be done sensitively as well. Truth-telling also depends on a hierarchy of pre-empting principles. There will be cases where higher moral duties or goods trump truth-telling as an obligation. It is not something that we can determine ahead of time, beyond ascertaining our moral obligations to truth-telling and other dutiful acts.

Similarly, we know that we are obliged epistemically to maximize contextually significant truths and avoid falsehoods, but how these are realized depends on the particular facts in any context and on a hierarchy of principles and values determining significance. It is not something that we can determine ahead of time beyond ascertaining our epistemic obligations to believe the significantly relevant truths. That epistemic obligations are situational, in that what is required depends on the facts of the particular cases or on the specific principles, leads us to suspect that there are no general criteria that provide an algorithm for determining what those contextually significant truths are. Human deliberation, assessment, and wisdom are called for as one discerns what propositions are true or false in the relevant context.

Moral structures for actions have two other categories—permissibility and special praiseworthiness—that do not fit under obligations, since we are not obligated to do what is merely permissible or especially praiseworthy (what is termed as being above and beyond the call of duty). However, they do further the analogy between the moral and epistemic. If I live in Oregon, I am permitted to use the physician-assisted suicide options the law there provides, whereby those who are terminally ill and of sound mind can petition a health care provider to assist them in obtaining life-ending drugs. But the facts that this is legally permitted and that I believe that the carefully circumscribed practice is morally acceptable in certain circumstances, such as when the terminally ill person experiences unrelievable suffering and there are no prospects for successfully addressing either the symptoms or the underlying malady, do not entail that I should employ this option if I were in this circumstance. Making the request is a morally permissible option, not a requirement. Similarly, if I am in an overcrowded bus, I am not obliged to give up my seat to an elderly gentlemen or a woman, but I might choose to do so, not only because it is permissible but also recognizing that such an act is especially morally praiseworthy (supererogatory).[24] The fact that an action is especially praiseworthy does not obligate us to do the action; we have the choice not to do the action (which does not leave us culpable) or to do it.

How, then, do permissible and especially praiseworthy acts fit into an ethical schema? In morals we are concerned not merely with fulfilling our moral obligations but with attaining moral excellence.[25] Fulfilling our obligations is necessary but not sufficient for being morally excellent. At the very least, as Kant pointed out, the motivation for the action plays a role in determining moral excellence. Doing the right action for morally suspect reasons is not a sign of moral excellence. But more than this, the way the action fits into the agent's habits, dispositions, goals, and objectives also contributes to moral excellence; engaging in sporadic actions that fulfill our moral duties fails to demonstrate the possession of the moral character characteristic of moral excellence. Properly handling what is permissible also contributes to moral excellence; morally excellent persons know the range, extent, and timing of permissible actions. Using their deliberative abilities, they are able to discern what is morally permissible and what is not permissible not only in general but in particular contexts. They recognize the extent to which they should go in their actions; they discern the proper limits even if permission allows them to exceed those limits. They know that exceeding those limits can border on the immoral in a particular context. Such persons might know, for example, that they have a legal right to claim government assistance given their condition, but they might also realize that if they claim it they would deprive someone else who is needier of those resources and would therefore forgo making the claim.

In epistemology, too, we strive for epistemic excellence.[26] Epistemic excellence at a minimum involves having contextually significant true beliefs and avoiding false beliefs. But it involves more than this; epistemically excellent persons form epistemic habits that demonstrate knowledge of the range, extent, and timing of truth-realizing processes and invoke these propitiously in acquiring and maintaining true beliefs. This results in understanding what is to be believed, how far one should pursue truth-realizing activities in a particular context, and what those relevant contexts are. Invoking truth-realizing processes concerns not merely believing what is true and not believing what is false, but believing or not believing these for proper reasons and engaging in appropriate truth-realizing practices. Regarding epistemic permissibility, epistemically excellent persons are permitted to hold a belief if it is true and where believing or not believing is properly related to the evidence or is properly warranted. The qualification regarding the basis for belief follows from cases where although what is recommended for belief is true, the believer either lacks sufficient evidence for its truth or possesses evidence suggesting that the proposed belief is false. Epistemic excellence is analogous to moral excellence in that the believing accords with the agent's epistemic habits, dispositions, goals, and objectives; believing on a mere whim may satisfy the truth condition if what is believed is true, but it fails to demonstrate the possession of the epistemic character characteristic of epistemic excellence. We will return to and discuss this in more detail at the end of the next chapter.

In short, epistemic *permissibility* is analogous to moral permissibility, where actions if done are to be moral but are neither required nor forbidden. To perform or not perform the act is a matter of our choice arising from conscientious deliberation about the facts of the case and the values involved. Similarly, persons are not obligated to believe every truth.[27] The characteristic of permissibility relieves epistemic obligees of the burden of having to believe all truths or even many truths, even if significant. Contextuality, present and future possible significance, and available or potentially available evidence all play a role. It might be true that Mars once had substantial surface water, but ordinary persons might not be obligated to believe this. Of course, they should not believe the denial of this if it is true; this would violate their obligation not to believe false propositions. But they might not be required to hold this belief about water on Mars since it is not significant for their particular context or for other contexts relative to them and their society. On the basis of permissibility, they could simply withhold belief, refusing to make any assertion regarding the presence of surface water on Mars, and be epistemically correct (though in virtue of this feature alone it would be improper to call them epistemically excellent). At the same time, that there is or was surface water on Mars would be a relevant belief for those who send rovers and landers to Mars or who might be planning a human Martian expedition to discern past and present climatic and environmental conditions. Permissibility, then, is also contextual to persons, their situation, and their social relations.

Since permissibility is also contextual with respect to the evidence or warrant that a person has, various persons may adopt differing attitudes toward these truths. Some are justified in being agnostic or withholding belief, while others are justified in believing them. This category of permissibility allows for the kind of "academic skepticism" that allows one to think critically about the evidence for a belief without the necessity of any immediate commitment, acceptance, or belief formation. That is, this justifies the view that suspension of belief is compatible with both epistemic obligations and epistemic excellence.

We can continue the analogy noting that just as there are acts that are not morally required but that persons are especially praiseworthy for performing, there is a host of truths that an epistemically excellent person would be *praiseworthy* for believing. These truths may not be significant for us or even useful, but at the same time they may enrich our personal or intellectual life. Educators often recommend—sometimes making beliefs obligatory by a demand conveyed through behavioral incentives—that their students learn such truths. They are significant for educators but might not have significance for their students beyond the immediate context of the academic class. Educators may even indicate that the beliefs or knowledge may not have any practical value but may enrich them as human beings nonetheless. Persons possessing this kind of extensive, liberal (in the sense of wide-ranging) set of beliefs, arising from their curiosity about the world or their desire to know, insofar as the beliefs are not merely disjointed but woven into the fabric of knowledge, can be called epistemically excellent. It is this kind of belief that, when part of knowledge, often falls under the category of wisdom. Wisdom, of course, is more than a liberal set of beliefs; it also involves being able to engage in careful, reasoned deliberation that leads to truth and to making sound judgments that bear fruit in successful practice. As Aristotle notes, since being practically wise is connected with being good, epistemic obligations connect with moral obligations.[28] (We will take up this connection in the next chapter.)

This analysis, conducted with an analogical eye to moral obligations, provides a reasonable way of understanding epistemic obligations. First, what this shows is that epistemic excellence involves more than mere epistemic obligations with regard to the truth of our beliefs. With regard to epistemic obligations, we need to not hold or to eliminate our false beliefs and maximize contextually significant true beliefs, both those of our immediate context and those of contexts that might relate to our personal, professional or occupational, societal, human, and environmental well-being.[29] But if we are to move from mere epistemic obligations to epistemic excellence, we need to consider also permissible beliefs and especially praiseworthy beliefs. Epistemic excellence will involve believing, with a dose of Aristotelian moderation, a wide variety of truths[30] that arise with human curiosity and enable us to function virtuously, humanly, and with more fulfillment in life, but will also allow us to suspend belief when epistemically appropriate.[31] The moderation with regard to believing is important because our lives have many aspects that need to be balanced, and while the devotion to acquiring a large number of true beliefs may satisfy our curiosity, if overindulged in it might produce a rather one-sided life. As my colleague puts it, some people are in danger of becoming epistemic junkies. Human lives are scarce resources, and though believing is an essential and important aspect of life, other features likewise need to be cultivated that might require or at least value withholding belief or not even pursuing belief in many cases. Epistemic excellence then goes beyond mere obligations and prohibitions. Since our concern in this book is with epistemic obligations, we will focus our considerations on the analogy between epistemic and moral requirements and prohibitions, though as we shall see beginning in the next chapter, the analogy extends beyond mere obligations to epistemic excellence when we attempt to ground our epistemic obligations and, later, discern true beliefs. We will not be able to isolate epistemic obligations from epistemic excellence.

It is important to note that we have not provided either a list of epistemically obligatory beliefs or an algorithm that will produce such. It is one thing to say that we have epistemic obligations to form contextually significant true beliefs and avoid false beliefs; it is another to discern what these beliefs are. This, however, is not unique to epistemic obligations; philosophers have been noticeably unsuccessful in delineating an unqualified list of moral obligations or developing a noncontroversial algorithm for producing them. What we can say is that since we have defined our obligations contextually, the obligations will be, to some extent, relative to individual persons. What the iron worker will be expected to believe and know will differ from what the chef will be expected to believe and know. At the same time, the obligations will not be completely relative insofar as we share common conditions of humanity, social relationships, and life on this planet; after all, the iron worker and chef will have much in common as well: they may be members of the same community, organizations, church, and so on. Put another way, the question of epistemic obligations can be discussed objectively and subjectively. That is, while there are truths relative to a given context that any person in that context should know, there are also subjective considerations regarding what one can expect persons to believe given their immediate interests, individuality, and background. We will have occasion to address these two perspectives in subsequent chapters. Finally, any attempt to impose a uniform set of beliefs would lead to the creation of such things as thought police and the removal of our liberties, neither of which is acceptable. We will return to this matter in the final chapter.

AN EXTERNALIST FORMULATION

Traditionally, the concept of epistemic obligations carries with it an internalist epistemic framework. William Alston inquires how epistemic obligations might be formulated in an externalist fashion. A deontological feature of belief is that the belief is formed and held responsibly. Interpreted in terms of an externalist account of knowledge, this means that "the causal ancestry of [the belief] does not contain violations of intellectual obligations."[32] Had we checked on the source of the evidence, had we done additional research, had we tested whether our faculties were operating properly, and so on, then we would have believed *p*, would not have believed *p*, or would have withheld belief from *p*. We are responsible just in case we did or did not fulfill our obligations with regard to the causal conditions that produced the belief. The epistemic obligations involved here concern not the holding of true beliefs but the engagement in appropriate practices or methods that reliably produce true beliefs. We have obligations to search for and evaluate new or contrary evidence and to properly exercise our belief-forming habits. For example, we ought to curb jumping to premature conclusions, to examine critically the testimony and credentials of those who testify, to assess the soundness or cogency of any reasoning offered, and generally to exercise our critical thinking skills and abilities. Where we have employed these in a causally proper fashion, we are blameless in holding or withholding belief. "S is intellectually to blame for believing that p *iff* if S had fulfilled all her intellectual obligations, then S's access to relevant considerations, or S's belief-forming habits or tendencies, would have changed in such a way that S would not have believed that p."[33]

Alston, however, is reluctant to adopt an externalist view of epistemic obligation, on two grounds. First, the obligations regarding causal ancestry are exceedingly vague. How much more information do we need or to what extent must we investigate before we can say that our beliefs are justified? The epistemic obligations would vary for different people in accord with their differing abilities, experiences, education, and tendencies. Second, and more significant, the causal conditions might be fulfilled without producing truth. For example, we often rely on authority for our beliefs, but though this is generally a reliable method, authorities can be unreliable and witnesses untrustworthy. But it is true beliefs that matter in epistemic obligations. In short, for Alston, causal methods are not truth-conducive enough to satisfy the requirement that we hold true beliefs. The causal processes invoked are fallible when it comes to producing true beliefs. Whereas Alston takes this as grounds to abandon a deontological notion of epistemic obligations, we suggest that what it shows is that an externalist view is by itself an inadequate basis on which to construct a theory of epistemic obligations. We will have much more to say about this in chapter 4. Before undertaking that discussion, however, we will turn to the question concerning the grounds for epistemic obligations as we have delineated them in this chapter. We take up this issue in the next chapter.

CONCLUSION

To summarize, what we have contended so far is that an analogy lies between epistemic and moral obligations. Thus, we can talk meaningfully about epistemic prohibitions. On the one hand, since our believing is directed to truth, we should not believe any propositions that are false. On the other hand, we can understand epistemic prohibitions in terms of the justification of our beliefs, where the obligations are relative to the agent's own knowledge, evidence, or context. We should not hold beliefs for which there is (or more weakly, we have) adequate evidence for their falsity or, more weakly still, where we lack adequate evidence for their truth. With regard to epistemic requirements, we should maximize the contextually significant truths we believe. If we move to epistemic excellence, then we should consider epistemic permissibility and epistemic praiseworthiness. As to the former, we are to form epistemic habits that demonstrate truth-realizing processes that we invoke to acquire and maintain true beliefs. In invoking truth-realizing processes, we not only believe what is true and do not believe what is false, but engage in belief-forming practices that successfully result in true beliefs. As to the latter, epistemic excellence involves forming and maintaining true beliefs about a host of truths that may not be immediately significant for us or even useful but that at the same time may provide enrichment of our lives.

3

Grounds for Epistemic Obligations

Supposing that we are correct that we have epistemic obligations and that they can be understood as we have just discussed, what is their ground? Are they grounded in the fact that true beliefs are intrinsically valuable, or are they grounded elsewhere? If the latter, philosophers have suggested several possibilities for their grounding: epistemic obligations might be grounded in prudence, morality, or human virtues. We will first look at their ground in the intrinsic value of true beliefs, and then turn to the various suggestions given for their being grounded elsewhere.

TRUE BELIEFS AS INTRINSICALLY VALUABLE

One response to the grounding question would be to suggest that we are obligated to have true beliefs simply because there is something intrinsically valuable about true beliefs. They are not means to anything else but rather are desired for their own sake. Just as moral human action aims at the good, believing aims at truth. And just as doing the right or achieving the good is its own justification, believing the truth is its own justification. As right acts are intrinsically valuable, so are true beliefs.

There is something attractive about this view because it extends the analogy between moral action and epistemic belief that we invoked in the previous chapter. It suggests a continuation of the symmetry, maintaining the correspondence of value between the good and the true. The good is something we aim at for itself, not because of something else. If we aimed at something else, that something else would be better, and to be better is to be a good. Similarly with truth. Truth is something that we aim at for its own sake. If we say, for example, with Bas van Fraassen that in our beliefs we aim at empirical adequacy rather than truth,[1] then we can ask whether if a proposition were empirically adequate but false, would we think that something was missing. We would because we really prefer having the truth.[2] We believe the truth because it is the truth, and hence it is the truth that obligates us to believe.

At the same time, we might raise doubts about this view. In particular, the having of true beliefs does not seem to be an end in itself. Accumulating true beliefs is something we can do with minimal effort and without any purpose. We do not praise individuals for the number of true beliefs they have. Merely adding true beliefs to our stock does not make us wiser, epistemically excellent, or persons of greater understanding. If it were so, we could realize the wisdom that comes from accumulation by sitting in our chair, analyzing our room, and forming true beliefs about its many contents and their relations to each other. Contrary to this, we have beliefs so that we can act wisely, excellently, intelligently, or prudently. Beliefs provide part of the condition, along with motivating desire, for action. Beliefs guide action. The addition of "true" to beliefs does not alter the fundamental purpose of believing but adds a critical ingredient to the believing's role in guiding. False beliefs tend either to be unsuccessful (not-pragmatic) or to lead to imprudent, if not immoral, acts. Adding "true" to the belief means that the belief is epistemically successful in that the belief will accurately, in some particular way, represent or correspond to the state of affairs in the world. Of course, that true beliefs are epistemically successful does not guarantee that acts that invoke them will be successful, although having true beliefs would enhance the probability of practical success. That true beliefs are successful only tells us that the beliefs correspond in some way with reality. But then true belief is not intrinsically valuable, but valuable insofar as it leads to successful or, in the normative realm, moral acts.

OBLIGATIONS GROUNDED IN PRUDENCE

Some philosophers ground epistemic obligations in the prudent. The purpose of holding beliefs is for engaging in prudential action, not arriving at truth per se; attaining truth is probably (or at least most often) the best way to attain other goals. Epistemic obligations are thus hypothetical: if one wants to achieve a certain goal, believing the truth most often provides the best way to attain that goal. Hence, we are obliged (hypothetically, not categorically) to maximize contextually significant true beliefs and minimize false beliefs if we want to achieve our prudential goals.

Jack Meiland, in the course of arguing against the evidentialist view that epistemic obligations are fulfilled only by acquiring sufficient evidence, sees our epistemic obligations as grounded in the prudential. Practical factors or extrafactual considerations should always be consulted to determine what we are obligated to believe or have the right to believe. What we believe—about the facts of the situation, our values, our goals and purposes—helps us determine whether we ought to adopt a particular belief.[3]

He creates the example of the business owner Jones who one day discovers that Smith, his business partner of thirty-five years, appears to be secretly siphoning off money from the business. The evidence normally would be sufficient to justify to anyone an accusation of theft. At the same time, Jones realizes that if he believes that Smith is dishonest, Jones cannot hide this from Smith and this revelation would not only seriously alter his behavior toward Smith but probably destroy the business partnership itself. Jones concludes that he cannot afford the demise of the friendship, let alone the business, and decides not to believe that Smith stole money from the business. Indeed, he decides to believe that Smith did not steal any money at all. Jones, Meiland concludes, is justified in believing that his partner did not steal the money because the price of believing otherwise would be too high.

The prudential view holds that we should form or hold beliefs that enable achieving our preferences or goals. That is, we are justified in holding beliefs if they have prudential value. One might note two forms of the prudential grounding.[4] The first is that we are justified in forming or holding a belief when, if the belief happens to be true, we are benefited thereby. The truth of the belief is central to our being justified in holding it, even though we don't know it to be true or it is unlikely that it is true. For example, it is very unlikely that we will purchase the winning lotto ticket. Yet the belief that the ticket we purchase has the winning number leads us to buy the ticket, and only if we purchase the ticket and it has the winning number can we win. That is, the prudentialist of this first sort would argue that we are justified in believing that the lottery ticket is the winning one because, if it is true that it has the winning number, we will be benefited thereby. On this view, truth considerations regarding the ticket are relevant to prudential concerns because only if the proposition that is believed is true will the belief prove beneficial. The second case of being justified in holding a belief is when we are benefited by holding the belief itself, regardless of whether the proposition believed is true. Richard Feldman gives the example of a person who is planning to take his doctoral oral examination from a professor known to pass only 10 percent of those taking the exam.[5] Those who are confident about passing have a 20 percent passing rate. In such a case it would be prudential for prospective candidates to be optimistic about passing, since this would double their chances, regardless of whether their belief about passing is true. It is the very believing, not the truth, that proves beneficial.

Meiland's view is an example of the second, for in his story of the two businessmen, Smith was stealing from the company. Hence, Jones' belief about Smith is false. Yet, Meiland holds, Jones is justified in holding the belief that Smith was not stealing because Jones wants to maintain the partnership that is essential to the success of the firm. Without this belief, it would not be possible to continue operating the business as a partnership. Jones, Meiland argues, does not merely pretend to believe Smith's innocence; he in fact really believes it—for prudential reasons.

The prudential view faces numerous problems, not the least of which is that it alters the connection of belief with truth. On this view, the function of belief is to achieve diverse goals, such as successfully maintaining a business, saving a marriage even when appearances indicate infidelity (another example Meiland uses), passing the oral exam, or winning the lottery. If the belief works in that it furthers our goals or objectives, we are justified in holding it. But especially in the second type of prudential consideration, this is countenancing self-deception and rationalization, which is contrary to the goal of arriving at truth. It is, as Louis Pojman suggests, "a type of doxastic suicide which may only be justified in extreme circumstances. If there is something intrinsically wrong about lying (making it prima facie wrong), there is something intrinsically wrong with cognitive voliting [believing against evidence], either directly or indirectly."[6]

Meiland, however, rejects the characterization of his view as involving self-deception and rationalization. In rationalization, we justify on pragmatic grounds holding certain beliefs that would successfully hide from us the real motive for our actions. Meiland holds that the case of Jones is not a case of rationalization because he is not withholding or hiding understanding of his motives—his desire to maintain the partnership and the business—from himself. Jones knows what he is doing and why he is doing it. Neither is it self-deception, since Jones knows that the evidence is sufficient for believing that Smith is dishonest. Jones both knows the truth about the sufficient evidence against his belief and also knows his desires to maintain the business relationship, yet believes that the truth is that Jones is innocent.

But even if Meiland is correct that this is not a case of self-deception, the fact that Jones knows what is happening and proceeds to craft his belief otherwise suggests duplicity of some sort. When Meiland goes beyond Jones' mere assertion that Jones believes Smith innocent to the contention that Jones actually believes what is not true, transcending the particular facts of the case, it seems closer to what Sartre called bad faith, for Jones both knows the truth and asserts otherwise. Even so, Meiland asks, why is self-deception—or bad faith—wrong? What obligations does it violate? We can hold to both self-deception and epistemic obligations understood prudentially.

One result of this would be the counterintuitive view that epistemic good (understood in terms of obligations) or excellence (as a kind of epistemic virtue) is compatible with lying to ourselves or with self-deceit or bad faith. These hardly seem virtues. Furthermore, the primary role of belief is altered. Belief now is directed to problem solving and no longer is connected to truth except perhaps accidentally, insofar as the truth often is the best way to resolve problems. But this consequentialist view of truth runs counter to the fact that Meiland holds to a deontological understanding of epistemic obligations.[7]

Prudential grounds may indeed lead to beliefs that prove beneficial. We have already alluded to Feldman's example of a person who plans to take his doctoral oral examination with only a 10 percent chance of passing but who finds that it would be prudential to believe that he can pass the exam since this would double his chances. Prudentially he would be justified in believing that he will pass, for this would motivate him to perform better and statistically double his chances of passing. A prudential belief here functions as a means to self-motivation, and the end justifies the means. But it works only in a utilitarian way, not in a way that is truth-conducive or even conducive of moral behavior, for on this view it is the practical success of the belief, not its moral quality or truth, that is decisive. This approach would justify any belief, even the most egotistical or selfish, so long as it is prudential.

In effect, though it may be prudentially beneficial for candidates to hold a belief that they will pass, the holding of the belief confidently is still irrational, for the truth of the matter is that though their odds are improved (in Feldman's case, doubled), it remains unlikely that the candidates will pass. The prudential considerations do not alter the fact that it is irrational in this case for the candidates to believe that that they will pass. Increasing the odds of passing in this case is not tantamount to making it likely that they will pass, only more likely; the probability remains far below 50 percent, making passing quite unlikely. Thus, *practically* the candidates might face a belief dilemma: believing that they will pass will increase their motivation, while at the same time rational considerations determine the epistemic issue regarding what they are justified in believing or ought to be believe. But the epistemic obligation regarding truth remains clear.

But, it might be objected, in what sense is the belief that he will pass irrational? It is irrational in the sense that it involves believing something for which there is inadequate evidence, perhaps something contrary to adequate evidence, and which is false. If one understands rationality in terms of evidence or in terms of truth, then clearly the person who believes that he will pass given the above scenario believes irrationally. But the rejection of this is precisely Meiland's point: in rejecting the evidentialist claim, he is rejecting the contention that evidence need be sufficient for believing. Suppose, as Meiland and Feldman do, one conceives of rationality differently, that is, in terms of the consequences of the belief. In this case it is not so clear that the candidate believes irrationally, for believing that he will pass increases his odds of passing, even though the odds remain inadequate to provide sufficient grounds for believing that it is true that he will pass. In this case believing might be considered rational because it is beneficial to the student; it improves the likelihood of a favorable outcome.

The question raised here concerns how one would show that having true beliefs because they are true is more rational than believing because the belief is prudential. The link usually is made via ethical considerations. The contention is that we should not subject moral concerns to mere prudential concerns. Clifford supplies the example of the shipowner who puts aside all qualms about whether the ship he sends on a voyage is seaworthy or not; it would not be prudential for him to investigate whether it can arrive successfully at its destination. To investigate might delay the voyage or show that costly ship repairs are needed. So he sends the ship out to sea with its cargo and passengers. But, Clifford argues, that it was prudential for him, in light of his goals, objectives, and personal interests, to send the ship sailing does not justify his doing so; in failing in his epistemic obligation he has failed in his moral responsibility to investigate whether in fact the ship is seaworthy.[8] As Stevenson writes, "If we have prudential obligations with respect to our beliefs because of prudential obligations concerning actions, but no moral obligations concerning our beliefs; then either we do not have moral obligations with respect to action or somehow there must be a split between thought and action in the case of morals which does not exist in the case of prudence."[9]

Trudy Govier responds that there is no logical link between epistemic and moral concerns. We are quite within our epistemic rights to hold that we should believe what will make ourselves or others happy, or what will enable us to function successfully in our society.[10] But although she is correct in holding that there is no logical link, there surely is a link, in that we rarely praise self-deception or the suppression of truth considerations for personal advantage. It is true, as Govier replies, that this presupposes a priority of the moral perspective. She asks, why not preference the prudential in cases where self-deception makes one happier or leads to a longer life? One might respond that another way of seeing the case of self-deception is that the conflict is not between the prudential and the ethical, but between two conceptions of the ethical, the deontological and the utilitarian. The prudential here is assessed in terms of good results, so that one invokes an ethical perspective that values good outcomes. Self-deception can be justified on act utilitarian grounds in that (or better, when) self-deception regarding one's beliefs actually succeeds. From a deontological point of view, however, the ends do not justify the means; self-deception remains suspect in that it involves a denial of the truth. In short, the prudential can be understood as a form of the ethical, interpreted in utilitarian terms, but the notion of epistemic obligations with which we are working is not utilitarian but deontological.

Even the utilitarian perspective is suspect. Suppose, as is likely, that the candidate fails to pass despite his belief. He will not end up being happy but will likely be unhappy when he discovers that his belief was false. His false belief improved the likelihood that he would pass, but it did not make it likely that he would pass. But his belief was the latter, not the former, and hence is not only false but disheartening when he discovers that it is false. And even if he passed, he must realize that though this belief improved the likelihood of passing, it was a false belief in that it did not make it likely he would pass. Reflection on this would show that his prudential belief was not a case of epistemic excellence.

If truth is understood in a utilitarian or pragmatic sense, it is no longer the primary concern; successful outcomes are what matters. The truth connected with belief is now understood pragmatically in terms of being a means. But our epistemic obligations are not about what we would like to happen: such "a policy of believing on the basis of preference would make wishful thinking the norm. It would not revise our rationality but play havoc with it."[11] If the deontological grounding of the obligation is to be preserved, a different grounding for epistemic obligations is required.

OBLIGATIONS GROUNDED IN MORALITY

A third view grounds epistemic obligations in morality. Those who ground epistemic obligations in morality contend that since we cannot sever beliefs from action, and since we are accountable for our actions, we are accountable for our beliefs. Beliefs influence our actions; "if a belief is not realized immediately in open deeds, it is stored up for the guidance of the future."[12] Yet exactly how beliefs affect actions is a matter of disputed philosophical discussion. Whereas some hold that beliefs by themselves motivate action, others, following Hume, argue that rational belief by itself cannot motivate action. Jane might believe that this bus will take her downtown, but unless she desires to go downtown, the belief alone will not get her to enter the bus. Desires must accompany beliefs to bring about action.[13] At the same time, desires alone do not produce action, for her desire to go downtown does not indicate which actions Jane is to take to realize the desire. Belief supplies that guiding element. She might believe that taking the bus, although slower than taking a taxi, is cheaper, and she has time but not a lot of money. Her beliefs about time and money guide which action she will take. Thus, although beliefs influence our action even if in no other way than that we would take the action of asserting or affirming that belief if asked,[14] the relationship goes far beyond asserting to affecting how we behave.

Precisely how epistemic obligations relate to moral obligations is a matter of some controversy. Roderick Chisholm treats the relation between epistemic and moral obligations differently in various places. In "Epistemic Statements and the Ethics of Belief," he treats the relation between them as analogical, as we did above.[15] In "Firth and the Ethics of Belief," he treats epistemic obligations as a subspecies of ethical beliefs.[16]

Suppose one follows Chisholm in holding that epistemic obligations are a special case or subspecies of moral obligations. On this view epistemic appraisal is an instance of moral appraisal. One might object that this cannot be the relationship holding between the two types of obligations, for one could fail the epistemic obligation while satisfying the moral obligation.[17] This might occur in a variety of ways. June might hold a false belief (in which case she failed in her epistemic obligation) but still act morally: she might falsely believe that you are drowning and then jump in to rescue you, an action for which she is praiseworthy. This false belief might be justified (she sees you thrashing around in the water practicing your water ballet) or unjustified (she just happens to spot you in the water and jumps in). She also might hold a false belief about something that is quite trivial and then act or not act on that belief: she might falsely believe that a pen lying on your desk is yours and consequently not take it because she does not want to offend you, though the pen is not really yours at all but an orphan pen. She has satisfied her moral obligation by leaving it in place—she did not yield to the temptation to personally appropriate it, but not taking the pen is quite trivial. Or she might hold a false belief and act on it, but the action is morally inconsequential: she might believe falsely (since, unknown to her, heavy rains are expected in the afternoon) that today is a good time to sealcoat her asphalt driveway, but whether she then does so today or tomorrow seems not to matter in any moral sense. In effect, she might entertain any number of false beliefs that lead to moral actions, lead to actions that are basically moral trivial, or have no moral import.

Clifford responds that such individual cases, while harmless in themselves, contribute to a pattern of "credulity that weakens the epistemic fiber." Our beliefs are public, not private matters. Even the most seemingly trivial or obscure belief can have moral effects. "It is not only the leader of men, statesman, philosopher, or poet, that owes this bounden duty to mankind. Every rustic who delivers in the village alehouse his slow, infrequent sentences, may help to kill or keep alive the fatal superstitions which clog his race. Every hard-worked wife of an artisan may transmit to her children beliefs which shall knit society together, or rend it in pieces."[18] Clifford's point is that our obligation to believe on sufficient evidence is grounded in our general moral obligations to society. In making myself credulous, I "must sink back into savagery." Failing in our epistemic obligations leads "to habitual want of care in others about the truth of what is told to me. . . . The credulous man is father to the liar and the cheat; he lives in the bosom of his family, and it is no marvel if he should become even as they are."[19] "No real belief, however trifling and fragmentary it may seem, is ever truly insignificant; it prepares us to receive more of its like, confirms those which resembled it before, and weakens others; and so gradually it lays a stealthy train in our inmost thoughts, which may some day explode into overt action, and leave its stamp upon our character for ever."[20] The particular belief may be harmless, but believing in general without sufficient evidence—as a general practice—is not harmless.

More practically, and in less purple language, one might put Clifford's point with respect to the last case above: if it is false that this is a good day to sealcoat her driveway, Jane might waste the coating. This action contributes, however slightly, to global warming because she has to buy another petroleum product to redo it. And how one contributes to global ecology is a moral issue.

But even in such a case the remote potential for harm is insufficient to establish that epistemic failure yields moral culpability: "if it were, not only drunken driving, but owning a car, would be morally culpable."[21] There are just too many cases where failure to believe the contextually significant truth does not lead to harmful or immoral actions. Though one may form bad epistemic habits, not all failures of epistemic obligations lead to or reinforce bad epistemic habits. The best one can say is that many instances of epistemic obligations are instances of moral obligations, in which case moral obligations would provide at best a partial grounding for epistemic obligations, and then only in those cases where epistemic failure leads to moral failure.

A second view is that epistemic obligations are correlated with moral obligations. When persons fail in their epistemic obligations, they are not necessarily thereby morally at fault. However, there is a significant correlation between the two, so that failing epistemically correlates with failing morally. What we have just said in criticism of the view that epistemic obligations are a subspecies of moral obligations applies to this view as well.[22] Someone may believe a proposition unjustifiably but not be morally at fault. The unjustifiability of the belief might arise from that for which the person is not accountable, for example, cognitive inadequacy, where the person has sincerely misjudged the significance of the evidence or accepted the apparently but not actually well-grounded beliefs of the community. Furthermore, as above, the case may be trivial, where no one is hurt, or the failure to meet the epistemic obligation is not one for which we would hold the person morally accountable.

A third option, espoused by Susan Haack, is the overlap thesis. On this view epistemic obligations sometimes overlap with moral obligations in that when one fails in one's epistemic obligation, one might also fail in one's moral obligation because of the harm done in the epistemic failure, and thereby that person incurs moral blame for the epistemic failure. The Milam example in chapter 1, as well as Clifford's case of the irresponsible shipowner, are cases in point. So understood, the overlap thesis would provide only a partial ground for epistemic obligation. It is only a contingent fact that epistemic obligations may incur harm in any given case. The overlap view leaves a basis for only those epistemic obligations whose failure to be actualized would result in harm, for then persons are obligated to believe only when harm might result from failing to do so. In effect, although this view would not provide a basis for all epistemic obligations, it does provide a grounding for obligations where harm might result.

What underlies Haack's discussion, as well as both of the previous discussions on grounding epistemic obligations in moral action, is the reduction of moral obligation to utilitarian concerns about committing acts that result in no harm (or at least no overall greater harm than benefit). In the first two cases, what the objector can show is that there are instances where persons have failed in their epistemic obligations but where no discernible harm is done. But this utilitarian approach may compromise the character of both epistemic and moral obligations. When both are treated deontologically, the justification rests on more than the notion of moral responsibility for the harm done or not done. Although Clifford at times bends in the direction of harms done, still it is the deontological dimension of moral obligations that remains critically central to the comparison.

Objections to Basing Epistemic Obligations on Moral Obligations

Philosophers have raised serious questions about basing epistemic obligations on moral obligations. One problem with grounding epistemic obligations in general on moral obligations is the possible conflict between moral obligations and epistemic obligations. For example, suppose I have a moral obligation to my society to quell a widespread epidemic (in 2009 pandemic flu was the medical worry; recently it is cases of drug-resistant TB) that brings slow but agonizing death. To accomplish this I need to discover quickly the causal pathogens. But suppose that the only person who knows this information will not reveal it. The question then arises as to how I am going to obtain the needed information. Some have held that it is reasonable to use what recently have been euphemistically termed "enhanced interrogation methods" to gain the information. The willingness to use such methods, the objection continues, indicates that the epistemic obligation to know the truth outweighs the moral obligation to treat the person not merely as a means but also as an end or as intrinsically valuable. Only if I refuse to torture that person to get the needed information, on the ground that it would be immoral to do so, would I affirm the precedence of moral obligations over epistemic obligations.

Yet this is not a clear countercase, for interrogators might hold that their need to know the truth about the pathogens is itself based on a moral obligation to society, and hence what they really have is a conflict between two moral obligations, one to society and the other to the reluctant scientist. The epistemic obligation derives its sanction, in part, from being necessary for the greater societal good.

Feldman suggests another possible conflict.[23] We have a moral obligation to trust our friends and family, and trusting them means forming the belief that what they say is true. But epistemically we might not be so justified in believing that what they say is true; we might have overwhelming counterevidence to what they affirm. So a conflict might result between moral and epistemic obligations.

A reply to this objection cannot be straightforward, since it involves serious questions about the role and primacy of family obligations (what is termed in Chinese thought *xiao* or filial piety) in determining our obligations to achieve the highest good. On the one hand, there are solid traditions that hold family obligations in greatest esteem. Kongzi says that filial piety ranks higher as an obligation than public justice.

> The Duke of She said to Confucius, "Among my people there is one we call 'Upright Gong.' When his father stole a sheep, he reported him to the authorities."
>
> Confucius replied, "Among my people, those whom we consider 'upright' are different from this. Fathers cover up for their sons, and the sons cover up for their fathers. Uprightness is to be found in this."[24]

When fundamental societal relationships are jeopardized, we have a moral obligation to hide the truth from others. Similarly, Socrates is aghast that Euthyphro would consider taking his father to court for murdering a slave through negligence. Only a person of superior wisdom, who was absolutely certain about his knowledge of religious truths like piety, would even consider initiating such a prosecution.[25] Socrates is quite skeptical that Euthyphro possesses such knowledge and attempts to convince him (albeit unsuccessfully) that he lacks the qualifications he so proudly proclaims. Euthyphro's failure to know what piety is disqualifies him from making the appropriate judgment regarding the conflict between piety and justice. Thus, one interpretation of these texts is that important moral voices affirm that moral duties may well conflict with epistemic duties and that in some cases moral duties to family should take precedence. At the same time, as the Duke of She comments, there are voices that say that a moral obligation to trust and respect our family does not mean that we should put aside all considerations of truth and justice. Where we take the evidence to the contrary to be sufficient and the trust is not warranted, considerations of truth win out. We have obligations to trust others, but these can be overridden by obligations with respect to believing the truth.

As we noted above, it is not at all clear with respect to these cases that the kind of conflict Feldman envisions between epistemic and moral obligations is a generally observed one. Indeed, the conflict with regard to filial piety and justice is not so much between moral duties on the one side and epistemic duties on the other as between different conceptions of moral duties and the role truth plays in that conflict. On the one hand, Kongzi and Socrates rank our duties to our family as among our highest duties, leaving concerns for public justice to play a lesser role. In this case truth serves justice and is hidden to preserve the primacy of filial piety. On the other hand, other persons give preference to alternative duties such as upholding justice, where telling the truth plays a substantial role. In both cases, the primary conflict lies between two competing moral obligations, filial piety and public justice, not between moral and epistemic obligations.

Although these examples can be given other interpretations, other possible cases lurk in the wings. We might appeal to the behavior of Dr. Gregory House, the main character in the TV drama *House*. A hospital diagnostician, he has a persistent desire to know and often invokes this desire even when a pressing moral issue might indicate otherwise. For example, he might refuse to hand over a corpse to the family who desires to bury it intact, and proceed with a destructive autopsy, not because it is necessary for any moral or legal end, but just because he has a desire to know what caused the death of the victim. The conflict here is between House's desire to know (to have true beliefs) and the moral concerns of the family. Let us, then, grant that there are possible cases of conflict between epistemic and moral obligations, especially where knowledge or having true beliefs is treated as an end in itself and not as a means to anything else.

Feldman then raises a broader objection about connecting epistemic obligations with moral obligations. In the process of holding epistemic obligations unique, Feldman argues that while we may hold that duties of a particular kind, such as moral duties, may trump other moral duties, we cannot hold that there is a ranking between different types of duties or obligations. Duties within discrete categories can be compared, but we cannot comparatively weigh, for example, moral duties in importance with epistemic categories: we cannot judge duties between categories. Accordingly, he rejects the thesis that moral obligations ought to trump epistemic obligations.

But we can and do make comparisons or weightings between different types of duties. Consider, for example, the weighting a dictator undertakes as she considers whether to secretly and violently eliminate her opponents. She may say pragmatically, "I ought to eliminate the opposition if I am to stay comfortably in power." If Feldman is correct, she can compare but cannot weigh this pragmatic *ought* with the moral *ought* of whether she should kill them. But this seems wrong; surely she has grounds not only for comparison in this case, but also for weighing moral obligations over pragmatic obligations. It may be pragmatically useful for her to eliminate the opposition, but it is immoral to do it on the proffered pragmatic grounds. It may be useful, we might say, but still you should not do it, and the moral *ought* should take precedence as having the greater weight. Further, in basing epistemic obligations on moral obligations, we are not weighing them against each other in terms of some ultimate ought, but rather grounding the one on the other. We may do this in terms of individual acts or in broader terms of epistemic virtue.

This weighing of cross-category obligations is just an instance of the larger process of the weighing of cross-category values that characterizes daily life. When I shop for groceries, I ask myself whether I am willing to pay $4.49 for a bag of oranges. The value relationship holds between money and fruit, and the question that arises is how do I compare the values of these diverse types of objects. I lack any algorithm for calculation; I possess no set standard for the value of an orange. In each transaction I have to ask what I am willing to pay for an item. Even where prices reflect supply and demand, my own choice of how to spend my money invokes cross-category value decisions that often are independent of supply and demand. Yet the weighing is not entirely arbitrary; were the oranges priced at $25 for the bag, I would not hesitate to walk on by—though others more wealthy than I might stop and shop. The same consideration applies to comparing time with other values. How much should I be paid for my time? I set a cross-category value when I market my time and skills. In short, since value judgments across categories are a standard feature of economic and social life, the fact that we are connecting epistemic with moral obligations is not thereby faulted by the cross-category nature of the grounding.

Nicholas Wolterstorff entirely rejects basing epistemic obligations on moral obligations.[26] His general point is that whereas moral obligations have to do with accountability, such that the agent is praise- or blameworthy, epistemic obligations do not connect with accountability. They may connect with character but not with praise- or blameworthiness. To make his case he distinguishes between paradigm obligations and responsibility obligations. The former have to do with proper functioning or meeting a norm; what is involved is propriety or impropriety, not accountability. For example, "'You ought to be walking on it in two weeks'—said by a physician as he finishes binding up a person's sprained ankle. 'It should have black spots all over its shell, not just around the rim'—said by one person, ladybug in hand, explaining to another person what ladybugs look like."[27] The obligation in these cases is not one where failure leads to being blameworthy; neither the person nor the ladybug has failed in intent. They may have failed in measuring up to a norm, but they face no moral accountability for that. Failure to measure up to an expected standard may have nothing to do with intent, and when this is so there are no responsibility obligations. Responsibility obligations, on the other hand, are the type of obligation that one is accountable for meeting or not meeting; meeting or failing to meet them is a matter of intent and reflects on a person's moral character in a way that is praise- or blameworthy. They are moral obligations. Wolterstorff's point is that although all responsibility obligations are moral obligations, the converse is not true. Both paradigm obligations and responsibility obligations may involve moral character, but involving moral character does not by itself lead to accountability. Holding false beliefs, for example, about moral principles or having bad desires contributes to a bad character, but having a bad character is not necessarily blameworthy; it depends on intent of action.

Epistemic obligations, Wolterstorff holds, are paradigm obligations, not responsibility obligations. Although false beliefs—for example, the kinds of beliefs Milam has about black persons—contribute to or indicate a bad character, Milam is not accountable for them because he cannot and did not choose those beliefs. He might evince epistemic malformation in his failure to satisfy a norm, but he is not guilty of moral failure in holding these beliefs. Moral failure arises with the formation of intentions to act on his beliefs. Whereas we voluntarily adopt responsibility obligations with the intent to carry out the obligation, we do not adopt or fulfill epistemic obligations voluntarily. We may entertain false beliefs and beliefs arising from bad desires, but we are not at fault or blameworthy in holding these beliefs. We may have responsibility for our beliefs, but where we have responsibility for beliefs, they come indirectly through "practices of inquiry." It is in these practices that we are morally obligated to investigate thoroughly and carefully, but the responsibility is not for holding or not holding the belief itself.

As we shall see in the next chapter, Wolterstorff is correct in holding that we have responsibility obligations for practices of inquiry, though for him these are not epistemic obligations. But he is mistaken, first, in failing to see that these practices are themselves inherently connected with epistemic obligations. We have obligations to see to it that our beliefs are justified in terms of correct practices of inquiry *because* we have epistemic obligations to arrive at truth. These practices are not intrinsically valuable, but have a derivative value from the obligation to hold true beliefs. We focus on the practices of inquiry to arrive at true belief, not for the practices themselves. Hence, we are accountable not merely for engaging in proper inquiry, but also for the beliefs that result from the practices.

Second, Wolterstorff is mistaken, for, as Feldman points out, although Wolterstorff's paradigm obligations are oughts in virtue of being norms, they are not properly termed obligations. Unlike obligation statements, they cannot be paraphrased into sentences that express obligations.[28] They reflect norms, but there is nothing obligatory about them. The person might view the norm as being able to walk on his ankle and the ladybug having black spots, but these do not create obligatory actions to meet the norm; the ladybug is not obliged in any way with respect to the dots on its back, nor is the person obligated with respect to his ankle. Hence, paradigm obligations cannot constitute the proper category for epistemic obligations, for epistemic obligations are not mere reflections of norms but true obligations. Though he thinks they don't amount to much since they have nothing to do with accountability,[29] they do amount to much, for they invoke accountability. It makes sense to say that one ought to believe contextually significant truths; it is not merely a paradigm norm.

Third, although Wolterstorff is willing to grant that epistemic failures along with moral failures reflect on a person's character, he is unwilling to assign the blame to the former that he would assign to the latter. The reason he gives is that we don't have control over our beliefs in the way that we have intentional control over our actions. We are belief victims. Let us return to the case of Emmett Till we developed in chapter 1. Both Milam and Bryant had moral obligations not to harm Till. Wolterstorff would agree—responsibility obligations are moral obligations. But their immoral actions arose out of their racist beliefs, and though they might have held these beliefs through ignorance, one can reasonably argue, contrary to Wolterstorff, that they are responsible for the racist beliefs, for they are part of their defective moral character. Wolterstoff admits that both false ethical principles and evil desires contribute to defective moral character. He sees the perpetrators as mere victims, products of their environment, so that it is inappropriate "to *blame* them on that account, to hold them responsible and accountable, because they aren't. It would be right to do that only if one believed that they were not purely a victim in this regard."[30] But though in some cases we may not have some control over our beliefs, it is hard to see that Milam and Bryant (or anyone) are mere victims in regard to most of their (and our) epistemic beliefs. His retort is that they are cases of moral malformation, reflecting negatively on their character, but for that alone they are not blameworthy, since those beliefs were arrived at through no fault of their own, but only through ignorance. Only if they are culpable with regard to their practices of inquiry are they accountable, and then for that practice or their intentions and not for the resulting beliefs. But this is viable only if one takes a radically subjectivist view of epistemic obligations and holds that we lack any significant control over our beliefs, a view we will critique in chapter 5. Milam and Bryant should have (and could have) known better, not merely in that they should have had better practices of inquiry, but because they failed to hold to principles available to their fundamental moral intuitions.

Part of the critical contention here is to what extent we have control over our character and beliefs. Wolterstorff believes that we don't have control over our beliefs, and hence insofar as beliefs play a role in forming our character, we do not have responsibility for that character. Our responsibility grows out of our intentions, not our beliefs. To the contrary, we will argue in chapter 5 that we do have significant (though not complete) control over our beliefs and that this control is sufficient to hold people accountable for their beliefs. We have responsibility for both the epistemic and moral dimensions of our character. And indeed, it is to character that shortly we will turn to find a ground for our epistemic obligations.

In short, none of these objections to linking epistemic and moral obligations succeed. We do have epistemic obligations, and in many cases the two types of obligations are connected directly in that epistemic obligations have moral implications; upholding or failing to uphold them often, though not always, has consequences that are moral in nature. This grounds some epistemic obligations on moral obligations. However, this view is not fully adequate to account for the relationship between the two obligations, for since not all failures to fulfill epistemic obligations incur failures of moral obligations, the view is not a robust enough relation on which to base *all* epistemic obligations. The grounding is contingent, not necessary.

Relationships of Analogy and Consequences

We might summarize our discussion to this point. Our discussion of epistemic obligations in the previous chapter suggests that significant analogies hold between the two kinds of obligations, and in particular that an analysis of the types of moral obligations we possess helps us to understand our epistemic obligations. The analogy grounding goes further, suggesting that since epistemic appraisal is analogous to though independent of ethical appraisal, the ethical grounds the epistemic. At the same time, making epistemic obligations and ethical obligations merely analogous has the fatal weakness that the two are independent of each other.[31] If they are independent, the one cannot be grounded on the other; they simply lack any connection other than similarity. Thus, the relationship of analogy helps us understand the two obligations but is inadequate for grounding the one on the other. There must be some connection between the two types of obligations.

Above, we noted Haack's overlap thesis, which specifies a kind of connection. This needs specification, for not only is the overlap thesis ambiguous (which overlaps which?), but to say that they overlap again fails to provide significant specificity of the connection for grounding. What Haack, Clifford, and other defenders contend is that the specificity can be found in that beliefs can and do have consequences for our actions. Beliefs play a causal role in our intentional actions in that we act out of our beliefs, either consciously or subconsciously. These actions, in turn, can be morally evaluated. Since we have moral obligations with respect to our intentional actions, and since beliefs are causally connected to these actions, we have obligations with respect to the beliefs: in particular, that they be true. This applies not only to beliefs that are currently affecting actions, but also to beliefs that are stored up and have the potential for influencing future actions. This causal connection between belief and morally evaluable action provides a specific grounding connection between the two sets of obligations.

But if the consequence thesis is correct, the obligations are not necessarily or universally but only contingently connected with moral obligations. As we argued above, only some (though many) epistemic acts have moral consequences, and not all epistemic failures are morally significant. Many individual failures are trivial, though as Clifford points out, forming a habit of epistemic failure is quite a serious matter. At the same time, the connection is not trivial, for often believing falsely causes harm and, even more frequently, believing truly produces good, and present beliefs may have such consequences for future actions. Since we never know which of our beliefs will have an impact on future actions that are morally evaluable, it is critical that our beliefs be true. That is, the grounding applies not only to beliefs that cause harm, but more broadly to beliefs that could have moral consequences. This greatly widens the beliefs so grounded. We can conclude that a causal connection between belief and action and a possible normative evaluation of the action is sufficient to provide a significant grounding for epistemic obligations. We are obligated to believe the truth and avoid falsity because of the actual or possible moral consequences of doing so.

But we want to say more than make this utilitarian point. As Aristotle pointed out, close working connections hold between intellectual or practical virtue and moral virtue.

They are integrated in that believing the truth is necessary for making wise moral choices and ultimately for achieving moral excellence. One can, of course, make the right choice based on false beliefs, but in such cases the good result is more a product of good luck than of the realization of excellence in life. This suggests that we need to go beyond an act-causal relation to holding not only that epistemic obligations have direct or possible implications for moral acts, but that both epistemic and moral obligations connect to human flourishing, to what it is to be human. Only humans can have obligations of which they are aware, and the practices associated with fulfilling those obligations, whether epistemic or moral, are central not only to living humanly, but to realizing our humanness in ways that are excellent. That is, both obligations pursue excellence, whether epistemic or moral. This then brings us to the possibility of developing a concept of epistemic virtue that integrally connects with moral virtue.

OBLIGATIONS GROUNDED IN EPISTEMIC AND MORAL VIRTUE

A fourth option grounds epistemic obligations in the normative properties of the persons who engage in actions, hold beliefs, and seek to attain knowledge. Moral acts, justified beliefs, and knowledge follow from the properly motivated and successful exercise of a person's character or virtues. The objective is to be virtuous.[32]

In the previous section the obligation to hold true beliefs was seen to arise from the moral implications of our beliefs and the resulting accountability for acts. Virtue theorists point out that the primary objects of evaluation are not acts but the agent's inner traits; both morality and knowledge are to be assessed in terms of the respective personal virtues that characterize the persons doing the acts and holding the beliefs or seeking to attain knowledge. Hence, a more basic feature needs to be addressed, namely, the proper development, motivation, and successful exercise of the virtues of epistemic agents. Epistemic evaluation of any belief is not act-based but person-based, grounded in the underlying epistemic and moral virtues possessed by persons holding the belief.

In developing this view, Linda Zagzebski not only sides with those who connect epistemic and moral obligations but envisions an almost indistinguishable relation between epistemology and ethics. Rejecting attempts to differentiate intellectual from moral virtues, she provides an account of virtues that subsumes the intellectual virtues under moral virtues. This enables her to show the relations between and integration of these traditionally distinguished virtues.[33]

She defines virtue as "a deep and enduring acquired excellence of a person, involving a characteristic motivation to produce a certain desired end and reliable success in bringing about that end."[34] Her understanding of virtue emphasizes two critical aspects: both the motivational aspect (which initiates and directs the act) and the success aspect (achieved not through luck but resulting from the motivation). She applies this definition to both moral and intellectual virtues traditionally conceived. She develops a virtue understanding of belief and knowledge parallel to a virtue understanding of ethics; epistemic judgments address the virtue of the agents, the agents' motivation, and the success of the cognitive act. "Right cognitive acts are, roughly, what persons with intellectual virtues would or might do in certain circumstances."[35] When acting with proper motivation and when this successfully leads to true beliefs, the person acts with intellectual virtue.

What has this to do with grounding epistemic obligations? Since epistemic virtues are a form or forms of moral virtues, and since we have moral duties with respect to both being virtuously motivated and acting virtuously (so that the virtues have a successful outcome), we likewise have moral duties with respect to both being virtuously motivated intellectually and engaging in epistemic practices that are truth-conducive, practices that will successfully result in true beliefs or knowledge. The mere holding of the belief does not fulfill the duty; it must be held in a virtuous matter, that is, "from the right motive and with the right understanding."[36]

People who want truth, or, more broadly, have a desire to have cognitive contact with reality, should be motivated by intellectual virtues in their belief-forming processes. The central or foundational motivational component of the intellectual virtues is the motivation to know, a motivation that includes holding true beliefs. This motivation is not valuable because of its outcomes or because of other external goods; it is an intrinsic good. One might say that our epistemic obligation is to form the appropriate virtues, rooted in the intrinsically good motivation to know and understand.

What, then, of beliefs? Does holding true beliefs in and of itself constitute a duty? Is being motivated toward the truth a conditional or categorical imperative? Zagzebski says that we have a duty to hold true beliefs if and only if it is unjustified to disbelieve them. And a belief is justified when it is "what a person who is motivated by intellectual virtue, and who has the understanding of his cognitive situation that a virtuous person would have, might believe in like circumstances."[37] She does not abandon justification of beliefs. But beliefs are not justified in themselves, apart from agents; persons are justified in holding beliefs when motivated by intellectual virtues that include "intellectual carefulness, perseverance, humility, vigor, flexibility, courage, and thoroughness, as well as open-mindedness, fair-mindedness, insightfulness, and the virtues opposed to wishful thinking, obtuseness, and conformity."[38] Since intellectual virtues are undifferentiable from moral virtues, those who fail in obtaining intellectual virtue have failed also in their larger, moral virtue, for they have failed to develop beliefs from the proper motivation.

Epistemic obligations, then, are grounded in morality, not in terms of particular outcomes or duties, but in terms of the excellence of agents who have and exercise the appropriate intellectual virtues. A belief is not justified apart from the agent but rather through the virtues of the believer. The evaluative property of beliefs derives from intellectual virtues, and since intellectual virtues are a form or subset of moral virtues, their evaluation is a moral evaluation.

Our epistemic duty is not simply to hold true beliefs and avoid false beliefs but to believe or know in a virtuous manner—successfully from the right motives and right understanding. Epistemic obligations are grounded in the greater good of knowledge or connecting with reality. Developing the proper motivations and successful epistemic practices are part of achieving both moral and epistemic goodness or well-being.

Questions about a Virtue Grounding

Many philosophers argue that most, if not all, of our beliefs are formed involuntarily; we simply do not have control over our beliefs. Whether the stronger thesis—that we exercise no control over our beliefs—is true we have good reason to question, but suppose we grant that many of our beliefs are formed passively. They result not from an agent's conscious action but from events that happen to us. Seeing a dog in the corner simply leads to the belief that a dog is sitting in the corner. I might not have exercised any of my intellectual virtues—open-mindedness, courageous persistence, analysis of detail—in order to arrive at this true belief. Lack of control over our beliefs, however, raises a problem for Zagzebski's account, for her account requires virtuous knowers to actively exercise their intellectual virtues. So though she might be correct with regard to beliefs that result from virtuous acts, her analysis will not cover all beliefs, in particular, beliefs over which we have not exercised voluntary control.

Of course, this objection will continue to leave epistemic obligations in place. One can argue that the agent still ought to exercise proper epistemic motivation and arrive successfully at true beliefs, realizing that in some cases belief control is not only impractical but impossible. But it does suggest that where belief control is possible the obligation remains incumbent on us. (Although we will question and reject the stronger skeptical claims made in this paragraph in chapter 5, we will work with the commonly held view here as a criticism).

Zagzebski is less bothered by this objection than would appear, for two reasons. First, even if the belief itself is not in our control, the intellectual virtues are in our control to fundamentally the same extent that the moral virtues are in our control. "There is no reason to think that intellectual courage, perseverance, honesty, or sincerity are any less voluntary than courage, perseverance, honesty, and sincerity considered as moral virtues."[39] Responsible control thus is not an issue with regard to the exercise of intellectual virtues, for it does not differ from responsible control over moral virtues, of which the first are a subset. Second, she is concerned with justified belief in the context of knowledge. Thus, the kind of passive beliefs that she sees as often presented as paradigmatic counterevidence to her view, particularly perceptual beliefs, are not an issue for her, for she is dubious that these function as the paradigms for knowledge. Perceptual beliefs are located toward the same end of the scale of voluntariness as are actions that arise without choice or deliberation. Voluntary control is not so much a matter of choice as of responsibility. In the case of morality, if one is morally responsible, then the action is voluntary to the degree of responsibility. Similarly, if one is epistemically responsible, then the holding of the belief is voluntary. Following what she takes as Aristotle's view, she wants to reverse the relation between responsibility and being voluntary; responsibility, not choice, is the key factor.

A second concern is that the nature of the epistemic obligation found in the virtue epistemic account is not really an obligation. As we have seen, we want to hold that persons are accountable not only for their actions but also for their beliefs. They are to believe contextually significant truths, not hold false beliefs, and believe truths that will enhance their lives as part of liberal learning. The virtue account alters this; our epistemic duty is not to hold true beliefs and avoid false beliefs, but to believe or know in a virtuous manner—from the right motives and right understanding. For Zagzebski a belief that satisfies an epistemic duty is a belief that a person motivated by intellectual virtue and possessing understanding would have in that situation. And this is rooted in the general motivation to know.

But why are intellectual virtues to be valued? Zagzebski suggests two responses. The first is that intellectual virtues might be valued because of their role in creating human happiness. Intellectual virtues are either a constituent part of the flourishing life, or else they are the means to such a life. In the first instance, human flourishing is a complex notion that allows intellectual virtues to be a part of it. Persons who are motivated by intellectual (and moral) virtues and are reliably successful in bringing about their ends are thereby living a life that achieves its end of happiness or human flourishing. The very motivations themselves are part of human happiness. In the second instance, the intellectual (and moral) virtues provide the means whereby we flourish. On either of these views we can recommend that the individual develop intellectual virtues, because they are essential in one way or another to human flourishing and, since they are defined as being reliably successful, they bring about true beliefs.

Zagzebski's own preference is for a slightly different take. The goodness of intellectual (and moral) virtues is not derived from its connection to other goods, such as happiness, human flourishing, or knowledge, but is to be found in their motivational features. The very motivation to open-mindedness or to benevolence is itself a good thing. The virtues are also to be valued because good motives are reliably successful in achieving their aims; this is part of their excellence. They are good, "independent of any good outside the agent."[40] They are not good as a means to anything else but as partially constitutive of the intellectual life.

The obligations attach to the motives rather than to the holding of beliefs. This might look like Chisholm's "trying" again, but it is not, for in Zagzebski's account the virtuous motivation is linked by definition with a successful outcome, so that an epistemically virtuous person will succeed in holding true beliefs or attaining knowledge. This specification of success—that they are truth-conducive—addresses the problem whether acts of intellectual virtue lead us back to truth, so that they can be part of our epistemic obligation. Intellectual virtues "lead to the use of reliable belief-forming procedures."[41] If they did not, she argues, we would not consider them to be virtues at all. It is because they are excellences—excellences in reaching truth successfully—that we recommend them as virtues. "Any evidence of an intellectual virtue that is not truth conducive (or knowledge conducive) is more reasonably interpreted as evidence that such a trait is not a virtue than as evidence that some intellectual virtues are not truth conducive."[42] They may not be truth-conducive in any particular given case, but one must consider their function in the long run, over time.

Can this account of epistemic virtue provide a basis for epistemic obligations? It provides an account of epistemic good or excellence, but do we have an obligation to have and exercise the motivation to know the truth or be connected with reality and to succeed at it? Zagzebski rejects the notion that achieving knowledge is a natural human desire, though being motivated to achieve knowledge or wisdom lies within our power. But though it is not a natural desire, it can be seen to be a part of human fulfillment or flourishing. Hence, the degree to which a virtue account provides a basis for epistemic obligations rests on the contention that we have an obligation to further that which enables us to flourish as human persons. And, prima facie, this is a reasonable belief. The connection between epistemic and moral virtues, however, differs from the previous account, for there is no direct obligation to hold particular beliefs. The obligation is more indirect, namely, to become morally and epistemically virtuous, a position from which in the successful employment of our virtues we will hold true beliefs.

CONCLUSION

When we apply the results of this chapter to our initial cases in chapter 1, as well as to traditionally highlighted cases, the complexity of determining epistemic obligations becomes apparent. The fact that Clifford's shipowner violated his epistemic obligations by holding a false belief is more than merely a matter of failing prudentially. His epistemic accountability is rooted in the moral accountability he has for what happened to the ship and its passengers, for had he exercised his epistemic responsibility to hold a true, justified belief, in all likelihood the passengers would have arrived safely, or if not, it would not have been due to the unseaworthiness of the ship. If we invoke a virtue account, we might hold that the owner is epistemically culpable because he did not manifest the virtues or act out of the motivations that virtuous persons would have had in this case. He exhibited neither intellectual concern to understand the state of the ship, intellectual sobriety to carefully inquire about its state, nor intellectual determination to press for a clear assessment of seaworthiness. Epistemic excellence goes beyond whether the evidence warranted sending the ship to sea; it extends to the epistemic excellences the shipowner should have manifested.

Whether there was a failure of epistemic obligations in the Neumann case is less clear. One might consider the case prudentially. It might be the case that people in Neumann's circle of friends have a better chance of being healed if they entertain the belief that prayer is the primary way to achieve healing. God responds to faithful prayers, so that prudentially their chances of being healed in this fashion are increased by adopting the corresponding positive outlook. Whether this has to do with achieving a positive outlook on the situation or with belief in the activity of God is beside the point if pragmatically this belief increases the chances of being healed. But despite this increase in odds having to do with belief, the question still remains regarding the truth of believing that prayer is a preferential substitute for medicinal intervention for diabetes. If one appeals to whether their belief regarding the best way to achieve healing was justified, one has to decide whether one should understand this objectively (in which case one has to ask whether they fulfilled what most people would consider to be a reasonable investigation of faith versus medicinal healing) or subjectively (in which case we would have to explore the extent to which the Neumanns believed that the evidence of past healing experiences provided adequate justification for their action). If we appeal to epistemic virtue, whether they entertained the appropriate intellectual virtues—perseverance, open-mindedness, diligence, thoroughness, etc.—might be difficult to discern, for again one might interpret this objectively or subjectively. Certainly their virtue did not succeed, in that they did not bring about the end that was the aim of the motivational component, though Zagzebski admits that we cannot determine success or failure from one instance, but over the long run. Whether a belief in faith healing is what an intellectually motivated person who has understanding would hold is far from a simple topic.

In the case of Milam, not only did he commit morally reprehensible acts, but these actions stemmed from his false beliefs about people of color. If we are to condemn his actions, we need to condemn his beliefs as well. His epistemic failure is not only moral but resides in his lack of virtue. His beliefs and actions did not grow out of a virtuous character. He evidenced no motivation either to arrive at a deliberate, courageous, and considered understanding of the facts of the case or to understand what it is to be a human being from the viewpoint of the one he tortured and killed. His epistemic failure remains a moral failure on this account; it extends beyond his lack of evidence for his belief to the qualities of character and motivation that he failed to possess.

Such an analysis likewise applies to Williamson, for as Clifford points out, it need not be the case that the bad consequences actually occur. It is sufficient that they *could* have occurred as a result of failure to provide a ground for the belief. Williamson's beliefs about the Holocaust might have an impact on future genocides, or at the very least on how he relates to Jewish people. But this then reintroduces the insights of a virtue understanding of epistemic obligations. Epistemic excellence goes beyond acts to the virtues individuals manifest. The excellences may, as Audi points out, extend to developing appropriate doxastic dispositions.

These multiple accounts suggest that one can provide a moral grounding for epistemic obligations conjointly in both an act and a virtue ethic. The first emphasizes that true beliefs often play a significant role in moral action, and although a particular false belief might not result in an immoral action in every case, as Clifford emphasized, the practice of forming false beliefs will indeed have such a negative impact in the long run. More broadly, our present beliefs may affect a host of future actions which even now we cannot anticipate but which when they occur can be morally evaluated. Conversely, the practice of forming and holding true beliefs will have positive moral consequences for our lives and society. And practices are developed by meeting our obligations one at a time, by developing the appropriate epistemic habits. The second emphasizes that there are intrinsic goods that are fulfilled when we develop the appropriate epistemic and moral virtues. Epistemic virtues lead us to use reliable truth-conducive belief-forming procedures. Where epistemic virtues are understood as successfully truth-conducive, epistemic obligations involve more than having true beliefs and avoiding false beliefs; they also connect with having and employing certain skills, dispositions, practices, and motivations that lead to the successful achievement of wisdom. And these are either intrinsically good or part of a fulfilled human existence.

4

Epistemic Obligations and Justification

In chapter 2 we developed a view of epistemic obligations according to which we need to minimize, if not eliminate, our false beliefs and maximize contextually significant true beliefs. We also suggested a broader concept of epistemic excellence that includes believing a wide variety of truths that enable us to function well in life and enhance our overall well-being. We patterned this after how we understand moral excellence, which includes the categories of prohibited, obligatory, permitted, and especially meritorious actions.

But the obligation to hold true beliefs and avoid false beliefs faces two serious difficulties. First, how can we fulfill our epistemic obligations when our access to the truth is limited, perspectival, fallible, uncertain, and, especially with respect to general and theoretical propositions, often disputed? If we are to maximize contextually relevant significant truths, we must be able to know what is true. If we are to shun error, we must know what is true to be able to distinguish it from what is false. Although our appeal to epistemic obligations sets a high objective standard, the subjective problem of determining what to believe remains. How do we determine what is true and what is false? We can appeal to perceptual experiences, testimony, memory, rational arguments containing inductive and deductive inferences, but these are all disputable sources. It is not that they are unimportant; surely they play a critical role in our arriving at true beliefs. But they often are fallible sources for determining what to believe.

The difficulty is that from having epistemic obligations it does not follow that I have to believe what you believe or that you believe what I believe, for we might disagree about what is true. Our obligation to believe the truth does not guarantee uniformity of beliefs. But how do we go about resolving disputes about what to believe? And if we cannot resolve these disputes, what is the value of appealing to epistemic obligations? If we cannot agree about what is true, we might as well allow people the right to believe what they want.

The claim that there is difficulty and disagreement in discerning the truth is not the same objection as proposed by those who assert that there is no truth. This latter objection fails from the outset, for one might inquire of its advocates whether their claim that there is no truth is true or false. If true, it contradicts the original thesis. If not true, we need not worry about the claim. If neither true nor false, what then is the epistemic status of the advanced claim, and why should we take it seriously? Thus, the issue here is not whether there are any truths, but rather the potential disputability of truth claims.

The second difficulty is that simply having true beliefs seems inadequate for meeting our epistemic obligations, for we might hold true beliefs by accident or even for bad reasons. What we desire, it is argued, is not mere true belief, but belief arrived at by rational methods or that is rationally grounded. We want beliefs that, as Socrates put it in *Meno* (98a), are tethered. But our discussion of epistemic obligations focused on belief, not on the rational grounds for the belief.

The common response to both of these problems is that epistemic obligations are less concerned with our obligations to believe contextually significant truths and avoid falsehood than with seeing that the beliefs we hold are justified.

Epistemic obligations are not merely about holding true beliefs; they are about holding true beliefs for the right reasons. With respect to the first problem, one way to approach our epistemic obligations to believe contextually significant truths is to discern what is true through justification; justification assists us to determine what is true and what is false by providing evidence or reasons for belief. When we disagree about the truth of a belief, we mutually inquire about the evidence that might be given to support that belief. Regarding the second, to avoid true beliefs formed or held accidentally, we should refrain from believing where we have inadequate grounds and accept only those beliefs that are or can be supported by adequate grounds or evidence.[1] We are epistemically obligated to hold justified beliefs.

This is the position of the most strident believer in epistemic obligations, William Clifford, though articulated on his own narrow evidentialist terms. "The question of right or wrong has to do with the origin of his belief, not the matter of it, . . . not whether it turned out to be true or false, but whether he had a right to believe on such evidence as was before him."[2] Clifford gives the example of a community where certain individuals are accused of misusing the laws in order to wrest children from their parents to teach them a particular religious doctrine contrary to that held by the community. He argues that even if the accusations are true, they should not be believed if they are based on inadequate evidence. What is significant is not whether the community's belief was true or false, but whether the community entertained it on the justified or unjustified grounds available to them.[3] This evidentialist view is echoed more recently by Jonathan Adler. "Any account of the ethics of belief should fit tightly with the crucial fact that it is not possible to regard oneself as both holding a belief and holding that one's reasons for it are inadequate. The explanation assumes that we grasp evidentialism's requirement of adequate reasons as a conceptual condition for believing properly."[4] Failure to so believe, he holds, is not an empirical inadequacy; it is a conceptual impossibility.

In linking epistemic obligations with justification of our beliefs, we move to a position where we fulfill our epistemic obligations when we are justified in holding certain beliefs (S is justified in believing *p*), or alternatively, the beliefs are justified for us (belief *p* is justified for S).[5] The duty has been understood as applying in at least three ways: we ought to believe according to the evidence or grounds we have for *p*, we have a duty to inculcate the proper sort of reliable belief-creating mechanisms that will bring about true beliefs, or we ought to develop the appropriate kind of epistemic virtues or dispositions from whose properly motivated implementation true beliefs and knowledge arise. John Greco terms the first of these options "perspectival internalism," according to which we are obligated to hold beliefs that are justified, and the justification must be possessed by the persons themselves.[6] The second represents a form of reliabilism, while the third arises from the virtue epistemology we considered at the end of the previous chapter. In the first two cases, our basic epistemic obligation will be fulfilled when our beliefs are justified or warranted; in the third case obligations are fulfilled when we have developed and employed virtues that when properly motivated successfully produce true belief.

OBJECTIVE AND SUBJECTIVE JUSTIFICATION

Justification helps us to get to the truth. Of course, justification provides no guarantee that we will get to the truth: we might be justified in our belief and still be mistaken. But justification provides at least some and hopefully good reasons for thinking that our beliefs are true. Put in terms of justification, our epistemic obligation, understood in nonvirtue terms, is to believe contextually significant truths that are justified and not to hold beliefs if there is insufficient reason to think they are true or good reason to believe they are false.

Although this advances the cause, it reintroduces the problem of subjectivity and objectivity, this time in the context of the justification of a belief. Consider the first clause.

It might be put: believe contextually significant truths that are justified, or alternatively, believe contextually significant truths that the person believes are justified. The first is an objectivist account of justification: there is some standard of justification that one ought to fulfill or meet in order to satisfy one's epistemic obligations. The second is a subjectivist account: what is justified depends on what information is available to the person holding the beliefs. The difference between these two constitutes a real difference. According to the objectivist approach, individuals have obligations to believe what is justified according to some standard or accepted norm of justification. We are obliged to believe truths that really are justified, not simply that we think are justified. If contextually significant propositions are justified, then we ought to believe them. In the case of the murder of Emmett Till, Milam has the epistemic obligation to believe not what he thinks is justified, but claims that really are justified about people who look different from him. If he is held merely to what he thinks is justified, we have no basis for holding him morally accountable, for he has acted on the best justified of his beliefs—what he thinks is true according to his own lights. To the contrary, we want to hold him accountable not only for his murderous actions but also because his actions were based on beliefs that he should not have held in the first place because they are unjustified.

Consider the case of a prosecutor who wants to present his case to the court. Based on the evidence he has accumulated, he believes justifiably that the defendant is guilty. But has he fulfilled his epistemic obligations with regard to the defendant? He is justified in believing the defendant guilty in light of the evidence he has in hand, but is he justified in holding this belief about the person's guilt in light of the total evidence available? The subjectivist might hold that the prosecutor should be satisfied in proceeding with the case, since he is justified with respect to the evidence he has in hand. The objectivist would hold that the prosecutor really should not be satisfied with his evidence until it is clear that he has evaluated all available relevant evidence for determining the case. He has an obligation to go beyond the evidence he has if that additional evidence, whatever it shows, is extant, reasonably available, and relevant.

But given the objectivist rendition, how does the prosecutor (or anyone else) know when he has obtained all the available relevant evidence with respect to showing the defendant's guilt or innocence? Such a requirement would seem to lead to interminable delays, for it is reasonable to think that the prosecutor could (or at least might) never know when he possessed all the available relevant evidence. This objectivist view of justified belief—in terms of the total available relevant evidence—is much too strong to satisfy epistemic obligations, for rarely would we know, at least in important matters, whether we have obtained all the available relevant evidence.[7] At the same time, a strictly subjectivist view that affirms that one's obligations are fulfilled simply by holding beliefs justified on the basis of the evidence one already possesses is too weak, for it fails to address the requirement that persons have evidence sufficient to persuade others and not just themselves, or that in certain cases they seek additional relevant evidence. It would allow the prosecutor with the weakest possible case to be justified in proceeding, so long as he believes that the evidence he has in hand is sufficient. In effect, the one view is too strong, for it appeals to a standard of justification that either does not exist or is unattainable; the other is too weak, for it provides no check on individuals' assessment of their own justificatory actions. Rather, our epistemic responsibility is best fulfilled somewhere in between the strict objectivist and strict subjectivist views. But what would this look like? To answer this, we need to attend to the concept of justification.

INTERNALIST CONCEPTIONS OF JUSTIFICATION

The importance of justification can be located most clearly in the internalist epistemology. "Almost all internalists agree that their general position is supported by a 'responsibilist' concept of epistemic justification, or a conception of justification which takes epistemic responsibility to be central to justified belief."[8] "To accept a belief in the absence of such a reason [a good reason to think they are true] . . . is *epistemically irresponsible.*"[9]

One place to observe such a deontological conception is in the writings of Roderick Chisholm, who takes the basic epistemic notion that "S ought to refrain from accepting *h*" as foundational.[10] On his account, a belief is unreasonable for a person if and only if the person ought to refrain from believing a certain proposition, that is, either not believe the proposition or withhold assent from it. And the person ought to refrain from believing a proposition if and only if there is adequate evidence for its contradictory. Chisholm thus spells out his deontological account of justification negatively. That is, he spells out the conditions under which a person ought to refrain from believing rather than conditions under which one has obligations to believe. Instead of speaking about obligations to believe, Chisholm speaks about epistemic permissibility. If it is not unreasonable to believe *h*, then it is acceptable or permissible to believe *h*.

On the one hand, this is a very broad notion of epistemic obligation, for a person is allowed epistemically to believe any proposition so long as no adequate evidence exists for its contradictory. Thus, contrary to the more rigorous conditions set forth by Clifford, since propositions are innocent until proven guilty, we are justified in believing any proposition whose denial lacks adequate evidence. That does not mean that we should believe all such propositions. Here Chisholm introduces the category of indifference. It is indifferent whether one believes a proposition or not if there is no adequate evidence either for the proposition or for its contradictory. In such cases it is acceptable to believe either the proposition or its contradictory, though of course not to believe both.

As we observed in the previous chapter, Chisholm sees epistemic obligations as an analogue of moral obligations. But Chisholm's employment of the analogue is incomplete. Whereas we have acts that are obligatory and forbidden, epistemic obligations for Chisholm are only analogous with the second. Chisholm does not spell out any particular positive epistemic obligations. Thus, though it appears that Chisholm has an exceptionally broad notion of epistemic obligations in terms of permissibility, one might also say that he presents a very narrow conception of epistemic obligation, for there are no positive obligations to believe propositions for which there is adequate evidence.

Feldman's Deontologically Justificatory Account

A more robust internalist deontological account is provided by Richard Feldman, who defends his own version of the Cliffordian thesis that belief should be based on sufficient evidence. Feldman suggests the following formulation to capture epistemic obligations directed toward justification.

> O2. For any person S, time t, and proposition p, if S has any doxastic attitude at all toward p at t and S's evidence at t supports p, then S epistemically ought to have the attitude toward p supported by S's evidence at t.[11]

The epistemic obligation is not a general obligation that holds all the time. Rather, it occurs when one takes an attitude toward a proposition. The attitudes that are relevant to O2 are believing, disbelieving, or withholding or suspending belief. Feldman notes that O2 "conjoins three principles: if a person is going to adopt any attitude toward a proposition, then that person ought to believe it if his current evidence supports it, disbelieve it if his current evidence is against it, and suspend judgment about it if his evidence is neutral (or close to neutral)." In all three cases, persons should follow the evidence available to them and believe on the basis of that evidence. This principle is parsimonious: "It does not instruct you to believe logical consequences that you don't entertain or to otherwise squander precious resources."[12]

Epistemic Duty to Acquire More Evidence

There is much to be said in favor of Feldman's position. Yet several questions arise when epistemic obligations are understood in terms of beliefs that particular persons take as being justified for them in terms of the evidence available to them. *First*, although we have stepped back from having to directly connect our beliefs with truth, we still face the earlier question concerning which beliefs need to be justified. All of them? The important ones? Here, moral and epistemic obligations seem to differ. With moral obligations, all our moral actions should be morally justified either as being obligatory, permitted, or forbidden. But with epistemic obligations, we cannot justify all of our beliefs (note Clifford's exhausted skeptic), and if we cannot justify all our beliefs, at a minimum those who defend epistemic obligations would need some decision procedure to determine which beliefs need to be justified.

Feldman resolves this by specifying that epistemic obligations apply only to cases where one already is considering a proposition, not to propositions in general.[13] Obligations only apply synchronically, not diachronically. When one considers a proposition, then one should follow the evidence by either believing it, withholding belief, or not believing the proposition. This frees one from squandering one's epistemic resources while creating no obligations regarding future beliefs.

But Feldman's view leaves untouched any obligations that we might have toward believing propositions that we have never considered. Many, including educators, politicians, salespersons, advertisers, talk show hosts, sports enthusiasts, editors, and religious believers, think that we do have such obligations and take active steps to bring others to particular beliefs about what the advocates think is true. Political candidates, for example, engage in oratory, dialogue, persuasion, and debate to convince potential voters that their platform contains true propositions that the voters should affirm, and that because of this they should not only vote but vote for them, regardless of whether the listeners have previously considered them as viable candidates or shown an interest in their candidacy. As for religion, some Christians contend that people have an obligation to believe in God, regardless of whether or not they have considered God's existence or taken an attitude toward or have an interest in beliefs in God. One's future destiny might hinge on whether one has the proper beliefs.[14] Similarly, educators generally assume that students have an obligation to believe contextually significant true propositions and disbelieve contextually significant false propositions in the teacher's field, regardless of whether the students previously had or currently have an interest in them or not. True propositions, especially those that professors have presented in lectures or students encountered in their texts, ought to be believed, and indeed, educators take it upon themselves not only to introduce students to these propositions but to test their knowledge of, if not beliefs about, certain personally affirmed allegedly true propositions. Teachers would not tolerate students who responded that they did not need to know the answer or the concept because they had no interest in discerning the truth of the propositions presented. The function of the roles of educator, politician, scientist, advertiser, editorial writer, religious evangelist, counselor, and many others calls for a broadening of epistemic obligation beyond merely the propositions that one considers, attends to, or has an interest in. Significant propositions exist that one is obligated to believe, not only because they are significant, but because they are true in a significant way, either in general or in a specific context.

The parsimoniousness of Feldman's view also leaves untouched what seems to be a present duty. Feldman produces a case where an individual, say myself, believes that a certain supplement is beneficial to my health but comes across a magazine article that possibly questions this view. Am I negligent, he asks, in not reading the article? Not necessarily, he notes. What I should do is follow the evidence I currently have until I actually come across contrary evidence.[15] Just because someone else might have contrary evidence does not mean that I should depart from my current belief.

But don't I have an obligation to gather relevant evidence, whether supportive or contraindicative? Cases like the ones we introduced in chapter 1 suggest that people should put themselves in the best position to determine whether belief is justified or not. It may not be sufficient merely to follow the evidence one already has. If additional evidence would be available to them that would show that the belief they have is unjustified or that what they do not believe really is justified, if implications or leads could be developed and followed, they should pursue that evidence. On the parsimonious view, people like Bishop Williamson could meet their epistemic obligations by presenting the evidence they have to support their belief about the relative lack of severity of the Holocaust without having any epistemic obligation to pursue other leads or worry about additional evidence that does not interest them. Their critics would want to point out that they have availed themselves of circumscribed evidence, but with their appeal to evidence of interest, the critics could be ignored. Yet, although the evidence they possess may justify their view, what they possess may be inadequate, arise from tainted sources, ignore critical facts, be biased, or suffer other epistemic ills that may be discoverable by pursuing further investigation. Unless a wider view than current interest is taken, it is unreasonable to think that Bishop Williamson or any others have satisfied their epistemic obligations in their believing when possible contrary evidence is available to them for a reasonable amount of effort.

It may not be sufficient merely to follow the evidence one has. Questions can, indeed must, be raised about the epistemic quality of the evidence used for justifying one's belief. A sign of epistemic excellence in critical thinking is looking at the question from different perspectives, trying as much as possible to procure all the available relevant evidence, and being open-minded about the possibility of additional and possibly contrary evidence, so that whether belief truly is justified can be adequately determined. This is simply to say that we are epistemically obliged to attend to our practices of inquiry. It is a relevant question, in considering whether our beliefs are justified, whether additional relevant evidence is available that might tip the scale, so that we would see that our belief really is justified or not justified given the evidence we have in hand (subjective conditions) but also that which is extant (the objective conditions) and attainable.[16] My guess is that Feldman would not be satisfied to attribute epistemic excellence to Milam if Milam contends that his view of African Americans is justified by the evidence he has. Surely Milam has not done his epistemic best to gather available relevant data to justify his belief.

Feldman replies that "it's surely true that there are times when one would be best off finding new evidence. But this always turns on what options one has, what one cares about, and other non-epistemic factors. As I see it, these are prudential or moral matters, not strictly epistemic matters."[17] Epistemic obligations, he holds, best apply synchronically (at the given time) rather than diachronically (over time), whereas diachronic issues involve moral and prudential obligations. In effect, morally Milam is suspect, but not epistemically.

The primary purpose of justification is to arrive at truth. But what is true may stand independent not only of what we have an interest in at the time (it might be about something we are not interested in) but also of the justifying evidence we have in hand. The evidence we have in hand may not be adequate or sufficient for or relevant to the truth of what we are seeking. In effect, there are not only subjective conditions of justification (conditions of which we are currently aware) but objective conditions as well (conditions that hold regardless of the information we possess), and as we noted above, our epistemic obligations must lie in between, taking account of both. Feldman's rejection of the epistemic duty to seek more evidence and his making it merely a prudential consideration ignore the objective requirement. Returning to the case of the prosecutor, whether or not the prosecutor has an interest in the additional information regarding the accused, if his beliefs are to be directed to the truth, he is obligated to go beyond the information he has—what he may narrowly circumscribe as his interest—to discern what is contextually relevant to determining the truth in this case. Finding new evidence is not as optional as Feldman suggests, for to make it optional drives a wedge between what we are obligated to believe and truth. Though we have turned to justification rather than truth per se, the point of this turning is still to get to the truth: to believe contextually significant truths that are justified and not to hold beliefs if there is reason to believe they are false or there are insufficient reasons to think they are true. If belief is directed toward truth, then the matter of attaining truth is not merely a prudential matter or a matter of interest but an epistemic matter as well. Of course, our epistemic obligations may be a moral matter as well; the prosecutor has a moral obligation to society and to the potentially accused to make a justified case. As we argued in the previous chapter, there is good reason to think that epistemic obligations often are connected to or in specific cases grounded on moral obligations. The obligation to maximize evidence is not only moral but epistemic as well, and to this we now turn.

Justified Believing

Second, what is it to be justified in believing? One proposed definition is that "S is [deontologically justified] in believing that *p iff* in believing that *p* S is not violating any epistemic obligations."[18] And to satisfy our obligations, which are to maximize significantly relevant truths and minimize our false beliefs, "we want to know whether S had *adequate grounds* for believing that *p,* where *adequate* grounds are those sufficiently indicative of the truth of *p.*"[19] Justification here is understood in the sense of being permitted, which raises the question of what grants us permission to believe. Alston suggests that one internalist view is that we are epistemically justified in believing *p* when we have not violated any of our "'epistemic,' 'cognitive,' or 'intellectual obligations' in believing."[20] But so understood, it appears that we are caught in a vicious circularity: we are epistemically obligated to hold justified beliefs, and beliefs are justified if and only if they do not violate our epistemic obligations.

Feldman attempts to avoid this circular reasoning by specifying that one is justified in believing a proposition if the evidence the person has at the time supports the proposition. For Feldman, this means that one ought to follow the evidence. But following the evidence does not necessarily get one to the truth. In some (and perhaps many) cases, following the evidence will get one to false beliefs. For people living in the twelfth century, following the evidence would get them to the false belief that the sun went around the earth. Following the evidence that one thinks supports the proposition is neither necessary nor sufficient for arriving at the truth of the proposition. But then it is hard to see that we have an epistemic obligation merely to follow the evidence. In effect, this analysis of epistemic obligations in terms of justified belief drives a wedge between epistemic obligations and truth. I might have a belief that is epistemically justified based on the evidence available or on the adequate functioning of my belief-creating mechanisms but that still is false. Persons who rely primarily on their senses might have reliable reasons to think, falsely, that the sun goes around the earth. Contrarily, I might not be justified in holding a belief that is true. My belief that Pluto is composed of rock and ice might be formed unjustifiably by relying on the testimony of my ice-fishing friends, who, being from Minnesota and practically living on a lake during the winter, think that everything that is cold is formed from ice, and hence be unjustified but still be true (it is a matter of luck that they were correct about it being made of rock and ice).

But making this objection—that we have shifted the focus of epistemic obligations from truth considerations to justification—forgets the very reason why we introduced justification in the first place, namely, because our knowledge is fallible. This being the case, one has to live with the possibility that exercising our epistemic obligations might get us to falsity rather than truth, and that this is about the best we can expect.

This objection raises further questions about justification and epistemic obligation. If justification is not directly linked to truth, what degree of justification, or how much justification, is needed to satisfy my epistemic obligations? The question is clearly illustrated by Clifford's shipowner. Even having his ship inspected does not guarantee that the ship is seaworthy. The inspector might have been soused, dishonest, or incompetent. So, to be justified, should the shipowner pay for a second—and perhaps a third and fourth—opinion before he sends the ship to sea? The problem is that justification is a matter of degree, not easily measurable, so that to determine whether the grounds are *adequate* is problematic. To say that it is what a reasonable person would accept is not only unclear but comes close to begging the question. But if we cannot answer what is required for a person to be justified in believing *p*, we cannot determine when persons have met their epistemic obligations under this scenario, let alone for what they generally would be held accountable.

Feldman bites the bullet here, shifting the epistemic obligation from truth to having a "rational attitude." That is, we are obligated, not to form true beliefs, but rather that, if we have a belief, it be held rationally.[21] And to be rational is to conform to the supporting evidence. But how adequate, how supporting, must the evidence be, and from how broad a survey must the evidence be gleaned? Undoubtedly no clear general principle can be formulated, for what is required will be contextual; rather, we must ultimately appeal to formulated principles of critical thinking applied contextually. Application of appropriate critical thinking skills and techniques to the issue at hand will lead to the best results epistemically possible. In short, what makes for an adequate justification stands somewhere between the subjective (when we believe on the evidence we have at the time) and the objective (the total available evidence relevant for determining the truth). Clearly, it involves more than the first, but the second is unspecifiable, since it will vary case by case. We will return to this discussion in the final chapter.

In sum, epistemic obligations are directed toward believing the truth. However, because truth is sometimes elusive and because we can hold beliefs for inadequate or no reasons at all, it is argued that such obligations might have to be more indirectly connected with matters of truth than appears at first blush. When directed toward justification, they are directed to truth-aiming and truth-producing processes rather than directly to truth. That is, they address an aspect that at best only makes it *likely* that the belief will be true. And even here, some, like Chisholm, have moved from manifesting these conditions to *trying* to manifest these conditions. But moving from obligations to truth to obligations regarding justification substantially weakens the case that we have epistemic obligations. After all, it alters the obligations from the results to be achieved (holding true propositions and avoiding false propositions) to the processes used to often arrive at truth. But these processes might also arrive (justifiably) at falsehood in any given case. But we don't want to abandon epistemic obligations to believe contextually significant truths, for there is good reason to think that persons are not justified in believing or do not have the right to believe whatever they want. In effect, understanding epistemic obligations in terms of having justified beliefs is inadequate.

Yet we don't want to abandon justification either. Something more than true belief is necessary for epistemic excellence, something that gets us beyond epistemic luck. As with the ice-formed Pluto example, if we want to be epistemically excellent we want to be correct in our beliefs for the right reasons; otherwise it is a matter of chance that we correctly believe, and this cannot be accounted as epistemic excellence, for then sometimes we are correct and sometimes not and we have no careful procedures for delineating between them. Justification has been what rescues knowledge from luck. The Gettier problem has cast doubt on the sufficiency of justification when it comes to defining knowledge. Nonetheless, something like justification is needed to take the believer beyond luck to epistemic excellence, even if justification is not always truth-conducive. When we commend someone for having true beliefs, we commend them not only for their true beliefs but also for having arrived at them epistemically virtuously.[22]

AN EXTERNALIST CONCEPTION OF JUSTIFICATION

The reliabilist approach contrasts with the above internalist approach in being externalist in character. According to reliabilism, a belief is justified just in case it formed reliably, that is, formed not in a defective manner. Alvin Goldman rejects internalist views of justification on the grounds that they use the concept of justification in one form or another to provide an account of justification, a method that he claims is either circular or fundamentally uninformative. His goal is to have a theory of justified belief that does not employ epistemic terms when justifying a belief.[23] In place of internalistic epistemic criteria he constructs a view of justification that relies on causal relations that include both initiators and sustainers of the belief. Whereas an unjustified belief is formed by unreliable processes such as confused reasoning, wishful thinking, hunches, or hasty generalizations, justified beliefs are formed by generally reliable processes such as standard perception, remembering, good reasoning, and introspection. Belief is reliably produced when it results from causal processes that have a high tendency to produce true beliefs and where the input-beliefs are true, that is, when the belief "has an ancestry of reliable and/or conditionally reliable cognitive operations."[24]

The problem that results from an externalist view for a typical deontological theory of epistemic obligations is that we don't need to know whether or not the beliefs are reliably produced in order for us to hold a belief justifiably. We have the right, not to believe anything we want, but to believe what was reliably produced, but at the same time we need not know whether or not our beliefs are of this sort. The subjective considerations regarding what we do or do not know are irrelevant; what matters is that in fact the beliefs were reliably produced. But without the subjective cognitive conditions, epistemic obligations of the sort we have considered disappear, for they require consciousness of what we are obliged to believe.

This is not to say that a reliabilist account lacks epistemic obligations. Goldman notes that "failing to apply a reliable inferential process to evidence against reliability cancels justifiedness."[25] Language about persons "failing to apply" processes or methods introduces epistemic obligations. Though we may not need to know that the causal process or method used is reliable, we have an obligation to apply reliable methods if they are available and to avoid using unreliable methods. Obligations are not to the beliefs themselves but to cultivating the proper epistemic methods or practices that generally result in our holding true beliefs.

"Failing to apply" can be understood in at least two ways. One would be an objectivist account: the persons used reliable methods or processes to acquire their belief and thereby are justified in holding that belief, or the persons used unreliable methods to acquire their belief and thereby are unjustified in holding that belief. The other would be a subjectivist account, where the persons used reliable methods but despite this believe that they are unjustified, or where the persons did not use reliable methods but still believe that they are justified in holding the belief. Goldman considers the case of a person whose belief is produced by reliable processes but who has grounds for thinking that the belief is unjustified. It would seem, Goldman notes, that despite being produced reliably the belief would be unjustified for that person, for the person does not believe that the belief was reliably produced. Goldman rejects the view that someone would have to convince the person that his belief is reliably produced (which would be to resort again to an internalist view of justification—knowing that his belief was justified) in order for his belief to be justified. Instead, Goldman suggests that in such cases persons are justified in believing they are unjustified in holding the belief just in case the persons have no reliable process *available* that, if used, would result in their not having the belief.

Putting it this way still is ambiguous, as Goldman admits. Does it mean that objectively the person had no access to alternative processes, or that the person did not know that other reliable processes were available? The former specifies objective conditions; there is no way anyone in this condition or situation could know that the methods employed are unreliable. The second connects to the subjective view of the person. Goldman calls the first view strong justification and the second weak justification. On the strong view, the belief should be formed by a reliable method, the method should have been acquired in a suitable fashion, and the believer should believe in the method. On this view a person is (strongly) justified in holding a belief if no reliable method is objectively available to him that would show that it was not acquired suitably. On the weak view, although the method by which the belief is produced is (or may be) reliable, the person does not believe it is reliable and is personally unaware of another way of discerning whether it is reliable, and there are no processes or methods the person believes to be reliable that would show it is reliable.[26] Here the person is (weakly) justified in believing it is unreliable depending on what the person knows about alternative available methods such as acquiring testimony or gathering evidence that if pursued would give the person grounds for knowing that the methods used were reliable or unreliable. The person simply might not know that methods that would establish reliability were available, and in that case would be justified in his or her belief that the processes were unreliable despite the contrary objective conditions that show that the processes used were reliable. On either account, the person has an obligation to consider whether other methods are available that might show that the methods the person used were reliable or unreliable, and failure to do so would be blameworthy. The issue concerns whether the methods were objectively or subjectively available.

Goldman is willing to talk about blame.[27] Blame may be appropriate when persons have not made use of available reliable methods. But there is also blamelessness when persons use unreliable methods but do not believe the processes are unreliable or do not know that they have access to other methods. Goldman recognizes what he terms the cultural plight of the believer. We have already noted that Milam is rooted in his Southern mid-twentieth-century racist culture and that he formed his beliefs by generally reliable methods such as perception, accepting testimony, and making inferences. Objectively, the methods Milam used are generally reliable; we rely on these processes to make sound judgments. And it is easy to believe that Milam thought he had good reason to trust these methods, especially the testimony of his cultural peers, though in this case they and their testimony were unreliable. Yet he believed that they were reliable and subjectively believed that he had no access to methods that would show that they were unreliable. On this account, following Goldman's characterization, his beliefs are weakly (or subjectively) justified.

Goldman's point is that ignorance of a certain sort of the causal conditions provides an excuse. But can we agree that Milam is epistemically blameless even in the weak sense? On the one hand, this is a classic defense against blameworthiness; one cannot hold persons accountable for what they did not, and more strongly, cannot believe or know. Yet acceptance of this notion of epistemic blamelessness would allow all sorts of individuals—think of members of the Nazi organization who were following orders[28]—to claim epistemic innocence because they were acting from their own lights and did not know about other available methods that would have put their trust in the methods they used to arrive at their beliefs in doubt. But it is difficult to excuse or hold epistemically innocent Milam, the Nazis, and countless others whose horrible acts stem from their belief that they are innocent or justified. They are at fault, not merely for their actions but for the beliefs they hold. Perhaps the way to have both epistemic blamelessness and also accountability is to suggest that there are certain basic things that people should know, regardless of the cultural impediments. Just as there are fundamental moral intuitions, the argument goes, that are universal—it is wrong to torture, to kill innocent people, to cheat and defraud—so there are fundamental epistemic truths that should be known. That we have the first is evidenced by the fact that when people commit acts such as those listed, they do it secretly or covertly, hiding their identities. Perpetrators kill and rob wearing masks; they run away and hide or attempt to cover their paper tracks after committing the deed; they take steps like creating false identities or using pseudonyms to prevent identification; they commit their crimes at night or when people are not around to witness them. That there are universal epistemic truths to which people admit is more difficult to substantiate. We might agree that we have no generally accepted set of true beliefs because, as we already noted, what persons should believe is contextually (both present and future) significant. Contextualization, along with cultural diversity of language and interpretative schema, would make creating a list of such beliefs extraordinarily difficult (though educators and politicians continue this endeavor through standardization and setting political educational policy). Nonetheless, despite the contextualization of epistemic truths, we at base often do claim that people should believe or know differently. That there are such truths we can generally expect rational people to know follows from there being fundamental moral intuitions or principles to which we can hold people accountable, for those principles are expressed in propositions that accordingly should be believed. Fundamental moral truths, if such there be—and, some might hold, mathematical and basic scientific truths—at least provide a starting point for thinking about what someone should have known. In moral and in practical cases, we are not misstating when we say that "You should have known better." In effect, our obligations ultimately concern the truth of the belief, not merely its reliable formation.

One might also worry about the processes—perception, inference, testimony—Milam used, for since these are generally reliable practices they would seem to fit the description of causally generally reliable justificatory belief-forming processes. We rely on our properly functioning perceptual apparatus to give us accurate information about the world, we rely on making good inferences from information, and we often rely on testimony to make judgments about what we should believe and do when we are in a position where we personally lack or are unable to rationally process the relevant information. To hold Milam blameworthy, one would have to argue that despite the general reliability of these process types, in his particular case their tokens were unreliable. He relied on perceptions—for example, of skin color, living conditions, language usage, and educational level—to discriminate between individuals, and one can hold that perceptions gave accurate sense data. The problem is that these perceptual data are irrelevant to forming and holding beliefs about the worth of individuals or how they should be treated. The inferences he made from these perceptual data were flawed. He relied on testimony from his peers, but though the testimony of his peers might have been truth-producing in many other instances, their views with regard to race were greatly suspect and so in this case unreliable. He used inference or reasoning, but one might contend that contrary to what he might have believed, it was not good reasoning. The arguments employed might have been valid, but the premises were false, and this invalidated the appeal to logical reasoning.

Milam would undoubtedly respond that he had no reason to think that his beliefs about Black persons were unreliably caused. Take, for example, the inferential or logical part of his reasoning. "And when a nigger gets close to mentioning sex with a white woman, he's tired o' livin'. I'm likely to kill him." Since Till got close to mentioning sex with a white woman and persisted in his "poison," Milam did determine to kill him. The *modus ponens* reasoning is valid; the debate concerns whether the premises are true. Milam had his reasons for thinking that the premises were true based on certain causal processes such as testimony and inferences (equating asking someone for a date with mentioning sex; mentioning sex being tantamount to asking for trouble). It would seem that if we are to fault Milam, it would have to be in terms of some objective truth conditions, conditions that would involve rejecting his view that his premises were true. Goldman agrees, but in a reliabilist fashion; the beliefs on which the process is based should themselves be justified. Goldman's reliabilist view requires not only that the beliefs be formed by reliable processes but that the beliefs used in the methods (for example, as premises in inferential reasoning) be themselves justified because similarly formed. Otherwise, if the beliefs in the premises are not justified by being reliably formed, we have no grounds for thinking that the resulting beliefs generally will be true. Of course, the justification of the premises need not itself be in terms of inferences; it could be reliably caused in other ways, such as by perceptual experience. Hence, being reliably caused is not necessarily inferential, so that this reliabilist view is not caught up in an infinite regress of inferential appeals.

At the same time, for Milam to be justified in his reasoning, it is not enough that the premises be justified by being formed by generally reliable processes; for his reasoning to be sound, his premises must really be true. Whether the reasoning was good reasoning has to be adjudicated not merely procedurally but in terms of both logical validity and the truth of the premises. Having true beliefs is critical to being justified even from a subjective reliabilist viewpoint. But if the premises are to be true, does it matter how they are formed? It seems not, unless we take a subjectivist view. So again, the objectivist–subjectivist issue arises. We will return to the matter of objectivist and subjectivist accountability in chapter 7.

JUSTIFICATION ON A VIRTUE ETHIC

At the end of the previous chapter we saw that virtue epistemologists also talk in terms of justified belief but that their account differs from that developed above. Beliefs are justified when the propositions are "what a person who is motivated by intellectual virtue, and who has the understanding of his cognitive situation that a virtuous person would have, might believe in like circumstances."[29] Justification is provided in terms of the person who has engaged the appropriate virtues, not in terms of the evidence that the person has for them or whether they have been formed by a reliable mechanism. This account of virtue has an objective and a subjective dimension. The objective sense is found in the contention that a belief is justified if it is a proposition that a properly motivated person with understanding would believe. It is justified regardless of who actually does or does not entertain it; a justified belief is a proposition that an ideally virtuous person would or might believe. This has nothing to do with the individual actually holding the belief, but with some ideal virtuous knower. The subjective sense is found in the contention that persons have fulfilled their epistemic duty and are thereby properly praiseworthy when they hold a justified belief from the right motive and right understanding. If they hold the belief for the wrong motive, then the *belief may still be justified*, but *they are not justified* in holding the belief. When persons believe virtuously—for Zagzebski, from the proper motives with right understanding—the beliefs that they hold will be justified. In this case, being justified for a given individual has everything to do with the individual actually holding the belief.

Thus, whether individual persons are to be praised for holding a justified belief depends on how they hold the belief. Just as persons can perform a right or permissible moral act even if they are not virtuous, persons can hold a justified belief without being epistemically justified, that is, without holding it from the proper motivation and understanding.[30] If they hold it without exercising their intellectual virtues, they mimic what the virtuous believer would do but are not thereby praiseworthy for holding it. For persons to fulfill their epistemic duty, that is, for them to be virtuous, what is required is that the believers hold the justified belief virtuously, with the right motivation and the right understanding.

The problem of knowing what is true has been answered in terms of ideal knowers who properly exercise their epistemic virtues and understanding and thereby arrive at true beliefs. They are persons (not necessarily actual) who have developed and exercise the virtues out of the proper motivation, that is, to know the truth out of the motivations associated with the respective virtues. But if justified beliefs are defined in terms of such persons, how does one know what properly motivated persons with understanding would or might believe? One could say that the ideal persons would believe what the virtuously motivated person would believe, but this would be circular. And the virtue theorist would not reply that ideal knowers should believe what is justified by the evidence or formed merely by reliable mechanisms. So it is hard to see that we have advanced significantly in our understanding of what beliefs are justified, even when we are told that for such an ideal knower the virtues are successfully truth-conducive. For though we might know what makes a belief justified—it is held by a virtuous knower who successfully aims at truth with understanding or who believes conscientiously—it is not clear how we would recognize this ideal person in terms of whom beliefs are defined as being justified, and without this ability we cannot recognize which beliefs are justified.

It is hard to know how the virtue theorist like Zagzebski would reply to this, but one possible response might be pragmatic. Since virtuous knowers are successful in the motivated employment of their epistemic virtues, one could identify the ideal knowers by their success. The beliefs they hold virtuously would be true; they put knowers in touch with reality. But two problems surface. One is that this description is given in subjective terminology, but the ideal knower must be understood in objective terms. What is justified is what the ideal knower would believe, regardless of whether there is any such knower or whether knowing actions were actually undertaken. But if there is no actual ideal knower, one would not have actual results to evaluate as to whether the belief is true. Furthermore, the pragmatic justification supposes that one has access to the pragmatic results of the virtue employment so as to determine their truth, but it was the lack of such access to such results—the truth—that moved us to consider justification as a way of arriving at truth. So this direction leads to a dead end.

Another possible response follows from Zagzebski's discussion of the "generality problem." This problem is directed against reliabilist accounts of knowing, where a belief is justified just in case it was arrived at through reliable belief-forming mechanisms, regardless of whether the person was aware of these mechanisms. The problem facing reliability is that these belief-forming processes can be given a wide variety of descriptions, and these descriptions vary by degree. Zagzebski gives the following example.

> So if I read and believe a report in the newspaper on the increase in housing starts this year written by a person knowledgeable about the use of statistics in this area, my belief-forming process could be variously described as the process of believing what I read in the newspaper, the process of believing what I read in a particular newspaper, the process of believing what is written in the newspaper by an authority in the field of the report, the process of believing what is written in the newspaper by an authority who is merely reporting statistics that he is highly qualified to analyze, the process of believing an authority who has no reason to want the truth to be as reported, among many others. Some of these processes are more specific than others, but they do not all form subsets of more general processes. Clearly, the reliability of these different processes varies considerably.[31]

She goes on to argue that this problem does not affect the virtue theorist because one does not look at the mechanisms of belief formation but rather at the habits that are formed by virtuous knowers. If these habits are virtuous, they will be successful in forming true beliefs.

We might develop this to suggest that one would be able to recognize the ideal knower by the fact that such persons have formed habits that invoke the appropriate virtues, and by using these habits they would arrive at true beliefs, since to be virtuous is to be successful in one's epistemic and moral aims. But which habits should be developed? It would seem that we should develop the ones that are epistemically successful. But not only does this return us to the pragmatic justification, but it also goes against Zagzebski's contention that the virtues are not virtues because they are successful, but rather because they simply are intrinsically good. So the habits to be formed, since they are part of the virtues themselves, are intrinsically good. The ideal knower will have formed the habits of the intrinsically good virtues, and we should be able to recognize these virtues as intrinsically good, quite apart from their success (though in fact they will be successful). This response hinges, then, on our ability to know what intellectual acts and habits are intrinsically good.

John Greco responds to the problem of beliefs being subjectively justified by defining "justified belief" in terms of the cognitive "dispositions that a person manifests when she is thinking conscientiously." He does not define "thinking conscientiously" in terms of explicitly and consciously intending to find the truth. Rather, he understands thinking conscientiously in terms of the state ordinary people are in when they try to think honestly. Justified belief is thus found in the conscientious functioning of cognitive dispositions.[32]

But still, does this tell us which beliefs would be held by such a person with intrinsically good epistemic habits or cognitive dispositions? We can perhaps go from the habits and virtues to the beliefs, since by definition they are truth-conducive. But it is not clear that we can go the other direction, from the beliefs to knowing they are justified, for it is not clear how one would know with respect to any given belief that it is what a properly motivated virtuous person would believe or whether it would be grounded in conscientiousness. And without this it is impossible to know what our epistemic obligations are with regard to any given belief. The response, of course, is that we are not responsible with regard to particular beliefs but rather with regard to the formation of epistemically virtuous dispositions. But again, though we have obligations to become virtuous knowers (as we noted in the previous chapter), we also have obligations to hold true beliefs. It is the both-and that we want to maintain as being covered by epistemic excellence.

CONCLUSION

In the previous chapters we argued that epistemic obligations concern our obligations to believe what is significantly and contextually true and to avoid or minimize false beliefs. The problem is to discern what beliefs fit these categories. The other concern is that, to be epistemically excellent, we need to avoid believing merely accidentally or for the wrong reason. To these ends we have considered the role of justification. What we have seen is that on the traditional internalist account, shifting our obligations from true beliefs to justification does not guarantee true belief, so that we will have considerably weakened epistemic obligations if we alter or reduce our epistemic obligation merely to engaging in appropriate epistemic practices of critical thinking that tend to produce true beliefs. We need both true beliefs to fulfill our prima facie epistemic obligation and justification to achieve epistemic excellence, so that we can intersubjectively determine which propositions are true and that our beliefs are not merely accidentally arrived at. We have seen that on an externalist account, though we do not need to know the justification, to achieve epistemic excellence we still have obligations with regard to the justificatory causal process. But we noted that when blame was assessed, it was not assessed in subjective cases where persons did not realize that they had access to methods that would establish whether the causal processes were reliable. However, this appears unsatisfactory, for then the matter of having true beliefs and being accountable can disappear in critical cases; ignorance of accessibility provides an excuse, even when it is reasonable to hold that persons should have known. Moreover, the reliability of processes typically involved in knowing may be questioned; one might use processes that normally are reliable and yet not arrive at true beliefs. Again, one needs both reliable processes to arrive at true beliefs and true beliefs to satisfy our epistemic obligation, and one can reasonably argue that we need to engage in and facilitate reliable processes as means of arriving at true beliefs. Finally, we have also seen that on a virtue account, justification is defined in terms of what a virtuous person would believe, but that though we can agree that a virtuous person, defined as having employed the epistemic virtues successfully, arrives at true beliefs or knowledge, we cannot discern on this account what beliefs are justified and hence what we ought to believe since we do not have access to the ideal of a virtuous person. Yet we can also rightfully contend that epistemic excellence requires that we produce an epistemic character and that we develop and apply the virtues, since an epistemic character successfully employed leads to true beliefs. Thus, though epistemic obligations cannot be redirected to justification, they certainly will include justification. To put it another way, the epistemic obligations to truth that we promulgated in chapter 2 must be supplemented by concerns for the way that we arrive at that truth when we consider not merely having the beliefs, but being epistemically excellent. In the latter case, merely having true beliefs is not sufficient, for one might not arrive at them in an epistemically excellent manner. While epistemic obligations concern our obligation to have contextually significant true beliefs, epistemic excellence will include both *processes* of careful and persistent investigation, open-mindedness, and epistemic conscientiousness[33] that epistemically virtuous persons use, as well as *belief* in contextually significant truths that result from the successful use of those processes.

5

Belief Voluntarism

In the forcgoing we provided an account of epistemic obligations and suggested why they are significant. It is generally recognized that having epistemic obligations entails that we have control over our beliefs to an extent that we can be held accountable for them. The contention that we have epistemic obligations only if our beliefs are in our control arises, in part, from an analogy between epistemic and moral obligations. Obligations are standards for evaluating persons and thus create accountability on the part of the subject. And for agents to have accountability, "it must be within one's power to refrain from that action or avoid that state. Thus, not only does an obligation apply solely to [personal] agents; it applies solely to agents *qua* agents, i.e. in so far as they are responsible for whether they fulfill the obligation."[1] If I ought to do something and would be held accountable if I didn't do it, I can do it.[2] If I ought to return the money I found in a wallet on the street to its proper owner (and would be morally blameworthy if I did not do so), then I can return the money. Similarly, if I have epistemic obligations, I have the power to believe, disbelieve, or refrain from either believing or disbelieving. To some extent my beliefs are directly under my control. We will term this "belief voluntarism."

As we will see, this characterization of belief voluntarism needs clarification. What is meant by direct control of our beliefs, as over against indirect or other forms of control? How much control must we be able to exercise for something to be a case of belief voluntarism? What is the role of reasons and causes in an adequate account of belief voluntarism? In this chapter we will have occasion to respond to these questions in providing a reasonable and workable theory of belief voluntarism that is consistent with epistemic obligations.

Although belief voluntarism has had a long and distinguished career in Western philosophy, found notably in Thomas Aquinas, René Descartes, William James, and Roderick Chisholm,[3] among others, it has been the subject of significant, substantial criticism in recent epistemology.[4] It would not stretch the point to say that most recent philosophers who have addressed belief voluntarism have done so with an eye to rejecting it. To discern whether the doubters are correct and to seriously pursue the issue of whether we have epistemic obligations, we will look carefully and critically at how epistemic obligations connect to belief voluntarism and how belief voluntarism is to be best understood.

BELIEF VOLUNTARISM

Although contemporary philosophers are generally skeptical about belief voluntarism, it assuredly plays a role in real-world affairs in diverse quarters. For example, belief voluntarism commonly underlies conversionist religions like Christianity, where priests and preachers summon their listeners to voluntarily alter their beliefs—"to believe and be saved."[5] Many Christians hold that belief in God manifested in Jesus is necessary for salvation and that God at the final judgment will hold people accountable for their beliefs. But unless belief is in our control, one wonders how God can hold people accountable for having particular beliefs or failing to believe. The same applies to holding moral beliefs. Recall the case of the pope and Chancellor Merkel, who not only held Bishop Williamson accountable for what he believed but expected him to change his belief by his own volition. In law as well, we are suspicious of contentions that we have no control over our beliefs. In the case of Patty Hearst, who after being abducted in 1974 by the Symbionese Liberation Army fell in with them in their spree of robberies, her lawyers argued in her defense that she was coerced or brainwashed into advocating for and joining the S.L.A.[6] Yet the judge and jury rejected this defense, holding her accountable for her beliefs and subsequent actions. The rejection of her appeal to compulsion is not unique; it aligns with the common view that people have some control over many of their beliefs and that they can be held accountable for the beliefs that they adopt or refuse to adopt. If beliefs are forced on us by evidence or otherwise, if we are passive with respect to what we believe, or if our beliefs are mere products of our passions, then they happen to us and responsibility lies elsewhere than with us, if anywhere at all.

There are prima facie reasons for thinking that belief voluntarism is true. These reasons are grounded, in part, on certain similarities between beliefs and actions. "Both are commonly grounded in reasons; both are a basis for praising or blaming the subject; both are sensitive to changes in one's environment; both can appropriately be described as objects of decision and deliberation, and beliefs can appear quite action-like when conceived as formed by assent or by acceptance."[7] Just as our basic actions—moving our legs, lifting our arms, blinking our eyes—can be done voluntarily, so likewise a significant number of our beliefs can be arrived at (or our believing done) or maintained voluntarily. We can decide whether or not to move our limbs, and we can decide whether or not to believe that the president will look out for the best interests of our country.

Voluntarists and their critics alike point to language about belief that (allegedly, the critic will assert) provides evidence for belief voluntarism. Jack Meiland describes the voluntarist case in language about deciding to believe. He presents the case of the woman who is faced with evidence that her husband has been unfaithful. However, the woman wants to maintain the marriage and believes that this can be done by believing in her husband's innocence. "She knows that she cannot conceal her suspicions and hence decides to believe that her husband is not being unfaithful to her."[8] Although in this case she has sufficient evidence of her husband's involvement, she wants to maintain that marriage and so decides to adopt a belief that will sustain that marriage. Meiland's use of "decides" here seals the point: her decision to believe that her husband is faithful, in spite of significant evidence to the contrary, is voluntary.

We can speak about deciding what to believe in types of situations other than disbelieving contrary evidence. For example, there are cases where underdetermination best describes the situation. Someone might ask me what I think about whether Susan is guilty of embezzlement since she was so charged by the district attorney. I might respond that I do not know what to believe, since the evidence is really quite unclear. On the one hand, the attorney must have good and convincing evidence, else he would not have brought charges. On the other hand, I know Susan somewhat well and from my limited experience have no reason to doubt her integrity. In this case, I might decide to believe that she is innocent, although the evidence is somewhat evenly split. My belief in this case of underdetermination is a case of direct voluntary belief; lacking sufficient evidence either way, I voluntarily and directly form the belief—decide—that she is innocent. (Of course, I also have the option of suspending belief, but that does not affect the example. Susan's case might not be what William James calls a forced choice, but what I choose to believe might be momentous for my relations with Susan. Even suspending belief might destroy our relationship just as much as if I believed that she is guilty.)

We might also think about deciding to believe where we have evidence. A senator might look at the various proposals for solving a particular problem—for example, the pending social security shortfall—and, after evaluating them, decide to sign on to sponsor a particular bill designed to address the problem. The senator takes into account all the evidence, and although the evidence for adopting one particular approach is not compelling—does not definitively show that one proposal is undoubtedly far superior to the others in resolving the pending crisis, but rather leaves the success of the endeavor quite indeterminable—the senator decides that the evidence for this proposal is strong enough to warrant the senator's support to a degree more than the other proposals. The senator comes to the view—believes—that this was the best proposal.

We also might alter our beliefs because they are not working and adopt an alternative belief without evidence to show that the belief now adopted is reasonable or more likely to lead to success. One can see beliefs like this functioning in superstitious behavior. My luck has been bad, so I decide to blow on the dice before rolling them. This time I was lucky—the dice came up with the number I needed, so I decide to blow on them the next time as well, believing that some kind of causal connection holds between my blowing on them and the number that appears. The belief that blowing on dice to get a good number does not arise from reasoned causes, for any number of alternative beliefs might have been selected to change my luck. Instead of blowing on the dice, I might decide to believe that wearing my hat backwards or singing the national anthem will produce the desired effect. The beliefs I have with regard to this superstitious behavior might be reasonable while the practice works, but what other practice I change to and the beliefs I hold regarding that—believing that wearing the hat backwards rather than sideways or inside out results in better luck than wearing it in any other way—don't result from reasoned evidence and precede pragmatic success.

We likewise speak of withholding belief. In an example we will develop below, we might witness a magician engaged in sawing a woman in half. The evidence that he accomplished this feat is quite astonishing: one can observe the woman climbing into the box, witness his sawing motion, and see a resulting space between the top and bottom parts of the box that housed her body. At the same time, we may withhold the belief that the woman is now in two parts (and presumably dead), for we realize that the context is one of a magic show and believe that it is highly unlikely that the magician would risk prosecution for really doing what he gives the appearance of doing. It is true that when we form beliefs, the beliefs that we form may be false—the magician might really be a sadist—but the falsity of the belief is irrelevant to the contention that we can voluntarily withhold belief (though as we have already noted, we don't believe that the proposition is false).

We might even completely suspend belief about what we are experiencing. Given the ambiguity of the situation, we might be unwilling to commit to whether there is or is not a puddle of water in the road ahead despite our perception of what appears to be water. It may or may not really be water; we cannot tell at this distance. We might simply refuse to entertain a belief about what the situation really shows, given the ambiguity of the evidence. Or again, we might see a person and note that she really looks like someone we know. At the same time, however, we might think it would be a very great coincidence to see her in this place and consequently decide to suspend judgment about whether the woman we are observing was really our acquaintance.

Indeed, we can marshal any number of cases where we employ language about belief that is clearly voluntarist. We say that someone—for example, a particular Republican senator from Pennsylvania—decided to become a Democrat (to hold or advocate the beliefs of the Democratic Party). In putting it this way, we do not indicate that the person's action was caused or that it followed necessarily in some way from evidence he had, for example, about his chances for reelection, though reasons could be relevant to the decision. Rather, we simply affirm that the person voluntarily decided to adopt a belief in the Democratic platform or system of ideas. *Deciding* and *adopting* relate directly to belief formation and accord with the voluntarist case.

Other voluntarist language is not so narrowly connected with belief formation but rather extends to belief maintenance. The verbs *assent* and *affirm* can be used with belief formation. I can voluntarily assent to or affirm a proposition that I have not previously assented to or affirmed. I can do this on the basis of what I take to be good reasons that I have for the belief; but I also might be willing simply to assent to or affirm the proposition because the proposition expressing the belief seems to be true. At the same time, assenting to or affirming a proposition might have nothing to do with the formation of the belief. I might already have formed the belief, in which case the assent or affirmation shows that I continue to hold the belief.[9] Reaffirmation of one's belief is common in religious contexts and is becoming increasingly popular with respect to other activities, such as retaking wedding vows at later ceremonies such as the twenty-fifth wedding anniversary. In ordinary conversation it is not unusual for someone to inquire, "Do you still believe that?," looking either for a change in belief or an affirmation of an already formed and articulated belief.

In short, evidence for belief voluntarism is widespread. Many of our practices and much of our ordinary language with regard to belief formation and belief maintenance provide prima facie reasons for thinking that we can have and do exercise voluntary control over many, if not most, of our beliefs.

Belief voluntarists need not hold that *all* beliefs are voluntary, only that a significant number of them are, if the doctrine of epistemic obligations is to have any epistemological bite. In fact, those who hold to epistemic obligations might affirm a weaker position still, not that beliefs are voluntary, but that beliefs *can* be voluntary. That is, we have the relevant power with respect to forming or maintaining our beliefs, whether we exercise it or not. This might occur, for example, with perceptual beliefs, where we usually cede any control over our perceptually derived beliefs, though it remains possible, as in the magician and mirage cases above, that we can assume control over our perceptual beliefs.

The piece that connects this with epistemic obligations holds that only if a significant number of beliefs are or can be voluntary can we determine whether they should be either obligatory or forbidden, and whether we are epistemically obligated to believe certain propositions, to disbelieve others, or to suspend judgment.[10] Before we turn to the criticisms of belief voluntarism, we need to attend to the argument that denies that belief voluntarism is presupposed by epistemic obligations.

DO OBLIGATIONS REQUIRE BELIEF VOLUNTARISM?

Richard Feldman argues that epistemic obligations do not imply epistemic voluntarism. To develop his argument, he lays out the antiobligation argument as follows.[11]

1. If deontological judgments about beliefs are true, then people have voluntary control over their beliefs.
2. People do not have voluntary control over their beliefs.
3. Therefore, deontological judgments about beliefs are not true.

Contrary to most critics of belief voluntarism, Feldman denies premise 2. However, he thinks that though the control we have is indirect (nonbasic voluntary control), it is rarely exercised and thus of minimal epistemic significance. Among the elements missing is an intention to form a belief. We will return to the consideration of premise 2 later. Here we focus on Feldman's real concern with the antiobligation argument, namely, premise 1. Feldman contends that persons might still have an epistemic obligation even if they cannot fulfill it. The basis for this is that "oughts" can result from playing a certain role or occupying a certain position.[12] "Teachers ought to explain things clearly. Parents ought to take care of their kids. Cyclists ought to move in various ways. Incompetent teachers, incapable parents, and untrained cyclists may be unable to do what they ought to do. Similarly, . . . forming beliefs is something people do."[13] These, he takes it, are responsibility oughts. And although parents, in their role as parents, ought to take care of their kids, it does not follow that they can. Similarly with teachers; they might not be capable of fulfilling the role their profession specifies they ought to undertake. Similarly, he claims, epistemic obligations are responsibility oughts that arise from roles we play or positions we hold. They tell us that we ought to form beliefs in the right way, that is, in the way specified by the role. But from the fact that we should form beliefs this way it does not follow that we can form beliefs voluntarily. "It is our plight to be believers. We ought to do it right. It doesn't matter that in some cases we are unable to do so." Thus, for Feldman, people have epistemic obligations even though they cannot exercise voluntary control over them. In short, he concludes, "ought" implies "can" with respect to moral obligations, but not with respect to legal, financial, and especially epistemic obligations. And if "ought" does not imply "can," epistemic obligations do not imply that we have voluntary control over our beliefs.

But contrary to Feldman, if the roles he cites have responsibilities attached to them, then persons in those roles, if they are obliged to fulfill those roles, must be able to fulfill them. Incompetent teachers can be trained to be good teachers; those who plead that they cannot teach (suffer from incurable pedagogical incompetence) should not take on the role of the teacher. It is wrong for them to do so. Similarly, parents can be educated to be good parents; help is available and should be accepted. Those who plead that they cannot parent should either not take on the role of parent or have their children removed, as social agencies do to protect children in cases of extreme parental incompetence. It is not that such teachers have the responsibility despite their inability to communicate or manage the classroom; it is that the inability to communicate or manage the classroom should render taking on the role of teacher as irresponsible behavior. Similarly, the inability to properly parent should render taking on the role of parenthood as irresponsible behavior. There are responsible and, unfortunately, irresponsible parents and parenting. In short,

Feldman's examples fail to show that "ought" with regard to roles is disconnected from the "can."

Further, do epistemic oughts merely describe the right way to play a certain role, the role of the proper believer? Should one be able to adopt or not adopt this role of believer at will, as one can choose to be a teacher, parent, or cyclist? The obligation with regard to beliefs is not a role or conditional belief. Epistemic obligations are absolute. They are more than mere "recipes for getting at truth"[14] or role descriptors. Since beliefs aim at truth, achieving epistemic excellence is not a conditional aim that depends upon our wants. It is not like: if someone wants to be a good teacher, she ought to be able to communicate effectively. Or, if someone wants to be a good cyclist, he needs to be able to maintain good balance and aptly shift gears. That is, it is not that if persons want, they should form true beliefs. It is not even that if persons want, they are permitted to form true beliefs. Rather, the relation of truth to belief is such that persons are obligated to form contextually relevant, significantly true beliefs and avoid false beliefs. So, epistemic obligations are more like moral obligations than they are like role obligations. It is not that if we want to do the good we should do such and such. Rather, we are obligated, not merely permitted, to do the right or the good. As we have obligations to realize the right or the good, so we have obligations to believe what is significantly true contextually and avoid what is false. This reiterates the points we made in chapter 3 regarding the ground or basis for epistemic obligations. In short, Feldman fails to show that premise 1 is false, and so we turn to premise 2.

VOLUNTARISM AND INDIRECT CONTROL

As most commonly presented in the literature, voluntarism comes in two forms: direct and indirect control over our beliefs. Since the latter is less controversial, we shall begin our considerations with indirect control.

Most philosophers grant that we have what Alvin Plantinga and others term indirect voluntary control over our beliefs.[15] Richard Swinburne, for example, argues that although beliefs are passive states, such that we cannot have direct control over individual beliefs at a given time, we can have control of beliefs diachronically, that is, over time, by making adequate investigations.[16] Our epistemic obligations are to adequately explore, investigate, attend to, and assess the evidence, so that true beliefs will result. Hints of this exist earlier in John Locke.

> But, though we cannot hinder our knowledge, where the agreement is once perceived; nor our assent, where the probability manifestly appears upon due consideration of all the measures of it: yet we can hinder both *knowledge* and *assent, by stopping our inquiry,* and not employing our faculties in the search of any truth. If it were not so, ignorance, error, or infidelity, could not in any case be a fault.[17]

For Locke, one has to investigate the matter, and this investigation will produce a probability. One does not choose to believe or disbelieve on the basis of the probability. Rather, the belief will arise naturally when the probability is discerned. Failure to keep our obligations, then, arises not from believing or failing to believe but in wrongly calculating the probabilities that occasion the belief.[18]

William Alston suggests two ways in which voluntary actions may influence our beliefs. One has to do with actions we take regarding what influences our beliefs.[19] We exercise indirect control by engaging or failing to engage in activities that influence a situation. Examples of this include checking the relevant evidence, getting a second opinion, reflecting on the relevant evidence or the arguments for a position, or noting whether my perceptual or other faculties are working reliably. The other concerns the "activities that affect our general belief-forming habits or tendencies." This might involve forming mental habits and abilities such as becoming more skeptical about taking everything written as true or learning how to recognize, understand, and evaluate arguments. Such practices we can voluntarily undertake in the hope of arriving at true beliefs.

Suppose we adopt the first tactic by taking actions of one sort or another to occasion, cause, or develop a particular belief or set of candidates for belief. But in taking actions with regard to a specific belief or set of candidates, have we not in some sense either begged the question with regard to the truth of that belief or else resorted to prudentialism? Blaise Pascal, who addressed the matter of belief-creating mechanisms, noted that if one has difficulty in believing that God exists, appealing to rational proofs of God's existence is unlikely to bring about belief. Rather, one ought to engage in certain practices, like attending Mass or taking holy water, that eventually will naturally make us believe.[20] But since actions stem from belief, if we take actions in order to bring about belief in a particular proposition, we must already believe either that that proposition is true (since belief aims at truth) or at least that we would be better off believing that it is true.[21] If we already believe that the particular proposition is true, then engaging in the action might be necessary to strengthen the belief but not to form it. And if we believe the proposition simply because it is prudent or in our best interest, we have grounded beliefs on prudential rather than truth concerns. But we have already seen in chapter 3 that prudentialism is not concerned with the truth of the belief per se but with whether it is beneficial, and thus is unable to provide a solid ground for epistemic obligations.

The second option is to take actions that we can describe more generically as becoming a better critical thinker (checking the relevant evidence, getting a second opinion, carefully assessing the logic of the arguments, keeping an open mind). We should "look for more evidence under certain conditions and train [ourselves] to be less credulous."[22] From an externalist point of view, we do our best to make our belief-forming processes as reliable as we can. From an internalist point of view, we develop the habits of more carefully attending to evidence or arguments that will bring us to believe.[23] These actions also are accompanied by beliefs, but not the particular true beliefs aimed at. Rather, the beliefs required are that these activities have the best chance of producing true beliefs. So understood, we now direct epistemic obligations to processes that we have some reason to believe generally will produce true beliefs in us, and they are processes over which we have substantial control. We can control the degree to which we attend to evidence, learn how to reason with cogent and valid arguments, keep an open mind, not rush into judgment, and check the proper functioning of our epistemic faculties. In short, we have the power, required by the obligation, to be conscientious thinkers.

But will granting indirect control over our beliefs save epistemic obligations? Alston finds this view wanting as a basis for epistemic obligations. For one thing, how much critical thinking, investigation, or weighing of the evidence is necessary before we can say that we have satisfied our epistemic obligations? For another, "what would be reasonably expected along this line will vary for different people in accordance with their abilities, experience, education, propensities, and so on."[24] We have already stressed the contextualization of belief, and here it involves the contextualization of the methods for arriving at belief. The levels or degrees of critical thinking expected of a professor of philosophy will differ from those expected of the professor's students when it comes to believing that, for example, Kant's categorical imperative will satisfactorily resolve moral issues. The problem here is the same problem that Clifford faced over a century ago when he wrote, "It is wrong always, everywhere, and for anyone, to believe anything upon insufficient evidence."[25] He never did—and never could—define what he meant by "sufficient," and if one cannot provide the criteria for "sufficient" in the context of what critical thinking activities will bring about true beliefs, epistemic obligations for merely indirect voluntary control are problematic.

Third, I may engage in proper belief-forming habits and still not hold a particular belief.[26] For example, with regard to Pascal's recommendation, taking holy water or attending Masses will not guarantee that I will come to believe that God exists. No clear causal relation exists between engaging in belief-forming habits and the result that I will entertain the belief habituated for. Sometimes engaging in critical thinking frustrates coming to have a belief, in that it leads to delay and more investigation rather than belief. Or someone might have done her best in trying to find out the truth about whether so and so is guilty of the murder, but she is such an incompetent detective that no matter what she tries, her beliefs are based on the wrong evidence and thus never turn out to be true. Or she might be the best detective around, but her beliefs might not have been formed reliably because whenever she considers evidence of this sort, she gets so emotionally attached that she cannot come to a sound or well-founded conclusion.[27] Or the evidence might be so convoluted that despite the best efforts of the investigator, the evidence points in too many directions to bring her to any belief, let alone a true belief.

The general point is that indirect voluntary control is clearly something we possess; this is not in question. We can take actions or enhance our critical thinking performance that may (or may not) bring about particular beliefs. However, understanding epistemic obligations in this indirectly voluntary sense presupposes a close causal connection between activities such as attending to evidence, assessing arguments, becoming a critical thinker, being open-minded, establishing good belief-forming habits, making sure that my belief-forming mechanisms are functioning properly—between these activities and attaining true beliefs. Justification is directed at enabling us to maximize truth and minimize falsity. Without this connection between what might be seen broadly as justifying activities and attaining true beliefs (what Alston terms "truth-conducivity"),[28] we might fulfill our epistemic obligations by taking the appropriate steps with regard to our belief-forming activities or habits without our arriving at or maintaining true beliefs. That we have attended to the evidence as best known to us (that our belief is justified in this sense) provides no guarantee that our belief is true. In fact, there might not be any constant connection, since we might have attended to the wrong evidence, mistakenly relied on unreliable authorities, misinterpreted or twisted the evidence, and so on. Similarly, that we have acquired the belief through what we take to be reliable belief-forming mechanisms provides no guarantee of the truth of the belief, for the mechanisms in any given case might have been unduly influenced, unbeknown to us, by emotions, desires, biases, or environmental factors.

Meeting our epistemic obligations by taking indirect action has shifted the obligation from beliefs to belief-forming processes. That is, cultivating epistemic obligations directed to attending to and assessing arguments, developing good belief-formation habits, and so on, commits us to saying that we fail in our epistemic obligations not if we fail to arrive at truth, but rather if we do not attend to proper belief-forming mechanisms. This is Feldman's considered position when he proposes

> (7) For any person S and proposition *p* and time *t*, S epistemically ought to believe *p* at *t* if and only if *p* is supported by the evidence S has at *t*.[29]

Feldman is concerned with the means of belief formation rather than with any obligation regarding the belief itself.

But without some truth-conducive connection between our belief-forming habits or mechanisms and truth, it would seem that we would not be obligated to hold or withhold a particular belief. Bishop Williamson can trot out that he has attended to the evidence that has confirmed his beliefs about the Holocaust. Those who say he fell short of his epistemic duties to carefully investigate because his belief is false presuppose truth-conducivity. Indeed, they go further by invoking their own (purported) knowledge of the truth to critique the critical thinking activities of the investigator. But if the obligation is to the method, not the belief, one cannot criticize persons for failing to come up with the belief one thinks the persons should have held. They fulfilled their epistemic duty in carrying out the evidential investigation. In short, epistemic obligations to engage in certain practices are some distance from where we started when we spoke about our obligations with respect to the truth.

At the same time, epistemic obligations to engage in certain practices are no less important, for as we saw in the previous chapter, since our belief-forming mechanisms are fallible, attention to justification often enables us to arrive at truth. And since these investigative and critical thinking practices used in justification often succeed in arriving at true beliefs, we have epistemic obligations to engage in them. I in no way want to be thought to be debunking critical thinking; it is indeed an essential part of epistemic excellence. However, although the epistemic obligations found in indirect control are relevant to the justificatory dimension, they are incomplete and insufficient when it comes to holding people accountable for the very beliefs themselves; hence, epistemic obligations cannot be made to rest solely on them. That is, proper emphasis on the obligations found in indirect control over our beliefs does not free us from thinking about direct control over our beliefs.

Epistemic excellence covers a variety of different obligations. It applies to holding true beliefs, to the processes used to arrive at those beliefs, and to the epistemic character out of which beliefs arise. The first requires some significant voluntary control over our beliefs; the latter two require significant voluntary control over the development, possession, and exercise of habits and skills involved in our belief formation processes. The former is necessary because the latter alone does not guarantee true beliefs; the latter is necessary because of our epistemic fallibility and hence our need to employ proper critical thinking skills and habits to arrive at true beliefs. Voluntarism is unproblematic for the latter; we can exercise the relevant control over these processes. However, it is more problematic for the former; to that we now turn.

VOLUNTARISM AND DIRECT CONTROL

If indirect voluntary control is possible and important but inadequate for a full accounting of epistemic obligations to believe contextually significant truths and not hold false beliefs, we need to attend to a kind of control that is more appropriate for epistemic obligations. The kind of control indicated here parallels the kind of control we have over many of our bodily acts or functions. I can have direct control over my breathing, lifting my arm to scratch my head, moving my fingers on the keyboard, moving my legs to walk, rolling my eyes, and so on. I can will or intend these actions to happen and they do. I do not think of what other actions I need to take to accomplish these basic actions; I do them directly. Alston terms this "basic voluntary control."[30] Similarly, some argue, I have direct control over my beliefs. I don't have to take other actions to bring about the belief; I directly can will to believe (or not to believe). In this way I have basic voluntary control over at least some of my beliefs. And if I have direct voluntary control over (at least some of) my beliefs, I can be held accountable for these beliefs, for I have chosen either to have the beliefs I have or to reject significant beliefs that I should hold. Direct voluntary control is what those who hold that we have epistemic obligations are looking for.

The phenomenon of having direct control over our beliefs can be manifested in various ways. Where the evidence for *p* is not compelling, we can decide to believe *p* rather than *not-p*, decide to believe *not-p*, or suspend our belief in *p*. Where the evidence is quite strong but runs counter to our intuitions, emotional constraints, background knowledge, or control beliefs, we might decide to go with or affirm our intuitions rather than with to what the evidence points. For example, despite the reading on my G.P.S. that the house I am looking for requires a left turn, I might believe that it is to the right, given what I have noticed about the street layout in the town. Where there is no evidence one way or another, we might choose to believe *p* on the grounds that it seems to be true, perhaps because it accords with other beliefs that we have, is simpler, or is more aesthetically attractive. We might voluntarily maintain a belief even in the face of cajoling to reject it (as with the biblical Job). These are just some of the behavioral manifestations of having direct control over our beliefs. We will flesh these out in more detail as we respond to critiques of our view in what follows.

Critique of Basic Voluntary Control of Our Beliefs

The major objection to the contention that we have epistemic obligations is that most, if not all, of our beliefs do not lie in our direct power. They are formed automatically from perceptual events, reasoning, attending to evidence, memories, making inferences, and the like. If our beliefs are not in our direct power, if we cannot choose to believe or not believe, or choose to maintain or not to maintain a belief, we are not in a position to choose to believe only those propositions that are true, justified, or have warrant. We nonvoluntarily hold beliefs, some of which are true and some not. We come to believe; our beliefs follow from the causal or rational- or emotional-assessment steps that we take prior to their formation. Beliefs are produced in us by the evidence and reasons, emotions, and appetites, or by the functioning of our diverse epistemic apparatus. Since "ought" implies "can," and since we lack the "can"—the ability to have direct control over our beliefs—we cannot be subject to epistemic obligations. The theory of epistemic obligations "suffers shipwreck before leaving port."[31] Louis Pojman suggests that philosophers have presented two types of arguments to refute belief voluntarism, an argument from psychological impossibility and an argument from logical impossibility. We will consider the former in the next section before turning to the latter.

Psychological Impossibility

1. Argument from Forced Acquisition of Belief

Developing an argument from psychological impossibility, Pojman puts the argument, which he terms the phenomenological argument against belief voluntarism, as follows.

1. Phenomenologically speaking, acquiring a belief is a happening in which the world forces itself upon a subject.
2. A happening in which the world forces itself upon a subject is not a thing the subject does . . . or chooses.
3. Therefore, phenomenologically speaking, acquiring a belief is not something a subject does or chooses.[32]

Premise 1 is defended by several powerful arguments. First, he argues that we cannot choose to accept or reject perceptual beliefs; seeing is (or causes) believing. When I look out my kitchen window and see a brown sparrow eating safflower seeds at my green bird feeder, I do not choose to believe or disbelieve that a sparrow sits warily at my feeder. My perceptual experience occasions or causes my belief about the sparrow; the belief does not arise from an act of my will. In fact, on seeing the sparrow I cannot will the belief that the sparrow is not at the feeder. The belief follows the perception; it "is forced on me."[33] Although I have some control over my perceptions, in that I can direct my perceptual apparatus elsewhere (I could close my eyes) or take physical steps to curtail it (I could pull the curtains or look in a different direction), I lack control over my perceptual beliefs themselves. The beliefs do not reside in my power.

But consider the following, to which we alluded above. I attend a performance where the showman, dressed in gaudy black shirt and pants, puts a scantily clad lady into a long, narrow box and proceeds to cut the box in half. I see the lady enter the box and the showman saw the box in half; yet this experience does not force me to believe that the showman actually sliced the lady in two. The reason that I am not forced to believe this has nothing to do with the perceptual situation. My perceptual faculties are performing properly. If the showman had placed a log instead of the lady inside the box, based on the same perceptual evidence I could readily believe that the log was sawn in two when he noisily cut the box. Rather, the reason I reject my perceptual data in this case may have to do with nonperceptual, moral beliefs, for example, that I believe that the character of the showman is such that he would not saw an innocent woman in half; with general experience, in that no person in his right mind would kill a woman in public; or with previous experience—I might have been fooled previously in the show and resolve not to be duped again. Seeing is not necessarily believing.

One might object that since I did not directly see the lady sawed in half, my belief about the woman results not from perception but from inference. I infer from the context that my perceptions might be inaccurate. But consider the case where I gaze at a blue checkered tablecloth. If I stare at it in a certain way, unblinking, for a certain length of time, the squares appear three-dimensional (one can think of many "magic eye" images that follow this pattern). Yet I am not forced to believe that they really are three-dimensional. I can (and do) withhold my belief that this tablecloth possesses these three-dimensional squares.

Wolterstorff argues that such counterexamples do not show a role for the voluntary. "Whether or not the perceptual experience of seeing a tree produces in one the belief that there is a tree before one depends, among other things, on the beliefs one brings to the situation. . . . What one comes to believe depends on one's sensory experience *plus one's other beliefs*; it does not depend on whether one decides to believe, or on whether one decides or does not decide to withhold belief."[34] The disposition to believe simply is not activated.

Wolterstorff describes this failure to activate the disposition as coming about without the agent's active decision. But why must we omit the agent's deciding role, as the voluntarist holds? That is, must we interpret the contrary instances as cases where it is merely the case that the belief disposition is not triggered? There is no necessity that these experiences be understood in this fashion. It is true that in ordinary perceptual cases the disposition to believe is triggered by the perceived event, in our example, my belief is triggered by the sparrow eating safflower seeds at my feeder. But in the case of the magician sawing the woman in two, the same perceptual conditions fail to activate the disposition because they are presumably overridden by other beliefs. But we can describe this by saying that agents bring their other beliefs about the situation to bear on the perceptual experience, and, weighing the two sets of beliefs, we can conclude that the perceptual experience is best explained by the volitionally invoked beliefs that this is a magic show, that the performer is a magician of reputable character, or that women when cut in half should scream. That is, one is not required to describe belief formation merely passively; accounts where the agent is active in belief formation are likewise plausible. Indeed, they better accord with the way we describe the event: I chose not to believe that the woman was sawed into two parts; this time I was not going to be fooled by the magician and his assistant into believing that what I observed really happened. I overrode my perceptual information; I decided to believe she was still alive although hidden.

In short, though generally speaking a perceptual experience is sufficient to occasion belief without any apparent intermediary volitional act, and in these predominant cases belief formation is passive in that one happens to believe or belief is brought about, one can introduce many cases where the perception is insufficient to occasion the belief. Additional perceptual experiences, the introduction of background sets of beliefs, or even an act of will may be necessary (as in the case of woman sawed in two) for one to form a belief, either affirming or contradicting the perception. Though often seeing occasions believing, seeing does not necessarily occasion believing. I can bring other beliefs to bear on the situation and will to accept or reject the perception to form a different belief than that suggested or indicated by the perception. Wolterstorff's argument does not show that we cannot control perceptual beliefs to some extent; it shows that we don't in fact normally exercise active voluntary control over these beliefs.

Pojman makes an argument similar to the argument from perception with respect to beliefs derived from memory. When I recall something, I do not choose to believe it or not; "Normally, I cannot help believing it." What I remember comes on its own, not by my volition. But again, contrary to Pojman, although this is normally the case, this does not exclude cases where, though I seem to remember something, the memory is unclear or I have countervailing evidence or even an intuition that something is wrong, and so I choose not to believe what my memory presents to me. On seeing a particular person I might recall that I have seen that person previously, but yet choose to reject this belief, either directly or on grounds it would be too much of a coincidence. I might even acknowledge the memory, but note that the memory, though coinciding with my belief, is weak, such that it is firmed up by my choice to have the belief. I might even like the way the memory unfolds and choose to believe it as providing a true account of the event. For example, I might remember how a pretty girl gave me a farewell kiss before I moved to another town, and though the memory is distant and vague, choose to believe it really happened because thinking so brings pleasure—even though I am no longer certain it happened, or at least happened the way I recall it. Pojman recognizes such cases but claims that "the fact that we only weakly believe our memory reports does not imply a volitional element in the belief formation."[35] But why not, as we have shown? The weakness of our beliefs based on memory might not imply volition, but it can be relevant to delineating the role of the voluntary. His claim to the contrary begs the question at issue.

Pojman raises a similar argument from consideration of psychopathological cases. Persons who suffer from schizophrenia often form beliefs that are false and irrational. On the basis of their perceptions they believe things are present that are not or that things are different than they really are. Even when they want these beliefs to change, they are incapable of altering them. A chemical imbalance in the brain, not their will, causes these beliefs. But again, although this shows that some beliefs or beliefs held by certain people in an abnormal state lie beyond the range of basic voluntary control, it by no means shows that all beliefs are beyond the range. In short, appeals to perceptual or memorial beliefs or beliefs held by people in dysfunctional states fail to show that we lack basic direct control over some or many of our beliefs.

2. Argument from Impossibility of Willing False Beliefs

Alvin Plantinga, along with others before and after him who make a similarly structured argument regarding false beliefs,[36] contends that if someone offered him a million dollars to believe that he is under thirty years of age, Plantinga could not honestly collect.[37] If our will controlled our beliefs, he argues, we should be able to do this, if for no other reason than prudentially to collect the offered money.[38] What we find, he argues, is that we simply cannot bring ourselves to believe what we know or have evidence to believe is contrary to the evidence or to what we believe to be false.

But this argument is much less persuasive than it first appears. To say that I don't have control over my beliefs because I cannot will myself to believe true something that I already believe is false provides no relevant counterexample.[39] For one thing, as Sharon Ryan points out, there are many things that I cannot do, but that fact does not establish that I don't have control over them. She gives the example that she could not run over a mother and her child walking down the road. She just could not do this. But this inability does not show that she did not, in some sense, decide not to run over them or that she did not have control of her car. Her freedom is not removed by this moral inability. The "cannot" here is controlled not by physical conditions but by normative conditions: she cannot bring herself to act contrary to moral norms.

She notes that Plantinga might respond that she really could run them over; it is just that she would not do so since she "has not been given a good enough incentive." That is, she could do so provided she had adequate reason. But, she notes, this modification could then apply to Plantinga's case, in that if someone gave him not money but good reason or evidence—say a properly authorized birth certificate—he could believe he was under thirty. "The mere fact that I cannot just believe anything in the face of what I consider to be enormous evidence to the contrary, does not show that my beliefs are not under my control. At most, it shows that we cannot believe a proposition willy-nilly. What's so bad about that?"[40] Probably Plantinga was simply given the wrong incentive. To make their case, belief voluntarists do not have to commit to forming or holding their beliefs randomly or to willing beliefs true that they believe are false.

Plantinga's argument fails for the simple reason that beliefs aim at truth. It is contradictory to say that I believe that *p* is false but I believe *p* nonetheless. Since beliefs aim at truth, and the point of my epistemic obligation is ultimately to maximize contextually significant truths and avoid falsity, it is no objection to the voluntary control of my beliefs that I cannot will myself to believe something true that I either believe is false or that seems to be false. Such would require a mental contradiction. This inability to believe something that I already believe to be false or seems to me to be false is one trait that differentiates epistemic obligations from moral obligations, for whereas I can do something wrong even when I believe that I should not do so, I cannot believe something to be true that I already believe to be false. Nevertheless, the lack of an exact parallel here fails to affect the claim that some or many of my beliefs are voluntary.[41]

In a conference presentation Plantinga suggested that there are varieties of evidence that one might have for a belief, including forensic evidence, propositional evidence, and evidence from perception. To this list he added what he termed *impulsional* or *doxastic* evidence: I might believe *p* on the grounds that *p* seems to be right, acceptable, natural.[42] Beliefs that you think are true feel different from those that you think are false. Plantinga, however, refuses to call this voluntarism, since he holds that one does not have control over one's beliefs; they follow from the evidence. Two responses to this suggestion are in order. First, it is strange to term seeming to be true or right "evidence," since doxastic evidence would apply to every held belief: one cannot believe propositions that seem to be false, since belief is directed to truth. Second, this would be a case of voluntarism if the doxastic evidence is not belief compelling, that is, if one could still withhold belief even in cases where what is proposed seems to be true. One could not, of course, believe it to be false if it seemed to be true, but one could withhold belief even though it seemed to be true. Seeming to be true is necessary for holding a belief, but not sufficient. For Plantinga to deny that this is a case of epistemic voluntarism, he must hold that seeming to be true is not only necessary for holding a belief but also sufficient. It is necessary for holding a belief, since it is contradictory to believe what seems to one to be false. But I see no reason for thinking that it is sufficient, that belief simply follows from *p* seeming to be true. One could hold that *p* seems to be true without believing *p*.

3. Argument from Error

A third argument for the psychological impossibility of willingly forming beliefs is the argument from error. The argument is that although avoiding error can be deliberate, in that one can take steps not to be mistaken, error itself is not deliberate. Any willfulness of error would conflict with the contention that to be in error involves ignorance. One cannot deliberately purpose or intend to be in error, since when I am in error I don't know that I am in error. Rather, I think that what I believe is true. The mistake might have been avoided, but it is not willful. As J. L. Evans puts it, "If [the historian] considers that he has solved the problem and is in fact mistaken, he falls into error. But it is absurd to say that he takes this step willfully. It is something which happens to him rather than something which he chooses to do."[43] Will, then, is not connected to having beliefs, since beliefs can be mistaken.

But Evans' argument commits a crucial confusion. Since beliefs aim at truth, one does not intend to be mistaken or willfully enter into error. About this Evans is correct. However, although one does not intend to be in error one does intend to hold a particular belief that one thinks is true but, as it so happens, may be erroneous. But intending the belief is not intending the error. Evans has confused one's intention of holding a belief with intending a property of that belief here, that it was mistaken. One might intend the belief without intending a property of the belief. This is an instance of the more general principle that to intend something does not imply intending all its properties. I intend to remember my deceased mother but do not intend to have the accompanying sadness of her death. I intend to drive to work but do not intend that my car emit CO_2. This confusion between intending to believe a proposition and intending its properties mitigates Evans' argument against voluntarism.[44]

4. Conclusion

In reflecting on the psychological argument against belief voluntarism, Pojman suggests that at best this argument shows, and should be altered to read, that acquiring beliefs is *typically* not accomplished voluntaristically, that *typically* belief formation occurs when in one way or another the world forces itself upon us and the appropriate belief happens.[45] The voluntarist can respond that this conclusion would refute only a radical voluntarist view that holds that all beliefs are within direct control, and we are not concerned with defending such a radical view. But the voluntarist can go much further. Even if we typically do not exercise control over our perceptual beliefs, that would not show that we *cannot* do so. That typically I do not control the thermostat on my furnace but let the automatic setting sensor determine the temperature does not show that I cannot control the thermostat. If I believe that my perceptual apparatus is working fine, no reason exists to question what I perceive or to doubt that beliefs formed thereby are true, but my ability to take control remains. Similarly with memory. Thus, even if the above arguments worked and voluntarism were not typical, that would fail to refute voluntarism, for it confuses what is the case (we typically yield control) with what is possible (we could exercise control).

Furthermore, the voluntarist will be justifiedly wary of the word "typically," for though we usually do not exercise active control over many perceptual and memory beliefs, a large number of instances remain where we actually do determine our beliefs. We might return to Meiland's example of belief voluntarism that we considered in chapter 3. Meiland speaks of two partners in a business, where substantial, if not sufficient, evidence exists that the one partner is cheating, but the second partner decides not to doubt the first partner but to maintian his belief in the first partner's integrity. The reason is that he wants to preserve the partnership and the company. This looks like a belief based on a volitional act, for the second partner goes against the apparent contrary evidence. One can provide an adequate voluntarist account of this, as Meiland does.

Or consider instances where the evidence underdetermines the belief options. The weather report sugggests a 20 percent chance of rain today. I might look at the sky and wonder whether it is going to rain. The evidence is ambiguous: clouds glower, yet the sun peeks between them. Since the evidence for what will happen weather-wise is underdetermining, I might decide to believe that it will rain today and take the precautionary step of carrying an umbrella to work. Believing that it will rain is not forced on me, but I form a belief that becomes the basis for taking a particular action.

Pojman replies that belief voluntarism fails to provide the best explanation of these types of events. Where the evidence is ambiguous, we can accept a proposition (that it will rain) and even act on it (take an umbrella) without believing it or assenting to its truth.[46] We can simply act on it as an experimental hypothesis. But surely experimental hypotheses require beliefs, beliefs that we select or choose. Alston takes a line similar to Pojman, holding that where the data are ambiguous one neither believes not disbelieves that it is going to rain. He suggests several alternative explantions that he thinks provide a better account than appeals to basic voluntary control.[47] For example, in picking up the umbrella one might hold that at *this moment* the considerations for deciding that it will rain prevail, so that the belief that it will rain follows directly from the momentary conclusive considerations. Or again, it might be that the person makes a working assumption that guides his subsequent actions.[48] The person has to take some action, either taking the umbrella or leaving it behind. So the person might act without actually believing that it will rain, only *as if* believing it will rain. Or again, a person does not want to spoil her new dress and so takes the umbrella as a precaution, without having any belief about whether it will rain. In short, one can act in ambiguous situations without forming beliefs about what action to take.

Alston is correct that alternative hypotheses exist that can explain cases of underdetermination, but this in no way conflicts with the claim that a voluntarist's account also might explain the belief lying behind the action. These alternative hypotheses do not circumvent the need for forming or employing beliefs. Working assumptions involve or contain beliefs on which one takes actions. Believing *as if* is itself a form of belief. If someone asks me, "Do you believe it will rain?" I might reply, "The weather report was ambiguous, but because it seems as if it will rain I will take the umbrella." Taking the umbrella is an action that follows upon the forming of an as-if belief that it will rain. Several years ago, when I boarded a subway in Budapest, I saw a crowd of men get on and surround me. I had an intuition (formed the belief) that they would try to rob me; so I jammed my hand into my pocket to cover my wallet. My "working assumption" was an intuitive belief that guided my action, even though I had never had any such previous experience (the belief turned out to be true). Alston's alternative readings neither show that they pose better alternative accounts nor that the alternative readings do not invoke voluntarist beliefs. That is, Alston's arguments do not establish that belief voluntarism does not adequately resolve cases of underdetermination or ambiguity; they only show that in some cases one may suggest reasonable alternative hypotheses. But since these other accounts also invoke beliefs, they are fully in line with belief voluntarism. In short, belief voluntarism is not threatened by the psychological argument.

In sum, the psychological case against belief voluntarism fails. However, the critic may reply, isn't the concession that some of our beliefs are not in our control ultimately fatal to voluntarism and hence to epistemic obligations? Alston writes, "The voluntarist has already abandoned vast stretches of the territory. He has given up all propositions that seem clearly true or false, and these constitute the bulk of our beliefs."[49]

Alston's point, if it is to be telling, has to be more carefully put. Belief voluntarists have "given up" all beliefs that they think follow necessarily from the evidence or from belief-forming mechanisms. They have "given up" all beliefs they already think are true because the relevant propositions seem to be true, and the point of belief is to arrive at truth. Belief voluntarists also have "given up" all beliefs that they already think false, since they want to avoid holding false beliefs. But does this prevent voluntarists from changing their mind about beliefs they now think true or false? Not really. Belief voluntarists might address these beliefs directly, holding that what they once thought true they now think false or what they once thought false they now think true. That is, they may affirm the contrary belief as true because it now seems to be true and belief is directed to truth. Or they may address the beliefs indirectly in terms of relevant evidence, attending to accumulating sufficient evidence that will result in changing the beliefs. But these "sacrifices" are hardly fatal in the way Alston thinks. Even in cases such as perception and memory where we have given up control, it does not follow that we cannot exercise control. We exercise passive belief formation because it is the most efficient way to operate, just as allowing my thermostat to control the house temperature is the most efficient way to heat the house. But giving up control of belief formation or maintenance to efficiency does not mean that we cannot exercise control over it at some point.

Belief Voluntarism Is Contradictory

Others have advanced arguments to show that belief voluntarism is what Pojman terms conceptually impossible. The arguments have a common thematic structure: belief aims at truth, but in direct believing or "just believing" the person has no connection (except accidental) with the truth. Hence, believing directly or at will is impossible. Let me begin with the argument advanced by Pojman, namely, that the logic of belief argues against basic belief voluntarism.

1. Pojman and Beliefs Caused by Willing

Pojman maintains that, although voluntarism is not strictly contradictory, in the broad sense it is. That is, there is a broad inconsistency in holding the propositions espoused by the voluntarist position, for whereas beliefs are formed in terms of truth considerations, the voluntarist forms beliefs independent of evidential or truth considerations. One cannot, with full consciousness, believe *p* while at the same time believing *p* for reasons other than truth. Pojman puts the argument this way.

1. If A believes that *p*, A believes that *p* is true.
2. In standard cases of belief, the truth of *p* is wholly dependent on the state of affairs, S, which either corresponds to *p* (and makes *p* true) or fails to correspond to *p* (and makes *p* false).
3. In standard cases of belief, whether or not the appropriate state of affairs S that corresponds to *p* obtains is a matter that is independent of A's actions and volitions.
4. In standard cases of belief, A subconsciously or consciously believes or presupposes premise 3.
5. Therefore, in standard cases of belief, A cannot both believe *p* and that A's belief is presently caused by his willing to believe that *p*.[50]

In short, a contradiction obtains between the standard analysis of belief and the volitionist's contention that beliefs are formed or caused by a person's will, independent of truth considerations about the relevant states of affairs. The person must believe that there is some evidence for the belief, evidence in virtue of which the belief is true.

The conclusion (5), however, does not follow, for Pojman has confused conditions for the truth of a belief with conditions for believing. Volitionists are not maintaining that "I believe *p* merely because I want to believe *p* and therefore *p* is true," but rather that "I believe *p* because *p* seems to be true, and I want to hold true beliefs." For example, in cases where one has insufficient evidence regarding the belief or its contradictory—evidence that does not determine belief—volition plays a role. I might not have any or sufficient evidence for *p*, but since I want to believe the truth and *p* seems to be true, I believe *p*. My choosing to believe *p* does not affect the way I view the ground of the truth of the belief, that is, that *p* seems to reflect the way the world is. Pojman is thus mistaken in holding that volitionists hold the belief solely because they want to. They hold the belief because the proposition believed seems to be true, despite the absence of sufficient evidence, and it seems to be true because that is the way the world seems to be. The cause of their holding the belief includes, significantly, their volition and their desire to believe the truth. Hence, it is perfectly possible to believe *p*, that *p* is true because of the states of affairs in the world, and also to believe that the will plays a significant causal role in forming the belief.[51]

2. Williams and the Self-Contradictoriness of Belief Voluntarism

In an oft-discussed piece, Bernard Williams also suggests that belief voluntarism results in a contradiction, presenting a version slightly different from Pojman. Beliefs aim at truth, for we use truth and falsity to assess belief. If I know that beliefs are directed toward truth, and if at the same time I believe that I can consider a proposition that may be true or false and voluntarily affirm a belief, then I am engaged in a contradiction. On the one hand I am affirming that beliefs are directed toward truth, but on the other hand I hold at the same time that they may not be directed at truth. "If I could acquire a belief by will, I could acquire it whether it was true or not; moreover I would know that I could acquire it whether it was true or not."[52] And I would know I could do this before willing it as a belief. But then, Williams argues, before I believed it I could not think of it as a belief to be willed by me, since beliefs by their very nature aim at truth.

That is, I cannot simultaneously hold that I consciously intend to will it as a belief (something I hold to be true) and also know that I acquired it at will (since this is accomplished independent of truth conditions).

Williams' argument, however, is problematic. Williams contends that if I am to will to believe something, for it to be a belief I need to know that what I am believing is something that purports to be true, since belief aims at truth. But acquiring the belief at will does not mean that my belief does not aim at truth (at what is really the case). The aim does not change; what changes is how the belief is acquired. It is not acquired through perceptual experience, and hence, as Williams notes, it not an empirical belief. But not being an empirical belief does not mean that it does not aim at reality; whether the self-willed belief is true or not still depends on reality. It is just that the evidential, rational forming procedures that automatically create or bring about belief are supplanted by features relating primarily to the will.

One can see that his argument is problematic by noting that it would likewise hold against any theory of belief acquisition. Williams' contention—that if I am to will to believe something, not only could I acquire it whether it was true or not, but I would know that I could do so regardless of whether it was in fact true—would make almost all believing by finite beings contradictory, for since nontautologous propositions may be false, and since I can know that they may be false, I can acquire them whether they are true or not and would know that I am doing so. This even applies to indirectly acquiring a belief or believing. If I can acquire a belief indirectly based on justification, I can acquire that belief regardless of whether or not it is true, and moreover I would know this to be the case. Before obtaining the belief, while seeking indirectly, through investigation of reasons or grounds, to acquire a true belief, I would know that the resulting belief, whatever it is, might not be true. Once I believe it is a justified belief, it still does not follow that it is true, for even though it is justified it may be false, despite the fact that now I take it to be true. Thus, any acquisition of belief (other than in tautologies) falls prey to Williams' argument if his argument is sound, yet clearly we do think of these as possible beliefs "purporting to represent reality" before we believe them. So clearly something is amiss.

What is amiss is that Williams has confused objective and subjective conditions for knowing truth. Williams' purported contradiction arises only if one fails to disregard the distinction between whether the proposition is true and whether the person takes the proposition to be true. As Williams affirms, when persons acquire a belief, it is in the context of being concerned about the truth of the proposition. They aim at truth. In believing that they should aim at truth, the truth they aim at is truth belonging to propositions in respect to the proposition's relation to the world. Prior to their coming to believe *p*, they would not hold *p*, the belief in question. It is possible, for example, that to this point they have suspended judgment on the grounds that they do not have sufficient evidence for its truth or falsity or were unconvinced of the evidence, or perhaps they have never thought to entertain *p*. However, when they come to believe, for example voluntarily, they now believe that the proposition expressing the belief is true. The proposition might still be false; it is just that now they believe *p* to be true. But in coming to believe, they have not contradicted their claim that belief is directed toward truth. Their voluntarily assumed belief is directed to truth, and hence if they think that the proposition is true, it is appropriate that they believe it. It is only when one presupposes that the aim of belief (truth) and cause of the person's actual belief (what the person takes to be true) are determined to be the same that Williams' criticism holds. But there is no reason to think that the aim of belief and the cause of the person's belief are to be determined in the same way. The former is determined in terms of objective truth conditions; the latter in terms of what the believer takes to be true.

Merely believing something by volition neither means that one believes it apart from it seeming to be true nor that the belief formed in this fashion is not true. One believes it volitionally because it seems to be true, and it can seem to be true now even if it did not seem true previously, and one might believe apart from evidence (though as we shall see, that need not be the case). The latter might not be a recommended or even, as Pojman pointed out, a typical procedure, but the subjective basis with regard to the truth of the claim remains. And the belief formed in this fashion could in fact be true. The way one forms the belief is independent of determining whether the belief is actually true or not, though the aim is the same.[53] One wants one's belief to be true and believes it because it seems to be true, but whether or not it actually is true is another matter.

Williams' worry here is that one can get oneself to believe whatever one wants to believe. And in this case, it is as likely that we will arrive at falsity as at truth. But the voluntarist is not claiming that mere belief, apart from evidence, is desirable. Surely possessing evidence leading to justification of the belief is most desirable. Only in such cases can we make progress against self-deception. But the fact that persons responsibly use and, indeed, require evidence is not an argument against belief voluntarism. Rather, the belief voluntarist's objection was that having epistemic obligations solely directed to justification is inadequate because it requires that justification be truth-conducive when in fact it is not always so.

3. *Swinburne and Reasons for Belief*

Richard Swinburne, in defending his view that beliefs are passive states arrived at involuntarily, develops an argument that attempts to circumvent our response to Williams, maintaining that we can hold that *p* is true only because we have reasons for *p*. We might formalize his argument as follows.

1. Suppose that I can bring about [my beliefs] intentionally.
2. To do something intentionally involves knowing that you are doing it.
3. [But] if I knew that what I called "my beliefs" were the result of my choice, I would know that they were not forced upon me by outside forces, that what I

"believed" was in no way influenced by what was the case in the outside world; what I "believed" was simply what I chose to believe.

4. But then I would know that I had no reason or grounds for believing "my beliefs" either to be true or to be false; they would be just as likely to be false as to be true.
5. But if I thought that my beliefs were such, I would not really believe them.
6. Thus, we believe our beliefs because we know that . . . they are forced upon us by the outside world.[54]

Clearly, the problematic premise is 3. Swinburne apparently thinks that the second part of the consequent of 3—that they were in no way influenced by what was the case in the outside world—either follows from or unpacks the first part of the consequent—that beliefs are not forced upon me by outside forces. However, the first part of the consequent does not entail the second part. That I was not forced to believe *p* does not entail that I was not influenced to believe *p*.

To return to the umbrella case, it is surely the case that my taking the umbrella is influenced by the outside world. If I were not going outside, if I did not mind getting wet, if I were not going to work or didn't believe that I should walk to work, or if an umbrella was not handy, I would not pick up the umbrella. Picking up the umbrella is not forced on me, but that is not to say that I am not influenced in my decisions. Voluntarists need not isolate themselves from information, they need not decide or choose to believe in a vacuum, and they need not decide or choose to believe willy-nilly. Indeed, they cannot do this. Such assumptions are not necessarily parts of the voluntarists' case.

To return to the magician example we used earlier, that I am not forced by my perception of the magician sawing in two the box with the woman in it to believe that the woman was likewise sawed in two does not mean that I cannot advance reasons for my counterbelief. I might suggest that the magician would not risk prosecution for such a public act, the magician is a person of known high moral character, illusion is an accepted part of the magician's trade, and so on. That I choose not to believe or override my sensory evidence does not mean that my sensory evidence, and other countervailing evidence, are irrelevant to the belief. Indeed, it is this evidence to which I would appeal to show that my withholding or not forming a belief that the woman is in two parts has some justification. Swinburne assumes mistakenly that reasons here are causes such that if I consider reasons for thinking the belief true, unless those reasons are determinative or sufficient, I have no grounds for that belief.

Since premise 3 fails, 4 no longer follows: I might indeed have reasons for adopting a belief, so that the matter is not 50-50. But the reasons need not be determinative. As such, premise 5 no longer follows as well: if my belief has reasons but not determining reasons, I still will have reasons for forming a belief on such grounds. I will really believe them. In short, belief voluntarists are not committed to conclusion 6 at all; they need not hold that the only beliefs we entertain are those forced upon us.

4. Scott-Kakures' Argument for Conceptual Impossibility

A fourth version of the impossibility argument has been advanced by Dion Scott-Kakures.[55] He contends that a conceptual impossibility lurks within the voluntarist notion that one can voluntarily believe something: that I can believe what I want. It is not merely a contingent matter that I cannot—a thesis we have doubted—but that it is conceptually impossible. Whereas Williams focused on the alleged impossibility lurking in the prior state of wanting to believe, Scott-Kakures focuses on the transition between states of not believing and believing.

As did Williams before him, Scott-Kakures distinguishes two states or cognitive perspectives: the state prior to the belief and the state of believing. In the prior state (1) I want to believe *p*, (2) I desire to believe *p*, (3) currently I do not believe *p*, and (4) my believing *p* is currently not justified—there is nothing in my current epistemic state that justifies *p* for me. In the anterior state of a self-fulfilling belief, (5) I believe *p*, (6) I produced my belief in *p* directly by an act of my will, and (7) my belief that *p* is justified.[56] (Although he does not strictly say this, it appears that he treats these as necessary conditions in order to make his conceptual incompatibility criticism work.)

Between the two states is what he terms the *belief state transition*. He argues that if this is to be a direct willing, it has to be a voluntary intentional act as over against a nonvoluntary or deviant event. To qualify as a voluntary intentional act, this transition should be a basic action, and to be such there has to be guidance, control, or monitoring of the intentional behavior. That is, the transition must be controlled by a mediating mental state that has a content that anticipates the new belief, so that when this belief appears it satisfies the conditions for the intention. The new belief cannot just appear; it must be connected to the original intention not merely causally but in terms of the content of the intention: the new belief is what the person intended to believe. But at the same time the willing or intending cannot have a reason; otherwise, one believes because of the reason and the belief is not directly but indirectly willed; it is willed through the reasons for or justifying the belief.

But for Scott-Kakures this is precisely the locus of the problem. If the willing must be nonrational in that it has no rational explanation or reason (though it has a cause), then there is no guidance as to how the belief is realized. And without guidance or monitoring, there is no satisfaction of the intentional conditions and thus no reason to think that the belief was arrived at intentionally rather than that it merely happened. And if one cannot determine that it was intentional rather than merely being a deviant result, one cannot say that the person voluntarily arrived at the new belief because he wanted or desired to. One cannot say that he did what he wanted to rather than that it merely came to pass. In effect, because an unbridgeable cognitive rift lies between the anterior state regarding belief in *p* and the subsequent state of belief, direct willing of belief cannot be a basic intentional action. "For if I aim directly at believing that *p*, then I must leave behind the intention to believe that *p* before I am to believe that *p*."[57] Direct voluntary belief is impossible.

Several clarifications are necessary here. First, it is important to note that (7) need not be the case for the belief voluntarist. The voluntarist can hold that I might now believe *p*, thinking that it is true, but have no justification for my belief. Indeed, if I had a justification for the belief, such that my belief follows from that justification, I might believe *p* because of those reasons and hence believe *p* indirectly—a point Scott-Kakures himself makes. Condition (7) begs the question by assuming that the argument against voluntary direct belief is successful. Accordingly, all that applies in the anterior state are (5) and (6).

Second, (4) is ambiguous between a strong and a weak sense of "not justified." In the weak sense, my belief that *p* is justified in that "nothing I do currently believe is sufficient epistemic justification for my believing that p." That is, I do not possess sufficient evidence to believe *p*. In the strong sense, something is "immediately available which rules out the belief that p."[58] That is, believing *p* is unjustified in that *p* is ruled out by other beliefs. But these two senses of not being justified are not equivalent; that believing *p* is currently not justified for me is not equivalent to it being ruled out by my other beliefs. Suppose I consider the belief that my college president is interviewing for a presidential position at another university. This belief might be unjustified in that it conflicts with, is ruled out by, the belief that he is happy being president of my current campus, morally keeps his promises, and has contractually committed himself to six more years of being president. I cannot consistently maintain both that he is interviewing and that he is contractually committed (and thus not interviewing) and morally keeps his promises simultaneously; to do so would be irrational. However, it also might be unjustified in the weaker sense where I have no rational reason to entertain the belief. I might have no reason to believe that my college president is interviewing for a position at another university, but I also might have no reason to think that such is ruled out since I am not privy to the terms of his contract. I might simply not have any evidence concerning his possible job searches and contract and hence have no reason to believe that he is or is not looking elsewhere for a job. In Audi's terms, I have the disposition to believe, but do not have the (dispositional) belief either way. Hence, the weak sense of not being justified is not equivalent to the strong sense of being ruled out.

So (4) is ambiguous. If it is the case that believing *p* is unjustified in the strong sense, then Scott-Kakures may be correct in his argument that a rift exists between the two states or cognitive perspectives. There is no clear way to move intentionally (given his analysis of intentional basic actions) from the view that *p* is ruled out to the belief that believing *p* is justified. But the belief voluntarist need not adhere to either (7) or the strong sense of not being justified in (4); the weak sense of (4) is perfectly possible. This allows that in the anterior state I might simply have no belief with respect to p. As above, I have no evidence either way regarding my college president looking for another position, so it is not necessary in the anterior state to believe either *p* or non-*p*; there is no justification for believing either. Believing it is the case that he is looking would be unjustified, as would believing it is not the case. Thus, (4) understood in the strong sense is not a necessary part of the anterior belief.[59]

But then there is no gap or fissure between the anterior belief state and the posterior belief state. The transition between them is guided by the desire to believe *p* and the intention to believe *p*, an intent that does not conflict with the fact that I currently have no justification for believing or not believing that *p*. The transition between the states is guided in that the intention will be fulfilled just in case I believe *p* by willing to believe *p*. That is, it is carried out in the way intended. Without condition (4) being understood in the strong sense, the move from not believing to believing is not impossible, for contrary to Scott-Kakures, the beliefs that generate the intention are not incompatible with my believing that *p*. The content of *p* has not changed, though the intention has changed in that the intention has been realized. The intention to believe *p* need not be abandoned before its satisfaction conditions are realized because there is no incompatibility.

No "cognitive blind spot" exists. Just as I know what it is to raise my arm and the conditions under which it is typical and appropriate to realize it, so as a voluntarist I know what it is to believe *p* and the conditions needed to realize it in a voluntarist way. Just in case *p* is not ruled out, it is possible for *p* to be believed, and my willing it realizes it, despite the fact that, as with raising my arm, I do not know how I do it. One might quibble with whether it is done in a "typical or appropriate way," but whether doing it voluntarily is one way of doing it is what is in dispute. If the "typical and appropriate way" required for action to be intentional requires rational justification, then just willing to believe fails in this regard. But to require such begs the very question at issue about the possibility of voluntaristic belief. Furthermore, absence of rational justification does not entail that the behavior of willing a belief is unguided or unmonitored. The plan is that I will believe *p* (whereas before I did not), and though believing *p* is not justified (just as raising my arm might not be justified but desired and willed), *p* is produced. And without the cognitive blind spot or unbridgeable gap, the alleged conceptual impossibility vanishes.

The All-or-Nothing Argument

What we have seen so far is that there is no definitive psychological or conceptual argument that rules out belief voluntarism. The arguments presented, although interesting and provocative, are not successful, decisive, or in any way telling against belief voluntarism. At the same time, they do strongly suggest that the beliefs formed in the manner they critique—belief by fiat—are probably not significant or plentiful enough to ground a robust view of epistemic obligations since they lack any rational or evidential grounding.

But should the belief voluntarist worry about this? The answer is no. What underlies many, if not all, criticisms and many of the discussions of belief voluntarism is a view of voluntarism that requires that the agent be completely unaffected by any causal or epistemic conditions. In effect, critics of belief voluntarism have reduced having control over our beliefs to belief by fiat and once that is done announce what they think is an easy victory. As Trudy Govier points out,

> Thinking of decision and choice in contexts of belief, philosophers have tended to turn their attention immediately to belief by *fiat*. Perhaps this is because many beliefs simply emerge naturally from presented evidence; decision and will might seem only to be needed when one wants to believe rather perversely, against evidence, for some non-truth-oriented reason. When one is epistemically and logically well-behaved, it appears, there is no room for choice and decision in arriving at beliefs; the question of these arises when one has some motive for ignoring epistemic and logical norms.[60]

This view of belief voluntarism is clearly present in Barbara Winters, who defines belief voluntarism as believing *p* in such a way that *p* neither originated nor is sustained in a way that has any connection with the truth of *p*.[61] According to her, "to constitute a genuine case of *believing at will*, three necessary conditions must be met. First, the belief [must] have been acquired directly and as a result of intending to hold it. . . . Second, . . . the belief must be acquired independently of any considerations about its truth," and third the agent must be aware of trying to arrive at the belief in this way (a consciousness requirement).[62] Given these conditions, she then argues that it is easy to hold that beliefs cannot be so sustained, since we simply cannot believe something that has no connections with truth considerations.

Winters, like Williams and others, is correct that belief is connected to truth considerations. It makes little sense to say that we intentionally believe things that seem to us to be false. The first condition, however, is not true. It makes two claims: the belief must be acquired directly and as a result of intending to hold it. The second clause may be essential to belief voluntarism: if the person does not intend to hold the belief, it would not be a belief voluntarily adopted or maintained (though we shall question any strong version of this subsequently). But the truth of the first clause depends on what is meant by "acquired directly." If acquired directly means exclusive of evidence or reasons—what are termed indirect considerations—then this need not be the case. As we shall argue, direct considerations (the person intends to hold the belief and wills to do so) are compatible with indirect considerations, so long as the indirect considerations are not necessitating or compelling: they do not make holding the belief compulsory, so that persons say that they cannot but believe. Or put another way, the conditions do not make believing something that happens to a person. This then speaks to Winters' second consideration; she takes belief voluntarism to be all (without any evidence) or nothing (if a belief has evidence, it is not voluntary).[63] For Winters, as for Swinburne and other critics whom we have overtly considered and many others we have not overtly considered, the connection between belief and truth is made only through reasons. She writes, "[The voluntarist] cannot regard himself as believing something while knowing that his belief did not stem from a source that made it in any way likely that the beliefs acquired from it were true."[64] Justification, she argues, is necessary for one to hold a belief to be true. Voluntarists have disengaged themselves from truth conditions because they have allegedly disengaged from reason.

But I see no reason to think that the second condition is true. In spelling out a fiatist interpretation, Trudy Govier notes four conditions.

(i) we want to believe p
(ii) we didn't believe p at time t_1
(iii) we believe p at time t_2, not very much later than t_1
(iv) we did not have access to evidence pertaining to p, or to anything we would take to be evidence pertaining to p, at times between t_1 and t_2.[65]

But, as Govier notes, belief voluntarists need not be belief fiatists at all. They need not advocate (iv), namely, that evidence is irrelevant to their holding the belief or that their belief is contra-evidential. Neither need they (nor should they) claim that they are unconcerned with truth. Rather, they only need to claim in cases of voluntaristic belief the evidence is not belief-compelling. Beliefs, considered in light of evidence, are not caused passively.

We have argued all along that meaningful analogies exist between epistemic obligations and moral obligations. Given these analogies, we might gain significant insight into belief voluntarism by looking at the conditions involved in voluntarism with respect to our actions. When we hold that persons perform an act voluntarily or freely, several conditions must be met. (1) The action results from the person's choices; the person chooses to act in a certain way. The person does it because he or she wants or desires to do it. The person intends to act in a particular way. (2) The person's action is not compelled by something or someone other than the person him- or herself. The action is unforced (but not unconditioned). (3) The person could have acted differently. [This third condition should be qualified, for there are cases where I can be said to have acted freely even though I could not have acted differently. In such cases, the action is free when persons choose believing that they could have acted differently and they did not choose the action that would have been impossible. Consider the case where I choose to stay in my office and work on this chapter rather than drive to the grocery store to pick up baked chicken for supper (as my wife instructed me). However, unbeknown to me, she has taken our only car to go to the dentist. In this case, though in reality I am not free to drive to the store, my action of working in my office rather than driving to the store is free, since it was freely chosen by me. That is, it meets conditions 1 and 2, and though it fails to meet condition 3, this condition does not come into play because I did not choose to actualize it. I was ignorant of that fact, but yet acted as I wanted, without compulsion.]

It should be noted that nowhere in these conditions is it required that causal conditions do not affect or influence our acting. Despite the presence of causal conditions that condition, limit, conscribe, and facilitate our actions, where we have significant choice to do something we want, we are thought to be free and accordingly are responsible for our actions. Indeed, only because there are causal conditions can we act. The action is free when the operative causal conditions do not strictly limit all but one possibility or compel a particular action, when in a limited sense one can do what one wants given the operative conditions. In effect, freedom is compatible with there being causes (as necessary conditions) for our actions; it is incompatible with being compelled by those causes to act in a particular way.

Furthermore, an action can be voluntary and intentional even where we might not know many of the limiting conditions. In choosing to act, persons have to consider some of the particular conditions that hold and the options available to them. That is, they need to be aware, to some degree, of the facts of the case and the general principles—including moral ones if one is morally evaluating the action—that hold. However, they need not be aware of all or even of many of the causal conditions that are operative and affecting their choice. Total awareness of all causal conditions of the action is not presupposed by the claim that one is acting voluntarily and furthermore is totally unrealistic. The point is that many of these causal conditions—and many other conditions, both facilitating and conditioning my action—might be unknown to me, but still my act would be termed voluntary. In effect, despite the presence of causal conditions that condition, limit, or conscribe our actions, where we have significant choice so that we can do something of what we want, we are thought to be free and accordingly responsible for our actions. Indeed, the situation is not merely "despite these conditions." It is also because of the presence of many causal conditions that it is possible for me to stay home and work. That I am breathing, my heart is beating, my brain is functioning normally, the electricity is working, atmospheric conditions are conducive to there being electrical power, and so on: these conditions facilitate my action.

But that I am currently not thinking about causal conditions or am unaware of them does not remove the fact that my action of staying and working is both causally conditioned and voluntary. In short, voluntariness or freedom is not completely noncausal, but occurs within the context of causes that limit and facilitate both decision making and acting, conditions about which we may or may not be aware. Full consciousness of all that is involved in my choices or actions is not a necessary condition for a voluntary action.

Neither is merely wanting sufficient to make an action voluntary. This applies not only to complex actions but to basic actions as well. As Ryan points out, to perform the basic action of raising my arm or hand, "it is not really true that I can just raise my hand if I want to. Lots of other things need to be true as well. For example, my brain has to be working correctly, my arm has to be working correctly, and so forth. . . . The mere presence of a want is not sufficient to make the action free."[66]

Much of what we have said about causes applies to reasons as well; reasons are relevant to voluntary action. The fact that I had reasons to stay and write this chapter rather than go to the supermarket does not remove the voluntariness of the action. Indeed, the presence of reasons helps make the action understandable and reasonable. But being reasonable is not contrary to being voluntary or free. This, contrary to some of the discussions, also applies to voluntary basic actions. If my arm just shoots up, this is not an action but a reflex (as when my leg jerks in my sleep at night or the doctor taps my knee with his rubber mallet). However, if I raise my arm intentionally, it is a basic action. This basic action occurs in the context of reasons. I might raise my arm to pick an apple, to ask a question, to signal a turn on my bicycle, to wave good-bye, or to respond to the philosopher's request to demonstrate a basic action. In effect, I raise my arm intentionally or purposively, which is represented by the preposition "to" that indicates the reason. The presence of reasons does not make my action involuntary but rather helps to make it rational. Both reasons and causes are consonant with voluntary acts, so long as they are not totally conditioning but leave us free to take different actions.

In sum, moral actions are never totally free in the sense of having no causal conditions. There are limiting and facilitating causal conditions, and there are reasons directed to making the actions rational. Our freedom lies somewhere on a continuum between being totally free of all conditions (which despite the protestations of Sartre never occurs) and being totally determined (in which case we are not acting but engaging in responsive or reflex behavior). The fact that we are somewhere in between indicates that we are more or less conditioned, more or less responsive to reasons, and more or less free. But none of this militates against holding our actions voluntary in most cases that fall within the broad middle range of caused but not compelled actions. Only as we approach the totally conditioned end, as with the schizophrenic, the psychotic, or someone seriously suffering from senility or Alzheimer's disease, can we begin to significantly question the voluntariness of the action. In short, even in the most basic actions, as distinguished from mere reflex behavior, causal conditions and reasons are meaningfully present in ways that still allow us to speak of voluntary action. Their presence allows us to be free enough to allow for accountability for our actions.

This analysis of voluntariness with respect to action is instructive when we turn to voluntariness and belief. Just as moral actions are not totally free (there are limiting or conditioning causes or reasons for our actions) but yet we are free enough to allow for voluntariness, responsibility for our actions, and moral accountability, so our beliefs when voluntary are not totally unencumbered—from the conditions that distinguish one belief from another to the presence of reasons relevant to but not determining beliefs. One can still hold that the beliefs are voluntarily held, that they aim at truth, that the agent has reasons relevant to them, and also hold that they are voluntary and that agents can be held epistemically accountable for forming or holding them.

So what conditions are we talking about when we consider that a person believes voluntarily? The three conditions parallel those given for voluntary acts on p. 157. (1) First, for a belief to be voluntary, the belief results from our choices, if not necessarily in being formed intentionally, at least counterfactually in that we could withhold belief if we wanted to. The belief does not arise passively, but we form the belief from the desire for truth. We may play a role in various dimensions of believing: setting the conditions in which the belief may arise, developing a good epistemic character that enables us to successfully believe, forming the belief in conscious evaluation and acceptance of the evidence, and at times consciously and intentionally sustaining the belief. In each case, the belief arises out of the desire for truth.

Some have held that since a voluntary belief is one that is held intentionally, one has to be *fully* conscious of our belief formation or maintenance in order that it be voluntary. This is reflected in Winters' condition that "the action of acquiring the belief at will be performed with the agent fully aware that he or she is attempting to arrive at the belief in this way."[67]

In voluntarily *forming* a belief, it is reasonable to hold that we have some degree of awareness of doing so. That is, the first time we voluntarily form the belief, some form of consciousness is involved. But it does not follow that we are *fully* aware that we are doing so. This does not make belief formation involuntary. Indeed, it is no different from voluntarily taking an action. That I choose to do an act does not require that I be fully aware of my choosing. For example, when I steer my car around a corner, I do so voluntarily but am not fully aware of what I am doing. I might be attending to a program on National Public Radio, listening to my wife who is carpooling with me, thinking about getting to school on time, or focusing on the upcoming class discussion. That I am making the relevant moves to turn the vehicle might be marginal to consciousness, at best. This was brought home to me when I taught my children to drive. When I attempted to show my son how to release the steering wheel to recover from a turn, I did not know—could not remember—whether I did it hand over hand or simply let the wheel slide. I had to consciously do it several times to recall what actions I employed. Clearly, releasing the steering wheel is a voluntary act done while driving, but it does not follow that I am fully aware of how I handle the wheel when I complete the turn.

Similarly with *holding* a belief. One might voluntarily hold a belief without being *fully* aware that one holds the belief. This follows from two things. First, I might have formed a belief voluntarily and even intentionally and still hold that belief, but not be aware that I continue to hold that belief. I might have forgotten that I formed that belief; many things might have happened since I formed that belief so that I am not aware that I any longer believe it. But if someone asked me whether I believed *p*, I would reply that I did. Many years ago I wrote a college term paper on the concept of Deutero-Isaiah. Interestingly enough, a half dozen or so years later, the subject came up in a job interview. I could remember that I wrote the paper but for the life of me could not remember how I argued or came down on the complex issue. When the interviewer asked my view, I gave him my current belief, which upon checking was the belief I had formulated, albeit with different reasoning, some years before. Hence, though I formed the belief at one time, I was no longer aware that I held that belief, though in fact I had evidence (my subsequent affirmation) that I did hold it.

Since on some accounts beliefs are dispositions, we are not aware of all (or indeed of many) of our beliefs. Though we formed the belief voluntarily and still dispositionally hold the belief, one cannot say that we are currently aware of the belief, let alone fully aware. Yet none of this militates against the belief being held voluntarily. Of course, it is reasonable to hold that we are or can be aware, to some degree, of our dispositions. If I reflect on the matter or observe my own behavior, I know that I am disposed to eat in a certain way (I eat my food systematically in a clockwise motion), to put on my clothes in a certain order, to start my car before buckling my seat belt rather than after buckling it, to sleep on my stomach, and so on. Of some of these dispositions I am aware, and I am free to choose to actualize them or not. I could start my car after I buckle up or eat all of one kind of food before starting on the next or eat in a counterclockwise direction. In fact, I have some control over the actualization of these dispositions and in this way over the dispositions themselves, for by acting differently I would develop different dispositions. If we did not have some control, then we would no longer be free with respect to actualizing these dispositions. Yet even of these common dispositions we often are not fully aware. I generally don't think about the fact that I eat following a particular pattern; I just eat that way. However, the pattern I follow remains voluntary, in that I could change it if it were pointed out to me and I wanted to and tried hard enough to bring about the altered behavior that would change the disposition. We might say similar things about dispositional belief. We might be aware of a particular belief, and indeed by taking action we can shape, form, or alter that belief. Not only by forming beliefs, but by altering them, we manifest a degree of control over them without necessarily being fully aware of holding them. However, where altering a belief is intentional, it is reasonable to hold that we are aware to some extent of it.

Second, we might be aware that we hold a belief without being aware that we believe the complex belief's component beliefs. But being unaware or not fully aware of the component beliefs does not make the having of the belief or even its formation involuntary. Again, one might think of a parallel with action. Right now I intentionally am typing on the computer keyboard. I am aware of my action, for I am also thinking about how soon I will be done so that I can go eat supper. My action of staying at the keyboard and typing is voluntary. However, I am not fully aware of all the component actions of the keyboard typing. I do not directly intend to move my right finger and then my left finger and so on during the typing. I simply move my fingers to facilitate the typing. So while the typing is voluntary and intentional, moving my fingers is part of that intention, though I am not fully or maybe at all aware that I am moving them, or moving them in the order in which I do. In intending to type the paragraph, I intend to do what is necessary to enable me to type the paragraph. So, although one cannot say that I am aware that I intentionally move each finger in a given order or pattern, I do move them intentionally in a pattern, and indeed voluntarily as part of the act of typing.[68]

Similarly, we might intend to hold a belief, and in doing so hold the belief voluntarily with the awareness that we hold the belief. At the same time, in holding this belief we might hold other beliefs that are implied by or presuppositions for holding that belief. However, we cannot say that, with respect to these other beliefs, we hold them with the awareness that we hold the original belief, though in holding the initial belief voluntarily we voluntarily hold the supporting or implied beliefs as well. Thus, we might be said to hold a belief voluntarily without being aware that we are holding the belief.[69] In short, contrary to Winters' requirement that voluntariness requires being fully conscious, we may not be fully aware and still the belief is voluntarily held.

(2) The belief must not be compelled: the evidence for *p* must not be belief-necessitating. The choice to believe or not must be an unforced choice. We believe not out of compulsion but because we want to and choose to believe, or because we choose not to suspend our belief. That is, we are not in a position where we could not but have believed.[70] The belief must not be something that merely happens to us, where we had no choice but to believe. At the same time, since evidence generally is relevant to the belief, the belief need not be acquired or held independent of evidential considerations. Thus, we might be said to have chosen a belief when we choose to accept the reasons or evidence for the belief and thus think that the belief is true.

Schizophrenia provides cases that illustrate compelled belief. Some schizophrenics experience hallucinations but are unable to understand them for what they are; instead they both form beliefs and take actions on those grounds. They hold false beliefs that, since not based on reality, are delusional but over which they have no control. Such individuals have no voluntary control over these fixed beliefs.

(3) If the belief is voluntarily formed or held, we could have formed or held a different belief. This is not to say that we would have, that it is likely we would have, or that the alternative position would have been reasonable. It simply means that alternative belief formulations were possible and that we chose the belief we did—either for no reason other than that the proposition seemed to be true or, more likely, for what we took to be good reasons for it to be true, or even possibly because there was no (compelling) evidence against it. Another way of putting this is that the forming or holding of the belief is, to some degree, in our own power.

Because we are dealing with belief, truth conditions are relevant to forming or sustaining the belief. Beliefs aim at truth; as Williams points out, "to say 'I believe that *p*' carries, in general, a claim that *p* is true."[71] Hence the person forming the belief in believing aims at truth. That we have control over a belief does not require that we believe by fiat or adventitiously, or that we are able to believe propositions we know to be or have compelling evidence of being false. We would be inconsistent in holding a belief in the face of evidence that we understood or believed to refute that belief. At the same time, the presence and use of evidence does not remove our choice with respect to believing or not.

Moreover, voluntariness need not occur only in cases where we go against the evidence. We can voluntarily actualize, adopt, affirm, or implement the evidence we already have. As Ryan notes, "beliefs are very much like just raising your hand under ordinary conditions. For example, suppose you are feeling a little down in the dumps. All you'd need to escape the funk is to start believing something nice about yourself. I'm your friend and I am here to help you. Suppose that you just won the New York City Marathon last week. I ask you to believe that you just won the NYC Marathon. I bet you *could* just do it."[72] You are embracing a belief you already dispositionally have but do not have the disposition to believe. Turning this disposition to believe into a belief is a voluntary act. The mere presence of a desire is not sufficient to make the belief voluntary; it might not even be enough to bring about the belief. As we noted above, the mere presence of a desire to lift my arm is not sufficient to make it happen or to make it happen voluntarily. Causal conditions and reasons are relevant to doing the action and indeed, to its voluntariness. Similarly, causal conditions and reasons having to do with truth are relevant to forming and maintaining beliefs.

One might object that by allowing reasons to enter into the formation of belief we are no longer talking about direct belief but about indirect belief. With direct belief, we do not use means to bring about the belief. With indirect belief, we do not believe something directly but manipulate something else to bring about the belief. The critic thus contends that we have reduced direct to indirect belief, such that the voluntarist is no longer talking about the belief but about what one does to further the conditions under which the belief is formed in us.

The direct–indirect distinction often is developed in terms that require the voluntarist to hold that believing is a basic action. If it is a basic action, then it is direct; if not, then indirect. With basic actions it is held that we don't consciously employ means when we raise our arm. We just do so. Any means used to raise the arm—e.g., physiological components necessary to implement the willing, such as neurons, nerves, muscles, and tendons—play no *cognitive* role in raising the arm. In basic actions, no intermediate psychological state exists between our willing and doing the action, such that we are not aware of doing anything else when we lift our arm. We concentrate on lifting our arm and do it. If believing is to be a direct action, there would have to be no intermediate psychological state between the willing and the believing. But the presence of reasons, it is argued, prohibits this, which means that believing, unlike acting, would not be a basic action.

But reasons for believing are not the equivalent of intermediate psychological states. In basic actions psychological intermediaries between our decision and raising our arm are not involved, yet reasons are involved insofar as we choose to raise our arm rather than not, or rather than our leg. Rarely do we just raise our arm, unless it is a reflex action or an unconscious habit—in which case it is no longer a basic action. We raise our arm when we have a reason to do so—when asked to raise the arm, to reach for something, or to signal. We do it *in response to* a reason. Reasons play a role in basic actions in that they address the intentional aspect of the basic action and through intentionality connect with voluntariness. Similarly with belief. In forming a belief we may not know how to form the belief; there are no psychological intermediaries; we just form it. Yet forming the belief may be *in response to* the reasons given for the belief. As such, just like with basic intentional actions, reasons may be involved in intentionally forming or maintaining the belief, but the reasons are not cognitive intermediaries between the desire to raise my arm and the raising of the arm or the desire to believe and believing. Just as the basic action of raising our arm can be voluntary insofar as we choose to do so when given reasons to raise it, so the basic action of believing can be voluntary insofar as we choose to believe when given reasons to do so. Insofar as believing is a basic mental action—the possibility of which we will address in the next chapter—its voluntariness is not removed by the introduction of reasons.

If we are going to talk about voluntariness with respect to the direct–indirect distinction, we have to ask toward what the attention of the agent is directed. If the attention is directed to the evidence per se and to the critical thinking skills needed to assess the evidence, such that by manipulating these we bring about the belief, then the belief would follow if these conditions are belief-necessitating. Choice is involved in indirect believing when we choose to engage in critical thinking, to extend the conversation, to select epistemic norms by which to judge or form beliefs,[73] to keep an open mind, or to continue the research or conversation.[74] The question then becomes whether we are directing our attention properly to what is needed to acquire, understand, and carefully assess the evidence, not to the belief itself. Our critical thinking activities are voluntary in case we choose to engage in critical thinking, our choice is not compulsory, and we could have chosen not to so attend. The resulting beliefs per se are not part of the scope of this voluntariness, yet they may result from the voluntariness involved in choosing to think critically.

If the attention is directed to the belief, the choice is not directed to critical thinking or steps that might facilitate belief but to the role of the reasons themselves with regard to the believing: given the reasons, should we believe? Choice is relevant both in believing and with respect to how we consider the reasons relevant to the belief. Belief is voluntary in case we choose to hold the belief, our choice is not compulsory, and we could have chosen to not believe or believe otherwise. The resulting beliefs are part of the scope of this voluntariness. The latter does not does exclude evidence; it takes account of the evidence in forming the belief. We use the evidence to help make the decision about believing because the evidence helps us to decide or is relevant to our deciding whether the belief is true. It only excludes reasons as being determinative or overriding the ability to choose.

In sum, just as actions are not totally free (there are limiting causes and reasons for our actions) but yet are held to be voluntary enough to allow accountability, so our beliefs usually are (if we are rational) and should be encumbered with reasons and causes. In cases of voluntary belief, we can hold that the beliefs are voluntarily held when we aim for truth, could abstain from holding those beliefs, and can be held epistemically accountable for them. Voluntarists hold that truth considerations and evidence are relevant to the belief; they are not to be excluded. Voluntarists only require that the evidence not be so compelling that it is determinative of the belief, that it does not make belief something that merely happens to us. In arguing for the possibility of belief voluntarism, we are not arguing for belief by mere fiat; those who have developed criticisms of belief voluntarism on this ground have in effect created a straw person. Choice is involved in believing in many ways, from choosing to critically investigate, to attending to the evidence, to adopting certain norms, to giving or being able to give reasons or evidence, to believing or suspending judgment, to not believing when one could very well have believed.[75]

INTUITIONS AND BASIC BELIEFS

One final consideration. We have argued that the voluntarist need not argue that we believe things merely because we want to. Neither do we believe by fiat. Reasons come into play, though in cases of belief voluntarism not determinatively. But, we might ask, are there beliefs we hold that we hold directly without evidential appeal but that are not mere beliefs by fiat? At least two types of candidates emerge. First, we have a (maybe large) number of intuitive beliefs: about ourselves (including our identity), what the world is like (that it is orderly), moral intuitions (that human life is morally protectable), and the like. We might believe that it is wrong to torture animals, but at the same time not have evidence for this moral intuition: we just believe that animal torture is wrong because it seems to be wrong. Ethical theorists might derive moral beliefs such as this from more basic moral principles, but ordinary people rarely make those inferences. When asked why they believe fundamental moral claims, they often reply that they believe them because that is the way it is—the claims are simply true—or at least that is the way it seems to them. But even if such moral judgments are derived from basic moral principles—for example, that life is sacred and ought to be protected, or that one should never intentionally cause unnecessary pain and suffering—these too are known or believed intuitively. One cannot proceed indefinitely with more fundamental moral principles. John Stuart Mill noted that although utilitarians might justify their moral beliefs about practical ends through experience, beliefs about ultimate ends, like all appeals to first principles, cannot be proven by reasoning.[76] Beliefs in the truth of fundamental metaphysical, epistemological, and moral principles do not hinge on providing evidence, but neither are they simply self-evident. We believe them directly without justifying evidence. However, these intuitive beliefs are not mere random volitions or results of mere desires; they are not chosen adventitiously. They arise from a concern for the truth, and the relevant "intuitions are convictions that certain beliefs are true, not merely desirable."[77] Some people might not choose to believe these intuitions or might not hold them as fundamental intuitions. Many others will. We are not constrained by intuition to believe them; they can be resisted and hence reflect our choice. Just as we can reject evidence, so we can reject suggested fundamental intuitions. One might simply not accept, for example, the utilitarian first principles of moral reasoning, holding that they conflict with other fundamental, perhaps deontological, intuitively held moral principles. Furthermore, persons might choose to uphold their moral or religious intuitions in the face of those who give, for example, Freudian explanations of their origin. Beliefs arising from fundamental intuitions, then, can be examples of beliefs voluntarily held, though not held evidentially or by mere fiat.

It might be thought that appealing to belief arrived at by intuition is irrational. If by "irrational" one means that one has no reasons for the belief, then belief based on intuition is irrational, but is nonetheless unproblematic, for that is just what is meant by being intuitively arrived it. The objection would be significant only if having reasons were the only basis for believing, but to hold this would be to beg the question (as we noted above in our objection to Swinburne). If by "irrational" one means acting insanely, contrary to evidence, against reason, then there is no reason to think that intuitive knowledge belongs at all in this category. The insane is someone who believes contrary to fact; intuitive beliefs need not, as we have argued, be contrary to evidence or held obstinately in the face of evidence. And since intuitive beliefs need not be of that type at all, there is no reason to reject believing on the basis of intuition as irrational.

Similar things might be said about properly basic beliefs. There are beliefs that we hold to be reasonable, even though they are not supported by evidence or inferred from other beliefs. But as non-evidentially derived, we can say we hold them, not because we have evidence for them, but because we think that they are true and properly basic. Of course, properly basic beliefs need not be true; they could be false. But this does not mean that the person is not warranted in believing them. That these beliefs are not evidential does not mean that nothing is relevant to them. Indeed, our experience might be relevant, but even this experience functions under the interpretative scheme of some paradigm that we hold or have adopted. As Plantinga, for example, points out, we might have these beliefs because of the worldview or commitments we have chosen or have, and we are warranted in believing them when we believe that our epistemic faculties are functioning properly or when we think them grounded in experience.[78] Insofar as choice can be involved in any of this, voluntary choice can play a role in adopting these basic beliefs.

The significance of beliefs as fundamental intuitions or as properly basic beliefs is that even here a voluntarist case can be made for believing without evidence (though not necessarily without grounds). In both types of belief, the goal is to believe the truth, and we adopt these intuitive or properly basic beliefs because they seem to be true. Truth is not divorced from belief on either account, despite the fact that like our other beliefs, they may be wrong. To the degree that we expand our list of intuitive and properly basic beliefs, and see that in many cases (though clearly not all) they are formed not passively but voluntarily, the significance and extent of a voluntarist account increases.

CONCLUSION

What we have seen is that many are willing to grant indirect voluntary control over habits, skills, or actions that may lead to or produce true beliefs. But even if this be granted, it is insufficient by itself to provide an adequate basis for epistemic obligations, for indirect control relates to activities that are not necessarily truth-conducive. To fully satisfy our epistemic obligations, we need to have some significant voluntary control over our beliefs. If the critics are correct, epistemic obligations face stormy weather. They argue that since we cannot have basic direct voluntary control over our beliefs, we cannot meaningfully assign epistemic obligations. We have no epistemic obligation to believe the truth, only obligations to engage in responsible critical thinking.

Consequently, it is true that if belief voluntarism is equivalent to belief by fiat regardless of truth, things look bleak for epistemic obligation. It is not that belief by fiat is impossible, for as we have seen, the critics' arguments are less than conclusive. The psychological impossibility arguments make an intuitive appeal; Alston notes that his "argument for this, if it can be called that, simply consists in asking you to consider whether you have any such powers. . . . It seems clear to me that I have no such power."[79] Or again, Wolterstorff writes, "I think it is as decisively clear as anything ever is in philosophy that when we find ourselves believing something, we cannot by act of will give up that belief; nor, when we find ourselves not believing something, can we by act of will begin believing. Such actions are simply not within our power."[80] But such intuitive appeals can be met by intuitive appeals on the other side, buttressed by the fact that it seems clear that we do have epistemic obligations and can provide a reasonable and persuasive voluntarist account of belief. The cognitive impossibility arguments likewise do not survive scrutiny; they too fail to show a contradiction and that voluntariness is not part of direct believing.

The evidence that we lack control over our beliefs is hardly indisputable. Indeed, we are able to exercise some control over our beliefs, not only in instances where evidence is not determinative or compelling, but also in cases of what is taken to be prime evidence that beliefs are formed passively: perceptual beliefs. And even here, the fact that we relinquish control in cases of perception does not show that we cannot exercise that control. Further, we have kinds of beliefs, like intuitions and basic beliefs, that might be nonevidential (though properly grounded) and yet adopted voluntarily. Voluntary control is much more common than the critics suppose.

Fortunately, there is no reason to equate voluntariness and belief by fiat, just as there is no reason to equate act voluntarism with randomly chosen, conditionless, or unreasoned acts. Just as voluntary acts take place among reasons for acting and relevant causal conditions, so voluntary belief takes place among causes and reasons for believing. To equate belief voluntarism with belief fiatism, as most critics do, is wrongheaded. The voluntarist need not opt for belief by fiat in order to hold that our beliefs are voluntary. What is necessary for the voluntarist is that the person chooses to hold the beliefs—the belief is what the person chooses to believe—that the choice is not compelled, and that the person could have chosen different beliefs. It is not required that the other possible beliefs be reasonable, as attractive, or as likely to be true; it is only that one is not compelled to believe, that believing is not an entirely passive state, that belief is not merely something that happens to someone. The voluntarist who holds to epistemic obligations need not exclude the obligations to think critically but would not think these are sufficient to establish epistemic obligations. To fulfill our obligations to hold true beliefs, we should both employ proper critical thinking methods of justification to develop the proper epistemic virtues, and believe what is true, all of which, to some significant extent, lie within our control.

To separate belief from truth and leave it only to will is neither promising, nor realistic, nor a sound basis for epistemic obligations. We have seen that the voluntarist is not committed to this position at all. One believes, if one believes seriously and not merely hypothetically, what seems to be true. That is, one believes propositions that seem to possess the property of being true. Hence the groundwork is laid for morally and epistemically responsible believing.

The discussion in this chapter hinges, to a significant extent, on the nature of belief. We have spoken about believing as a basic action and referred to beliefs as dispositions. To what extent is belief (as a verb, believing) a disposition or an action or at least parallel to an action, or possibly both a disposition and an action? To answer this we turn to a discussion of beliefs in the next chapter.

6

Belief

Those who hold to epistemic obligations maintain that both extremes, pure Humean passivism[1] and pure Cartesian voluntarism or fiatism,[2] are mistaken.[3] The truth lies somewhere between, which is undoubtedly more consonant with our ordinary way of looking at the world. But how do we delineate this middle ground? To answer this we need to attend to the concept of belief.

LANGUAGE ABOUT BELIEF

The first thing to note is that our language about belief is diverse. We believe that something is the case. We want to, refuse to, continue to, or decline to believe. We form, hold, have, affirm, maintain, avow, alter, or change beliefs. We cannot help but believe or are compelled to believe, choose to believe, would be willing to believe if, and suspend our belief. We assent to or withhold assent from particular propositions. Do these expressions have something in common, or do they express different things? Do all these indicate the same state? Does treating belief as a disposition, action, representation, pattern of interpretation, or something else best characterize believing or belief?

"Belief" (believing) can refer to a propositional attitude, a mental state in which one takes a stance about the truth of a proposition or holds an opinion about what it is that would make the proposition true.[4] "Belief" can also refer to a member of a set of propositions about which I take up this attitude. It is in this sense that I have a certain set of beliefs. That I am ill; that this road leads to the university, that my wife is cooking supper, or that the president will be giving the State of the Union address to Congress next month all properly constitute beliefs. What is believed are propositions, indicated by the clause that follows "that." They may be understood as the objects of belief understood as a propositional attitude.

However, though these propositions are beliefs, it is not appropriate to say that we believe beliefs. Rather, we say that we form, hold, or have beliefs about what is embodied in the propositions that are the objects of believing. Thus, while "believe" functions as a verb, its cognate dealing with the object of the doxastic attitude functions as a noun. This distinction, though often overlooked, is important, for whereas beliefs are something that we have, it is less clear, as we shall see below, how to understand believing.

Not all objects of believing are straightforward propositions, though they can be rephrased propositionally. We might say, "I believe you," where we direct our believing to persons and to what they have said. Saying "I believe you" is shorthand for saying I believe what you have said. It is true that what is believed is a proposition, but what is believed is not merely the proposition per se, but also the person who is putting forth the proposition. The belief in the proposition is derivative from or dependent on the belief I have in the person. Here belief begins to take on an aspect of trust; when I say that I believe you I am putting my trust in you, so that what you are telling me I can hold to be true. It affirms not only the propositional content but also the trustworthiness or reliable authority of the presenter of the proposition. I believe that you are a truth-teller and hence that what you say is true. Understood this way, belief has a personal or subjective dimension.

This usage is related to the statement "I believe in you." Here I put my trust in another, and whether or not I believe any propositions seems tangential, for whether or not the other person utters statements is not germane to the case. I might put my trust in a person to belay me down a cliff, to repay a large loan, or to get me to the right destination when I am lost. It is true that beliefs in persons can be put in the form of a proposition: I believe that you will not let go of the rope, I believe that you will not abscond with my money, or I believe that you will not mislead me with your directions. But such an analysis merely in terms of propositions fails to capture the entire sense of the belief in, for more is involved than believing a proposition. A personal dimension—trust in the person—is not only an essential part of the belief; it is the most important part, and trust in the person, though expressible in a proposition, is not believing a proposition. It may involve believing propositions about the person—that the person is honest, has integrity, is reliable, that what the person says she can do she actually can do or will bring about, but it involves more than this. Belief in persons (the sense of trust) involves some personal risk, which belief in propositions lacks. When I trust someone, I might be expressing my willingness to, as it were, put my property, interests, perhaps even my life, into that person's hands, something generally not considered or required when one speaks of believing propositions. As such, belief directed toward propositions cannot fully substitute for belief in persons. For example, I might believe that you can carry me on a chair across a segment of Niagara Falls to Goat Island while balancing on a tightrope (a propositional belief), but at the same time be unwilling to trust myself to you by sitting in the chair. I believe the proposition that you can do it, but I don't believe *in you* enough to entrust myself to your chair. The propositional belief, one might say, is a weakly held belief, not strong enough by itself to bring about my action, whereas believing in you (trust) leads to action. What these two senses—believing that and believing in—have in common is that to trust someone assumes that you believe certain propositions about the person you trust, and hence when we say that we believe someone or believe in someone, the propositional content is there. What is extended in trust is the willingness to move oneself into an action that in some way places one in relation to and in possible dependence upon another.

In order to address epistemic obligations, we will focus on the propositional type of belief—believing *that* rather than believing *in*. Our concern will be with what it is to believe in the sense of believing propositions. Even here, we have ambiguity. "Belief" can refer to something a person has: he has the belief that Shanghai has the third-tallest building in the world. Alternatively, one can say that he believes that Shanghai has the third-tallest building in the world, where the focus is not on what the person has (a belief), but on something more disputable: the nature of believing when one believes a proposition. Unfortunately, this critical distinction between propositions believed (beliefs) and believing is masked by our language. The term "believe" can be ambiguous. The query "What do you believe?" asks for a proposition. "Do you believe?" asks about a state, disposition, or action. Recognizing this diversity of uses opens the door for a richer understanding of belief.

When we say that "He believes . . . ," one thing it might mean is that the person who believes is in a certain (mental) state, where one takes an attitude toward a proposition, holding that it is true or representative in some form of the actual state of affairs. In this state persons have information or some stored representation of that information about which they take a particular attitude. It is a continuing state that often provides guidance to one's behavior. For example, when Jones puts $50 down at the betting window on a filly named Rosie, it would be appropriate to say that he is in the state of believing something about Rosie and her chances of winning the race. In fact, not only is he in that state when he places the bet, but he might remain in that state for a period of time, from when he put the money down on the horse until (or depending on how Rosie performs, nearly until) the end of the race. Evidence that he is in this mental state might be derived from first person accounts—"I believe that Rosie will win the eighth race"—or from Jones' behavior during the race—he urges Rosie on when she is lagging, jumps off his seat when she moves to the front, waves encouragingly as the race tightens in the stretch, though these behaviors are much more ambiguous in that one might give varying accounts of what Jones believes based on his behavior. It is appropriate to hold that during this time he is in the state of belief with regard to Rosie. (This does not exclude him from simultaneously having other mental states, such as hope, being greedy, regretting that he did not believe more strongly and put $100 on the filly, or that he did not follow his instincts and bet on Hands Down.)

The phrase "He believes . . ." might also be understood to refer to another state, this time an actually existing dispositional state: one actually has the disposition. On this account, having a belief or believing means that I am behaviorally disposed to act in such and such a way, that is, as if the belief were true. Although I am not now considering whether my wife loves me, I surely am disposed to think this and if questioned would respond that I believe it, regardless of whether or not I currently was consciously entertaining such a belief. My belief that my wife loves me is a disposition; that I have this disposition will be revealed in many ways by the actions I take, whether verbal or nonverbal, in the appropriate circumstances.

Others have understood belief (as believing) as an action of which we are capable: I believe that . . . In the previous chapter we saw that this view underlies the discussion of belief as involving a basic act of some kind. In this regard we talk about forming a belief or coming to believe; about having, maintaining, or holding a belief; and about avowing, affirming, assenting to, or asserting something. Some suggest that there are significant differences between these three. The first refers to originating beliefs, not to believing itself. Some have seen this as causing oneself to believe, where causing is the action, not the believing. As we shall see, though a difference exists between forming a belief and having a belief, both are cases of believing. Further, it is not clear that causing oneself to believe does not fit under the broad framework of believing. We will also have to ask whether affirming and asserting are instances of believing, or whether they are only manifestations of belief. This is important because it seems that avowing and assenting are actions, such that those who deny that believing is an action will have to distinguish them from believing, relegating them to an activity in which we engage once we have a belief.

There are other analyses of belief, including other forms of behaviorism where beliefs are understood as attributed behavior,[5] but in what follows we are particularly interested in whether believing is an action or a disposition, or a complex notion that accommodates both, and what the implications of this might be for epistemic obligations and belief voluntarism. We will begin with the view that beliefs are strictly dispositions.

A STRICTLY DISPOSITIONAL ACCOUNT OF BELIEVING

One contemporary view is that belief is only a behavioral disposition, such that I have a belief that *p* when I am disposed to act as if *p* were true.[6] It has its recent roots in the writings of R. B. Braithwaite[7] and H. H. Price, and before that in C. S. Peirce. According to Price, "It is absurd to ask what kind of mental occurrence believe is, or what kind of a mental act it is, because believing is not any kind of mental occurrence or act."[8] Entertaining a proposition is a mental act, but believing does not add another mental act to the entertaining of a proposition. What believing adds is a disposition.

Price distinguishes between coming to believe or ceasing to believe and believing. Whereas coming to believe and ceasing to believe are mental occurrences or processes, believing is not an occurrence or a happening. "A belief . . . is something which we have or possess for a period, long or short, not something which happens to us, or something which we 'mentally do.'"[9] Beliefs, as dispositions, are expressed conditionally, and it is appropriate to apply temporal predicates to them. We might have the disposition to believe something over a very short or a very long time.

Moreover, Price holds that we cannot know what our beliefs are; even the possessors of the beliefs are not in a privileged position to know their beliefs. Their knowledge is on a par with others' knowledge of our same beliefs; it is indirect.[10] A belief, then, has meaning only in reference to our actions. We discover what we believe from observing our actions or by entertaining counterfactuals about our actions. Thus, beliefs are a readiness to act, or, as Audi puts it, "a (state of) readiness to act in certain ways appropriate to its content."[11]

One advantage of this view is that it can account for the fact that we can be said to believe *p* even when we are not actively considering or entertaining *p*. I can be said to believe that my wife is now teaching at Southside ABE even if I am not currently thinking about her, the school, or even anything to do with her. I do not have to be continually reforming my beliefs or checking to see whether I am maintaining my beliefs. For Price, I can discover that I have this belief by observing my actions (I get in my car to pick her up when school is finished, hearing my assent to the question whether she is teaching at Southside ABE if you inquire where my wife is, or seeing whether I entertain the counterfactual that if she were at home I would be walking out to the parking lot to go home early from work). Thus, beliefs need not be, as they usually are not, some proposition present before my mind, and certainly they are not actions.

It also has the advantage, not strictly germane to our present discussion, of allowing us to attribute beliefs to nonlinguistic animals. Though presumably nonlinguistic animals cannot entertain propositions, it does seem reasonable to think that they as agents act out of beliefs of some sort. My daughter's cat sits, at the appropriate time, by his automatic feeder, waiting for it to drop the pellets into the dish. He seems disposed to act as if the feeder has a schedule into which he must fit if he is to be satisfactorily fed.

Criticism of the Strictly Dispositional Account

The "strictly dispositional" account faces several objections. One objection concerns Price's behaviorist contention regarding how we know our beliefs. For Price, knowledge of beliefs is arrived at inductively from our actions. Thus, on his dispositional view, knowledge of our beliefs is indirect. The problem with this account is that I might never act on something I believe dispositionally. For example, you might want to know whether I believe that Old Country Buffet is serving salmon this evening. But if I ignore you or, since I do not intend to eat out this evening, will not be taking any actions like driving there that are relevant to the proposition in question, how will you (or I) know whether or not I have the disposition to believe this? There are no behavioral equivalents.

But, it is replied, one can set up thought experiments, using counterfactuals, to determine how one might act and thus what one might believe.[12] For example, you might ask, If you were going to go to Old Country Buffet tonight, would you see salmon on the menu or choose it? However, thought experiments are notably untrustworthy in any case, not the least because the circumstances surrounding actual cases may vary greatly from those of the thought experiments, so that the counterfactual thought experiment would yield false results about what I do in fact believe. Or even if the circumstances are the same as the thought experiment, what actually gets played out might vary greatly from the armchair context in which the experiment is conducted. I might say, "No, I would not have chosen it," but had I gone it is possible that upon looking at what was served I would have changed my mind and chosen the salmon.

Moreover, to know what I believe, I don't have to wait until I act or conduct thought experiments, using counterfactuals, about what I would do if I were in such and such a situation.[13] We have significant, though certainly incomplete, immediate, privileged access to our beliefs, so that frequently we do not have to await behavioral or quasi-behavioral (thought-experiment) outcomes to determine those beliefs. Since we can have significant direct access to our beliefs, belief is more than a disposition whose content is determined behavioristically. I do not have to await any action or assent to know that I believe *p*; I can know this immediately.

But, the dispositionalist might reply, do I really know immediately what I believe? It might be the case that I think I believe something but do not really believe it. I can be mistaken about my beliefs. This can be illustrated by a thought experiment that some ethicists suggest. How do I know what I believe about what I ultimately value? One response is to ask what I believe I would be willing to die for. My reply indicates my beliefs concerning what I take to be my ultimate values. But it is one thing to report what I take to be my belief about ultimate values—what I determine them to be by introspection—and it is quite another actually to be in situations where the choice is one of life and death and where I have to make critical decisions regarding what I believe. The latter provides a truer representation of what I believe.

This objection, however, applies not only to those who hold that we can determine our beliefs directly by introspection, but also *ceteris paribus* to the dispositional view that we determine our beliefs indirectly by conducting thought experiments. Return to the example where I construct thought experiments that put me in critical life-and-death situations in which I consider what I would be willing to die for and thereby arrive at an opinion counterfactually regarding my beliefs about my ultimate values. In cases of belief both by introspection and by counterfactual thought experiments, doubt arises whether what I indicate I believe would correlate with what I would actually believe when placed in the real circumstances. Direct awareness of my beliefs provides no guarantee against self-deception or being mistaken about my beliefs. I might think that I believe *p*, but in fact I really do not. But neither does the dispositional account provide any kind of guarantee of accuracy in this regard, for the thought experiment is counterfactual, so I really don't infallibly know what I would really do in this case either. It is equally unclear what behavior might result in the thought experiment. In effect, the dispositional account provides no better, and in most cases a worse (since it involves the counterfactuals of thought experiments), way of determining my beliefs.

Second, on the behavioral disposition account of belief, to believe *p* is to act as if *p* were true. But to act as if *p* were true can be satisfied in a broad variety of ways, including inaction or not taking any action. Actions are ambiguous; a great variety of actions might satisfy the contention that I believe *p*. Actions don't just follow from a single belief but arise from a complex of beliefs, motives, and desires.[14] The fact that I am walking out to the parking lot at 4 p.m. can fulfill any number of beliefs: my wife is at school, it is about to rain, I have a meeting across town, I have to pick up a colleague at the airport, my car won't start if it sits too long in the cold, and so on. If the only or even primary way in which I come to have knowledge of my beliefs is indirectly through my actions, it would be impossible to determine precisely (or perhaps even generally) what my beliefs really are. Too many interpretations of the behavioral phenomena are possible. And there are too many background beliefs, which themselves would have to be treated behaviorally, that would have to come into play to discriminate between the interpretations to determine what belief it is that the behavior is indicating. To believe that strawberries (to use Braithwaite's example[15]) are indigestible could be manifested by a variety of eating behaviors and also by not eating strawberries at all. But not eating strawberries at all could manifest not the belief that they are indigestible, but an indefinite number of beliefs: that they are not ripe, that they taste sour, that they have not been cleaned, that they are too expensive, that I don't like them, that I am allergic to them, and so on.

The dispositional account also fails to account for weakness of will. I might believe that eating fried foods is not good for my high cholesterol but yet not have the necessary willpower to stay away from French fries, potato chips, fried chicken and fish, doughnuts, and the like. But observing my eating behaviors would tell neither another person nor myself what my true beliefs are, for the problem of actualizing the beliefs has nothing to do with the belief itself but with my inability to implement what I truly believe.

Indeed, relying on our behavior to determine belief makes it impossible to explain the phenomenon where persons act contrary to their affirmed belief or verbal assertions. For example, someone might believe that smoking endangers his health but at the same time continue to smoke. As one student told me, "I believe that smoking is harmful, and I will quit after I graduate." But his continued smoking makes it difficult if not impossible to tell what he believes. Is it that he believes smoking is harmful but has weakness of will to do anything about it? Or is it the case that his smoking belies his verbal contention that he believes that smoking is harmful and rather reveals his true belief that he is immune from smoking's harmful effect? Or does his smoking have nothing to do with his beliefs but manifests a habit about which he is now really unconscious? The dispositional account cannot distinguish them. In effect, actions and beliefs do not always tally.[16]

Finally, one might object to such a strictly behaviorist account on the grounds that the dispositional account is incomplete. In particular, the question can be raised whether one can ascribe a belief to persons if they have not, at some time or other, actually formed the belief, and by forming the belief I mean that they have thought about or been aware of that belief. It seems inaccurate to say that I believe that the pope is visiting Minnesota—in that if you asked me I would assent to the proposition or would go with you to see his motorcade pass by—if I had never thought or known about his visit before you asked, or if in a weaker sense, I don't even know what the terms of the proposition refer to—for example, who the pope is. It is inappropriate in such cases to say I believe this, despite my agreeing to go with you or exhibiting relevant behavior. To say I have a belief *p* requires that though I am not now thinking about *p*, at some time or other I formed the belief that *p*; that is, that I believingly thought about *p* or about propositions that are equivalent to or entail *p*.[17]

Indeed, the strictly dispositional account leaves us with an indefinite, if not an infinite, number of beliefs. It is far too generous to say that I now believe anything to which I would assent or which would be a basis for or involved in actions that I take. Taking actions requires delimiting beliefs.

In short, the strictly dispositional view faces significant problems in providing a completely satisfactory account of belief. Although beliefs are a significant part of the basis for taking action, beliefs also serve functions that are only indirectly or distantly linked, if linked at all, to actions. For example, beliefs serve theoretical functions, as for example in theology or philosophy. The beliefs that Aquinas expresses in his *Summa theologica* might not lead to any action at all but play a role in his working out a coherent systematic theology. These criticisms do not rule out a dispositional dimension to belief; indeed, there is much to be said for an account that includes a dispositional understanding of belief. But by itself a merely dispositional account is not fully adequate and needs to be supplemented.

Belief as a Disposition and the Disposition to Believe

Robert Audi has proposed a solution to the last of these objections, namely, to the objection that the dispositional account leaves us with a very large and indefinite number of beliefs.[18] We have seen that on a dispositional account we have, perhaps an indefinite number of beliefs that we have never in fact entertained and indeed, probably never will entertain because the appropriate conditions for their formation or expression are never realized. This result is not contradictory in any sense but leaves us with a view of belief that is highly counterintuitive. Indeed, it makes believing fairly trivial, since on this account we would believe so very much that never informs our actions. Moreover, the plethora of beliefs would make epistemic obligations extremely difficult, if not impossible, to fulfill.

Audi maintains that beliefs are dispositional states, but wishes to distinguish beliefs from the disposition to believe. Whereas a belief is a readiness to assent to a proposition or to act, a disposition to believe is a readiness to form a belief, given the appropriate realizing conditions. The latter requires the intervention of a belief-formation process. It is one thing to recall a belief already formed and quite another to be ready to form a relevant belief. For Audi, at least two factors point to the distinction between having a belief (as a disposition) and the disposition to believe. First, persons might be in the appropriate circumstance to manifest a belief that we are certain that they would have if they were the kind of person they are, but at the same time not manifest or act on that belief. The second concerns the puzzle about how persons form the belief if they are not now aware of that belief.

The example Audi presents to resolve this is a bit puzzling. It concerns Tom, who to Norma criticizes a politician who is Norma's relative. Given Tom's character, if Tom realized what he was doing, he would be the first to be embarrassed by his action and would consequently believe, contrary to what he seems to believe by virtue of his action, that he is offending Norma by this discussion. Audi puzzles how we can ascribe a belief to Tom—that he is offending Norma—when his behavior manifests quite the contrary. The answer, Audi proposes, is that Tom does not believe that he is offending Norma, but rather, given his character, were Tom in possession of all the facts, he would affirm that he is offending Norma.

However, a belief dispositionalist could respond that this is not counter to the dispositionalist's theory. The behavior contrary to the belief can be accounted for by appealing to overriding circumstances—Tom's forgetting who Norma's relatives are, just as the disposition of a glass to break if dropped is not realized if the glass is dropped into a deep pile of feathers rather than on a hard cement floor. At the same time, however—and this seems to be Audi's point—from Tom's behavior we could not ascribe to him that he would believe that he would offend Norma if he realized whom he is criticizing. This is the product of a counterfactual. Thus, we would be hard pressed to understand how Tom could form the belief that he is offending Norma without at some point entertaining the belief. The best one can say, Audi concludes, is that Tom is disposed to believe that he would offend Norma if he realized to whom he is talking (insofar as she is related to the politician), not that he actually believes this (in either an occurrent or dispositional way). That is, we can say that Tom has the disposition to believe but not the belief (as a disposition).

The distinction, Audi notes, though subtle, is apparent. Although both the disposition to believe and believing can result in the same manifestation (namely, the affirmation of a belief), they can be distinguished. "If I already believe *p*, then I need only understand the question in order to reply sincerely, whereas if I am merely disposed to believe it, I must instantiate one of the realizers for that disposition."[19] The difference, in effect, is the difference between the manifestation of a belief (the actualization of the belief as a disposition) and the formation of a belief (the realization of the disposition to believe).

Despite this distinction, it seems that Audi is still left with an enormous amount of beliefs. For Audi, we can acquire beliefs without being conscious of doing so, that is, without entertaining the propositional content of the belief. For him it makes sense to say that someone comes to believe something if the person has sensory input regarding it. He gives the example of someone, rapt in conversation, believing that an ambulance sounding its siren went by. Although the person did not think about its sounding siren or entertain the proposition that an ambulance went by blaring a siren, Audi holds that the person still formed the belief that an ambulance with a siren blaring passed the house this evening.[20] It is a (dispositional) belief.[21] What is unclear is to what extent for him this sensory experience must enter into the person's conscious state—must actually become conscious—in order to be considered the cause of a belief. Is it that the person heard (perceived) the sound but merely did not entertain any propositions with regard to it? Or could such belief formation extend even to cases where the person only subconsciously heard the sound—there was sensory input—but the sound never became part of the person's conscious experience? Audi's discussion is unclear at this point. His contention that the person was "absorbed in conversation" suggests the latter, as does his claim that in the case of the ambulance "the propositional object of the belief apparently does not come before the mind but is somehow 'implanted' by the perceptual experience: the siren leaves a doxastic trace."[22] If this is the case, the number of beliefs (as dispositions) again inordinately skyrockets.

Audi's later discussion appears to clarify the issue. Audi rejects what he terms *experientialism*, the view that since beliefs form in response to experience, we believe all the propositions that experience puts forward. Thus, he holds that not every perceptual experience results in a belief, but "seeing something disposes one to form various beliefs about it."[23] We are discriminative about perceptual experiences that bring about beliefs and those that do not. Rejecting belief voluntarism, Audi suggests that this occurs naturally: "perception, thought, inquiry, or testimony makes one or more propositions stand out, or engage our attention, in a certain way."[24] Thus, perceiving can both dispose one to form a belief or produce a belief, depending on the experience.[25]

Consequently, it is better in cases of perceptual but unrecognized and subconscious perceptual awareness such as the ambulance case to say that the person has the disposition to believe that an ambulance with a siren passed by on the street than to say that the person has a (dispositional) belief that never entered his consciousness. This, as we shall see shortly, has implications for those who criticize an act notion of belief on the grounds that it violates the close connection between perceptual experiences and the forming of beliefs.

This distinction between the disposition to believe and a (dispositional) belief helps to alleviate the apparent plethora of beliefs that might be ascribed to us on a dispositional account of belief. We have many but not an inordinate number of beliefs (understood dispositionally), but we all have the disposition to believe, to form beliefs in the presence of the appropriate realizers. However, helpful though Audi's distinction is, it still does not rescue the strictly dispositional account from the other telling objections raised against it.

BELIEVING AS AN ACTION

Throughout the book we have noted the analogy between the moral and the epistemic, both in the notions of obligation and justification and in the role of the voluntary in accountability. First, actions can be assessed or evaluated, and where moral actions are concerned, considered as prohibited, required, permitted, or praiseworthy. Similarly, one can view believing as incorporating epistemic obligations regarding what is prohibited or required in the ways noted above, and with respect to epistemic excellence permitted and praiseworthy. Second, in an action agents have some awareness that they are performing an action. Thus, for example, with respect to moral actions, where the agent has no awareness of the action the agent is generally morally excused on the grounds that it was not intended. Analogously, where persons are unaware of their belief, belief is best understood as a disposition to believe. Third, relating to the question of voluntarism, we have argued that for the most part our actions are to varying degrees within our control. Philosophers distinguish actions from mere bodily movements on the ground that people have some control over actions but not over mere bodily motions. We distinguish the reflex knee jerk from the act of our intentionally raising our lower leg. With respect to epistemic voluntarism, Chisholm writes, "if self-control is what is essential to activity, some of our beliefs, our believings, would seem to be acts. When a man deliberates and comes finally to a conclusion, his decision is as much within his control as is any other deed we attribute to him."[26] Chisholm's general point is correct, though he may be overly optimistic, as many are, about the degree of control we have over our actions. Since we are unaware of all the causal factors that affect our choices and actions and of the extent to which they influence us, control over our actions is something we have to a lesser extent than often we think.[27] Yet, except in the more extreme cases, we hold that people have significant enough control to have obligations (of varying degrees) with respect to their choices and actions. Correspondingly, our control over our beliefs is a matter of degree, though also perhaps less than we think. It too is a matter of degree. Nonetheless, we have a significant enough measure of control over many of our beliefs. While we may relinquish control over many believings, such as perceptual ones, in that we generally believe what we see or experience, control is exercisable, for example, by altering the way we receive the perceptual input (e.g., turning away) or by consciously refusing to believe what we have experienced. Thus, belief should be understood, not only dispositionally when we are not conscious of our beliefs, but also as mental acts or believings, involving the action of entertaining, adopting, or assenting to propositions. That is, we may treat believing in many cases as a psychological or mental act.[28]

We can distinguish among various aspects of believing. There is coming to believe, which involves belief formation. The opposite of this is withholding belief, where persons refuse to believe a particular proposition. In forming a belief or withholding belief, we may use language such as deciding to believe or not to believe, or adopting or acquiring a belief or not doing so. We also speak about having, maintaining, or holding a belief. The opposite of this is suspending or relinquishing a belief one already has. Finally, we speak about asserting, assenting to, or affirming a proposition. We do this voluntarily and can do this in contexts where we reaffirm a belief that we already have or affirm this belief for the first time. All three, at least initially, look like events that involve actions.

The question is whether initial appearances are correct, that is, whether any of these actually is an event, and if any are, whether these events involve an action on the part of an agent. With regard to the first category, belief formation or acquisition seems to be an event and may or may not involve action. On the one hand, one might say, "I have come to believe that Shanghai has the world's third-tallest building," where the coming to believe (the believing) involves no direct agent action. It is something that happens to one: I might have been passing the newsstand and have seen a headline to that effect that caused me to believe it. This is similar to "I have come to Shanghai," where I come to Shanghai without taking any action (since I was wheelchair-bound, I was put on the train and brought to Shanghai). On the other hand, forming a belief about Shanghai might be similar to having come to Shanghai, where the coming is the result of actions that I have taken—getting in a car and actually driving to Shanghai. I might intentionally look up on the Internet "world's tallest buildings" and consciously form the belief that Shanghai has the third-tallest building. That believing is an action over which I have control can be seen in that I could look up the information but then decide that the Internet site I consulted might not be authoritative, that the authors of the site are mistaken, or simply that I don't believe what the site says—in each case refusing to believe. So the phrase "come to believe," like the phrase "come to Shanghai," is ambiguous with regard to being an action, but it certainly allows, if not at times requires, for it to be understood as an action. Other phrases—"I have formed the belief" or "When I heard the candidate's stump speech, I believed that he was the best candidate"—are much more indicative of belief formation as an action that I have taken.

It has been suggested that a mark of an event is that it can be dated. Clearly, belief formation is a mental event that can be dated. Yesterday I did not believe that so-and-so was the best candidate for the job, but now I do. In fact, I might be able to date this change of mind, this belief formation, to the very time when the candidate gave the speech or to when I had to cast my ballot.

Regarding the second category, having or holding a belief is much less clearly an action, for in having or holding a belief I might not be doing anything.[29] That is, there is in me no conscious awareness of the belief or of the proposition believed at all. When I believe something, I am in some state, and if I am not consciously attending to that belief, a dispositional account of that state can adequately explain the doxastic features of that state and its accompanying language. That maintaining a belief involves a disposition to believe *p* accords with the fact that I would be willing to affirm that I have a particular belief when called upon or to act in a certain way, even if in the meantime I have not thought about or entertained it. And dispositions are not actions. But although a dispositional account is helpful in understanding maintaining belief, especially in cases where I am not or am no longer conscious or aware of the belief, cases where one consciously maintains a belief seem more like an action than a mere disposition. It is true that often one maintains one's belief without doing anything. I still believe that my wife is faithful, even though I have not thought about it, taken steps to continually survey the evidence, and so on. In this sense, maintaining a belief is best understood as having a belief disposition and hence is not an action. However, one also might actively engage in maintaining one's belief, especially in cases when one encounters contrary evidence or the peer pressure of frequent assertions to the contrary. For example, a person like the biblical Job might be said to actively maintain his belief in his innocence and in Yahweh in the face of his sufferings and the constant questioning and accusations by his friends. They suggest that it would be easy and preferable for Job to view his medical situation as hopeless and either to admit to his moral failings or to curse God and die. But Job resists this advice, actively maintaining that he sinless and that God is righteous. One might interpret Job's maintenance of his beliefs as involving mental action: he willfully and actively affirms his beliefs in himself and in

God in the face of obstacles set by others, and again his belief maintenance is dateable, an event occurring at a particular time when he faces and defends himself against his accusers. And even where one does not encounter contrary evidence, one might persist in believing something. When I maintain a belief, I may do something indirectly, such as continue to believe the evidence on which the belief rests, continue to believe the testimony on which I based the belief, and so on, so that the belief I have follows from these other actions. Or I may directly maintain the belief, affirming that I have looked at the evidence, and since it has not changed, I will continue to believe. Recall that just because I use evidence does not remove the voluntariness of the belief and hence that the believing is a mental act. The issue is whether or not the believing simply follows from the evidence.

The third group—affirming, avowing, and assenting to a proposition—requires volition that prefers *p* to another proposition, and this conscious preferring appears to be an action. The believing found in affirming is a mental action that can but need not be publicly confirmed by bodily actions, such as by raising a hand or making an utterance in response to a question whether one believes *p*.

Some respond that affirming, avowing, and the like are actions, but they are actions taken on what is already believed. They are manifestations or confirmations of a belief being held, not believing itself. In this case, the believing itself is not an action; only the assertion of the belief is. The action is performed on the belief; I affirm something that I already believe. They suggest as evidence for the claim that affirming is not believing the fact that we can affirm something that we don't believe. But this would be impossible if affirming were equivalent to believing. For example, we might suppose (affirm) that *p* is true for the sake of argument, despite the fact that we don't believe *p*. One finds this sort of affirmation, for example, in *reductio ad absurdum* arguments, where one ultimately wants to refute the *p* that one initially asserts.

But the affirming in *reductio* arguments is not the same as the affirming characteristic of believing, but something quite different. To treat p as a hypothetical is not to assent to p or even to non-p, but rather to assent to treating p hypothetically, as if it were true for the sake of the argument. It is to propose p as if p were true without actually believing or denying p. Consequently, this fails to establish that asserting a belief is not believing.

A similar argument is made regarding accepting. Pascal Engel contends that accepting is not believing. He makes his case on the grounds that beliefs are involuntary whereas acceptance is voluntary, that acceptance is contextual and relative to the aim at stake, that acceptance is categorical whereas belief is subject to degrees, and that belief is unconscious or tacit whereas acceptance is explicit and reflective.[30] But the first ground begs the question; as we showed in the previous chapter, one can provide a sound justification for the view that beliefs can be voluntary. Second, as we shall argue shortly, believing is likewise contextual and can be intentional. One might believe for a purpose, as in Meiland's cases regarding the woman who believes her husband is faithful to preserve the marriage and the business owner who believes his co-owner is honest to preserve the business, or if Williamson believes regarding the Holocaust to avoid losing his bishopric. Third, acceptance too can be a matter of degree; one might, for example, conditionally accept a proposition (as in the *reductio* argument) to see what the consequences of that acceptance are, but wholeheartedly accept that one's spouse is faithful. Finally, belief can be unconscious but also conscious (not simultaneously); tacit when the former and overt when the latter.

What Engel fails to see is that "acceptance" is capable of diverse meanings in different contexts. He repeats the example of a teacher who accepts a student's paper, giving it a good grade to encourage the student, but does not believe that the paper really deserves the good grade. But what is being accepted here? Certainly it fails to show that the teacher believes or accepts that the paper is a good paper or that it deserves a good grade. Rather, the teacher accepts (receives) the paper and accepts (believes) that deceiving the student by giving the student a good grade will improve performance. The first use of "accepts" is an action that says nothing about the quality of the paper; the second is equivalent to "belief." Thus, a proper parsing of the uses of the relevant terms undercuts such claims about acceptance. Indeed, after making his arguments about the distinctions between belief, acceptance, and assent, in the very end Engel concludes almost with intellectual despair about the significance of his argument. "But the distinctions do not mark, in many cases, sharp oppositions. All these states lay [*sic*] on a continuum. In many respects it seems to be just a matter of terminology, for sometimes it may be more economical to say that we are simply dealing with 'beliefs'. But in other cases failure to sort out the various kinds of states leads to a distorsion [*sic*] of the facts. This is why doxastic life is so complex."[31] How he can conclude that belief, acceptance, and assent lie on a continuum when he holds that belief is a passive disposition and acceptance is a voluntary, intentional act is hard to fathom. But it does show the failure of his arguments to differentiate belief from acceptance and assent in all cases.

In short, one can make a prima facie case for the view that while in many cases where one is not conscious or aware of one's belief, belief is properly and perhaps best understood as a disposition, in many other cases believing can best be viewed as an action. It is properly an action in cases of forming a belief, of maintaining a belief (especially in the face of opposition of some sort), and of avowing, affirming, and asserting a belief.

Critique of Believing as an Action

One objection to the action account of belief arises from the contention that it violates the close connection between perceptual experiences and the forming of beliefs. We form beliefs when we have perceptual experiences, say of the humpbacked bridge over the artificial pond I encountered when my wife and I first were shown our apartment in Zhuhai, China. I had no beliefs about ponds or bridges being in the huge apartment complex where we were to live, but upon my seeing the bridge over the pond, a belief about the pond, the bridge, and its shape and color was produced or formed in me. Note that it seems more appropriate to say that a belief was formed in me by the perceptual experience than that I formed the belief, since it appears that I took no forming action with regard to the belief. That I formed the belief that a bridge stood over the pond was evident in that I daily chose to take the path that crossed the bridge rather than walked on the road around the pond. But I am not aware that I actively formed the belief—and in any case it is unlikely that I had this kind of role in obtaining the belief. It was formed in me (caused in me) by my perceptual experience.

All of this those who hold that beliefs can be actions would concede. The voluntarist is not claiming that we form all our beliefs voluntarily or that an act of volition is involved in all belief formation or maintaining. The objector may be correct in noting that many beliefs, especially those of the perceptual variety, are formed without our conscious consent or awareness (though we have had reason to question this above). However, what is of interest is that I have the power of withholding belief in perceptual situations. We noted an example of this in chapter 5 when we considered the case of a person witnessing the magician's act of sawing a lady into two parts. Though I have perceptual grounds for forming the belief that she lies on stage in two parts, each half contained in a now-separated box, I have the power of not forming or suspending that belief, and this power suggests that, at least to some degree, a voluntarist account of belief as an action is a reasonable account of belief formation, including that involved in perception.

This account of suppressibility as providing evidence for the voluntarist perspective has come under careful criticism by Robert Audi, who looks at the purported evidence for believing as a form of acting and finds it wanting.[32] First, Audi looks at the proposed evidence of voluntarism found in suppressibility. As we have seen, voluntarists suggest that a parallel exists between our ability to form beliefs at will and our ability to prevent their formation at will. That is, the fact that we have negative control over our beliefs—the ability to prevent beliefs from being formed—provides reason for thinking that forming beliefs is parallel to this and hence a kind of basic action. Audi demurs; being able to prevent a belief is not parallel to forming a belief and hence does not necessarily imply that forming a belief is an action. Sneezes and twitches can be suppressed, and the actual suppressing of them is an action. But what is suppressed are not actions but may be mere behaviors. But, the voluntarist responds, we can suppress actions, like breathing or raising our hand, as well. Audi grants this; his point is that suppressibility is not an indicator of whether what is suppressed is an action or not and hence provides no evidence that beliefs are actions. What Audi's argument does is to remove "suppressibility" as a universal indicator that beliefs are actions.

Second, with regard to believing in general, Audi looks at the language that appears, at least prima facie, to suggest that believing is a form of acting. In the previous chapter and above we noted that verbs like deciding, adopting, accepting, asserting, avowing, and assenting seem to point to believing as an action. Audi, however, believes that this language is subject to better, alternative interpretations, so that, contrary to the voluntarist, this language does not indicate voluntary direct control over our beliefs. With regard to deciding, recall Meiland's case about the woman who has evidence of her husband's infidelity but who decides nonetheless to believe his innocence. Audi suggests that when she decides to believe, the deciding "designates not the voluntary *production* of belief or any kind of 'act of believing,' but a *manifestation* of belief formation in response to the preponderance of the reasons." If she confronts her husband, he must present the picture of a very hurt, falsely accused husband, such that she believes "he is not acting, but genuinely hurt to be doubted. . . . Here 'deciding to believe him' indicates [her] cognitive resolution of the matter," rather than any separate volitional act. She is drawn to it by a "non-voluntary process of rising conviction."[33]

The voluntarist can agree that this might be the case, that her belief in his innocence may be something that happened to her, but it might also not be (and probably is not) the case as well. Being drawn to the belief is a very different thing from deciding to believe it. If I am drawn to the belief, my agency is put out of play with regard to the belief, whereas if I decide to believe, agency is in play. To have something decided for one is different from deciding for oneself, and the description given is of her deciding to believe that her husband was faithful. Thus, though Audi has presented an alternative account, it is not clear that he has presented us with a better interpretation. Meiland's activist description is likewise cogent. Audi's account simply omits direct agency, and this seems incompatible with the many belief reports that invoke it.

Audi provides similar explanations for accepting, assenting, and taking a stance. With respect to accepting and assenting, to which the belief voluntarist also appeals to show that believing is an action, Audi contends that it is possible to accept a proposition (for example, in a *reductio ad absurdum* argument) without believing it. If acceptance were an action, then belief would follow upon it. Since we can accept or assent to without believing, these verbs do not entail belief formation. Again, Audi is not saying that acceptance is not an action of believing, only that it is not evidence of such. At the same time, Audi's argument does not show that acceptance or affirming is not an action. As we noted above, Audi is correct in pointing out that there are cases where we hypothetically assent; otherwise one could not test for their truth in a *reductio* fashion. But a difference exists between assenting to a proposition hypothetically (accepting it provisionally in order to work with it to understand it or test it for its truth) and assenting as taking a stance on or actually believing a proposition. In the latter case, the manifestation account seems quite implausible. Assenting to a proposition seems clearly a case where believing understood as an action provides the best explanation and hence is best accounted for on a voluntarist view. There is no reason to support Audi's suggestion that his nonvoluntarist account uniformly provides a better explanation.

Audi is well aware that providing possible alternative accounts of voluntarist language does not show that the voluntarist is mistaken in holding that in some cases believings are actions. He writes, "I make no claim for conclusiveness in the non-voluntarist (partial) account of belief formation presented . . . to deal with the kinds of cases that best support doxastic voluntarism. Indeed, I grant that despite all I have said there is still a tendency to think that in the context of our willfully concentrating on evidence—particularly when it seems to us equally divided—the cognitive upshot of the process, namely belief formation, looks much like an action we might take on the basis of practical reasoning."[34] What he is arguing is that the evidence does not require a voluntarist account, not that it rules such an account out. So having made the case that there might be (better) alternative explanations for the voluntarist language, explanations that suggest that forming a belief, taking a stance, accepting and assenting need not require a voluntarist account, Audi gets to the heart of his argument, which focuses on his contention that believing cannot be an action.

First, Audi contends that beliefs are simply not the sort of things that can be actions. Beliefs have truth values—one believes propositions that are either true or false—whereas actions do not have truth values. A belief is thus successful when it fits the world, whereas an action is successful when it changes the world (the world fits it). Beliefs function to truly represent the world, not to change it, and therefore are not actions. In the former case, a causal chain extends from the mind to the effect in the world, whereas in the latter the causal chain goes from the world to the mind. Audi's evidence for this critical difference between beliefs and actions can be found in the roles reasons play respectively in believing (theoretical reason) and acting (practical reason). Both beliefs and actions are guided by reasons, but reasons operate differently in the two cases. The reasons for actions are teleological—one acts *in order to*; the reason I raised my hand was in order to vote. Reasons for beliefs, however, are not formulable in terms of "in order to." Rather, reasons are expressed in propositions that are themselves believed not only to be true but to support or explain what is believed. Thus, instead of functioning teleologically, reasons have truth values and a grounding function (though as he points out, not all grounds for believing are reasons).

Audi is aware that not all reasons for actions point to actions, that one might do an action for its own sake. His point, however, is that one never believes *in order to*. But, the voluntarist might reply, there are cases where one also might believe in order to. We noted cases of this in chapter 5, where the businessman believes in the innocence of his partner in order to sustain the business, and the woman believes in the fidelity of her spouse in order to maintain the marriage. Audi rejects these cases, suggesting that here the "in order to" is a reason to cause or sustain the belief—that is, a reason for action, not a reason for believing.[35] And for Audi, causing or sustaining beliefs is not believing.

But the voluntarist need not assent to this reply. After all, it makes perfect sense to say that the woman believed in order to save the marriage, the Christian believed because he wanted to (in order to) get to heaven, the donor believed that her candidate was the best because she wanted him to provide her a job, or the patient believed that the medicine would work because she wanted to be healed. In these cases, believing in order to can apply both to belief formation and belief maintenance, and both of these, as we argued above, are cases of believing.

Audi's primary argument invokes the roles of practical and theoretical reasons. His argument might be put as follows.

1. Actions are events.
2. Events bring about change.
3. Beliefs do not bring about change.
4. Therefore, beliefs are not events.
5. Therefore, beliefs are not actions. And, with regard to our argument in the previous chapter,
6. Therefore, beliefs are not the product of the will.[36]

The voluntarist might agree with premises 1 and 2, though questions might be raised about 2, depending on how one understands "change." But the disputable premise is 3: beliefs do bring about change. It is true that the will through desires aims to change the world. But a person forming and having a belief also changes the world. Prior to the person forming the belief or the person having the belief, a description of the state of affairs in the world would not include the person having the belief, whereas subsequent to the belief formation the description would contain that fact. Believing produces a change in the property description of the person and thus of the world. The change is not physical, but there is no reason to restrict change to physical change. Whereas physical actions bring about property changes in the physical world, believing and its kin—imaging, wishing, and the like—bring about change in a description of the mental content of the world or a change in the mental properties of the persons possessing them. Hence, beliefs do, like actions, bring about a different state of affairs, but reports of physical changes differ from those of mental changes.[37] If physical changes are required for something to be an event, then it would seem that there are no mental actions whatsoever: deciding, choosing, imagining, wishing, selecting, and so on would not be actions, since they have only indirect physical or mental property effects. It is true that one does not form a belief with the intent to change the world in terms of its description of one's mental state; beliefs need not be intentionally productive. But this is neither part of Audi's argument nor necessary to what it is to be an event. At the same time, one might form a belief in order to act. What Audi has done is beg the question by restricting the definition of action to physical action and thereby excluding mental actions from being actions at all.

Audi replies to this objection. "To be sure, if a belief is added to my cognitive inventory, the world is changed; but *I* (or some event) would produce this change, not the belief. The belief cannot even change the world in the direction of one's believing more truths (though it can, given other factors, guide action)."[38] But desires and will also do not produce physical change by themselves; it is by *my* willing or desiring, implemented through the body, that I bring about the change. As with belief, some sort of agency is necessary to bring about real world change. The presence of an agent is required in both cases.

Furthermore, one may inquire about belief formation. Is not forming a belief an event? To reply, Audi distinguishes between believing ("coming to believe something") and causing oneself to believe. Neither of these, he claims, is an act of belief formation.[39] In causing oneself to believe, causing oneself to believe is an action and the belief is the result of an action, but the belief is not an action, just as one's arm rising is not an action but the result of raising one's arm. On the other hand, simply coming to believe is not an action because one had no part in it. It is the result of an action, of doing something else like engaging in critical thinking, investigating, attending to, and so on. If coming to believe is something more, he argues, it is "equivalent to causing oneself to believe," and as we have seen, causing oneself to believe is not believing. In short, believing is not an event and hence not an action. Belief formation is the result of something else, such as the inclining oneself by attending to the belief. It is a belief forming, not the forming of a belief. Audi's argument, then, is that either we come to believe, in which case believing is not an action, or we cause ourselves to believe, and here too belief is not an action but the result of an action.

Attending to the first part of Audi's dilemma, it is true that beliefs might arise as a result of something else, like attending to or pursuing additional evidence, and if beliefs simply result so that we have no part in forming them, then belief formation is not an action but a happening. The causal conditions are capable of producing the belief quite apart from our acting as agents. But Audi has not given us sufficient grounds to affirm that this is the only way that beliefs are formed. We can come to believe in ways in which agents play more than an indirect role. What about the other horn of Audi's dilemma? His argument makes a confusion that we noted earlier between belief as believing (taking up or holding a particular attitude) and belief as the proposition about which we take up this attitude. What results from the formation of a belief is a belief in the sense of a particular proposition *p*. Thus, one might distinguish between believing (as an act) and the belief (the object of the act or the proposition believed). When I cause myself to believe *p*, *p* is not an action but the proposition believed. But the formation of the belief *p* is an action. Once one sees this distinction, there is no reason not to see belief formation as an event. Much of this would be clarified if we dropped the phrase "causing oneself to believe something." Putting it this way invokes the homunculus that Audi criticizes elsewhere, as if there is someone inside us acting to cause us to believe. Rather, belief formation is simply believing or coming to believe. And this, like Audi's "causing oneself to believe," can be an event.

Audi's *second* argument is that if belief formation were an action, there should be a practical reason for it, since all actions have practical reasons. But no practical reasons for beliefs exist. "The form could not be that of 'to believe *q*', where *q* is some proposition the person conceives as somehow related to (perhaps supported by) *p*; for this is neither an act-description nor even an event-reporting phrase."[40] But why cannot one say that since we have a desire to believe truths, that *p* seems to be true is the practical reason for believing that *p* is true? Audi's response is that *p* seeming to be true implies that there is a reason for causing oneself to believe *p* provided one does not already believe it. So the only reason one can give for believing is theoretical, not practical, and if it cannot be supported by practical reasoning it is not an act. Hence, though causing oneself to believe is an action, believing is not.

But we are back to the distinctions between believing and causing oneself to believe and between physical actions and mental actions. We have already rejected the first distinction. With regard to the second, physical actions are characterized by having practical reasons for their performance, whereas mental actions are characterized by having theoretical reasons for entertaining them. But as we already noted, there may well be practical reasons for engaging in mental actions. In short, Audi's careful account fails to show that believing cannot be an action. It cannot be a physical action, but then the voluntarist has not made such a claim in any case.

Audi wishes to grant that withholding belief or trying to cause oneself to believe, or trying to retain beliefs, is each an action but contends that this does not imply that believing is an action. For him, this much is enough to support an ethic of belief. An ethic of belief includes several things. For one, it includes the permission to believe a proposition if the proposition meets a certain standard of evidence. It also extends to withholding a belief at will or trying to cause oneself to believe or sustain a belief. Failure to do so in the presence of relevant and sufficient evidence would be to violate one's epistemic duty.

Audi, however, is more comfortable with a nondeontological view of the ethics of belief. His view is that one has the obligation to be properly attentive to the evidence—"to be properly attentive both to logic (broadly conceived) and to the evidences of our senses, memory, consciousness, and reflection."[41] The ethic he describes has to do with obligations to inculcate the methods of critical thinking, not with the formation of the belief itself. It is an ethic of inquiry, an ethic directed toward indirect measures of belief production.

But here we are back to the very weak sense of epistemic obligation that we rejected in the previous chapters as not being entirely satisfactory. As we have noted, it is not sufficient to say that one has met one's epistemic obligations by developing or honing one's critical thinking skills, by seeking and attending to the evidence, or by being open-minded. These are indeed part of our concept of epistemic excellence, but our epistemic obligations extend beyond our obligations to critical investigation to beliefs about truth and falsehood and should not be reduced to an ethics of inquiry.

Indeed, in the very end it seems that Audi returns to a form of belief voluntarism. He notes that "a person can be criticizable for having an inadequate degree of confidence, say for high confidence where the relevant probability is low, as well as for unqualifiedly believing something unsupported by grounds or for not believing something supported by excellent undefeated evidence. None of these standards requires a commitment to voluntarism."[42]

But to the contrary, this does commit him to belief voluntarism. In developing this ethic of inquiry, though he speaks of our indirect obligations to be good inquirers and critical thinkers, he introduces language that indicates a degree of voluntary control over our beliefs themselves: we "accommodate degrees of conviction" "to avoid having a degree of conviction at variance with the strength of our grounds"; we "form beliefs only when our grounds adequately support them;" we should "tend to believe it on the *basis* of reason."[43] But it would seem that to accommodate degrees of conviction I need to have direct control over my convictions (my beliefs and their degrees); indirect control will not do because, as we have frequently pointed out, not only are indirect measures not uniformly truth-conducive, but there is no necessary link between these measures and degrees of conviction. I might have looked at all the evidence and still (properly, at times) lack any kind of conviction or belief in the matter. Indeed, Audi himself recognizes this when he says that "an ethics of belief may countenance, in special cases, not only the obligation to develop epistemic virtue but also something quite different: a moral obligation to induce in oneself certain false or unjustified beliefs or to unseat certain true or justified ones."[44] But the obligation is not simply to induce these beliefs; it is to have them, and this surely is voluntarist language. Similarly, to form beliefs or tend to believe only when they are adequately supported suggests that we have voluntary control over our beliefs, so that if they are supported we should and can form them and if not we should and can withhold forming our belief. Again, indirect measures do not provide the necessary connection with the forming belief or withholding belief.

I cannot help but think that this commits Audi to belief voluntarism. Audi contends that it is more proper to say that a belief is formed than that we form a belief. This is one argument he gives in support of his view that belief is not an action. But in that case, one cannot criticize someone for holding a belief where the grounds are inadequate, for they did not form the belief on such grounds, but the belief formed on such grounds. Neither can persons control the "confidence" they have or the degree of belief, since that likewise would be formed, not something the individual forms. We have control over whether or not and the degree to which we attend to the evidence, but without a necessary connection between the evidence and the holding of the belief, it would seem that one could not hold persons accountable either for having or not having the belief or for the degree of confidence they have in the belief.

Audi's view is important in that it accords well with the obligation to develop epistemic virtues, which involve developing the proper epistemic dispositions that include careful attending to the evidence. But it is insufficient in developing a complete ethics of belief, which requires that we have epistemic obligations not merely to the way we conduct our critical thinking endeavors (our investigations) but also to the beliefs that we hold. Furthermore, and more to the point, he has not shown that in no case can believing be an action.

CONCLUSION

From the above we can reasonably conclude that "believing" has both a dispositional as well as an occurrent use as an action. Clearly, one use of "believe" is as a disposition. Belief is dispositional when we are not aware that we are holding a belief we have at some time formed but would assent to the relevant propositions or act on them if asked to do so or given the proper opportunity in relevant circumstances. Only in this way can we account for the continuity of our beliefs and belief systems despite the lack of continuity of consciousness of what is believed. At the same time, "belief" has an occurrent use as well: we engage in acts of believing. We perform acts of belief formation when we decide to believe or adopt a belief. This can occur in diverse circumstances, for example where the reasons or evidence for a particular proposition are not compelling, where our intuitions run counter to the evidence, or where we are baldly faced with a novel option that seems on the face of it to be true. We actively maintain our beliefs; this is especially obvious in but not limited to cases where we encounter opposition to our beliefs or doubts that threaten to undo our beliefs. Believing can also be understood as an act when we engage in assenting to, avowing, or affirming. Although terms like *assenting* and *affirming* might be expressions of doxastic attitudes already held, they also are ways of talking about acts of believing. Hence, whether we consider belief formation, belief maintenance, or affirming or avowing, believings can be understood as actions. As such, though belief is best understood in terms of being a disposition when the belief is not before our consciousness, it is reasonable to hold that believing is an action when we are conscious of what it is that we believe, in particular, when forming, maintaining, or avowing propositions.

As we noted in the previous chapter, this conclusion must be stated carefully. We have already noted the analogy between moral and epistemic accountability. With moral accountability, philosophical discussion sometimes assumes that we are in some sense or other completely free with respect to our moral choices and actions, and that this provides the basis for accountability. The opposite extreme is that we are not free and hence not morally accountable for our moral actions. The truth, however, lies somewhere in between. We are free in varying degrees, sometimes more, oftentimes much less. No clear line stands between being free and not being free; there is a huge area where causes and reasons variously apply and coexist with moral accountability. External forces have impacted and still continue to impact our decisions; internal forces (emotions, desires, appetites, habits) also affect our choices. Voluntariness occurs within the context of causal influences and, indeed, because of them.

Similarly with respect to our beliefs. It would be a strange case indeed if we simply willed a belief without regard for truth. In coming to and holding a belief, we want to believe the truth, and it would be rational if we paid attention to the evidence, sought justification for the belief, and traced it to solid bases or grounds. Hence, discussion of belief voluntarism under the notion of fiat seems badly misplaced. The fact that we have varying degrees of control over both our beliefs and our belief-causing processes does not imply that we carry out believing by fiat. The voluntarist should not be interested in defending belief by fiat, though often the discussion is carried on with this lurking in the background. Rather, the belief voluntarist contends that to some degree or other we have control over our forming and maintaining beliefs, and this with respect to belief, just as with respect to action, provides grounds for moral accountability. This applies whether to beliefs as dispositions (where we can have indirect control) or to believing as action (where we can have direct control).

What is denied is that only indirect belief voluntarism applies, that in every case of believing the believer is compelled to believe by the evidence. In some cases presentation of the evidence may be sufficient for me to believe a proposition. Given the evidence it may be that I cannot but believe. But that this is the norm is clearly false, as Meiland's and others' examples show. One might be faced with overwhelming evidence and still remain unconvinced regarding the proposition. One might simply be pigheaded in believing that one's spouse is faithful. Or one might believe that though the assorted pieces of evidence seem damning, they are not really so; reasonable alternative explanations can be constructed although one is unable to do so at this time. Or one might have background information, as in the magician case we noted earlier, that overrides the current perceptual evidence. Evidence is much more tenuous in its connection to belief, as any trial lawyer might attest. With evidence must come persuasion, for we are not merely rational machines that crank out rational beliefs. Beliefs are affected not only by reason and evidence but by emotion and passion, imagination and wishing, and by our own willing selves, not where the will is an internal homunculus, but where we have agent roles in forming, holding, and sustaining our beliefs.

All of this is compatible with seeing belief as dispositions that we have that may or may not be actualized and also with viewing believing as mental actions that we take. We can exercise control over both our dispositions and our actions of believing. We exercise control over our dispositions both directly and indirectly. We can do it indirectly when by our actions we create, reinforce, or curtail dispositions. This is one way that we can interpret Pascal's recommendation to engage in religious practices to bring about belief. By acting in a particular way we eventually create a disposition to hold beliefs of a certain sort related to our actions. The more we take holy water and participate in Masses, the easier it becomes to believe in God. So our dispositions to believe are, to some significant extent, indirectly within our control. We can reinforce them by acting, or even curtail them by acting in ways that alter our dispositions. Further, we can alter our dispositions directly. A personal example might help. At one time I was a Coca-Cola drinker, enjoying the refreshing taste after a hard day. One day, as I sat in the dentist's chair, I saw on his wall a chart that listed both the sugar content and acidic power of soft drinks. Coke was closer to battery acid than any of the others—too close for dental comfort—and from that day on I resolved to abstain. My willpower was sufficient, based on that evidence, to alter my disposition to drink a glass of Coke when I came home from the office or I was hot and tired from working in the yard.

We also exercise both direct and indirect control over our acts of believing. The above example began with an act of belief about the dental danger of sugar-laden soft drinks. My deciding to believe that soft drinks were not good for me, based on the evidence presented in the chart, was the beginning step leading to a change in behavior and dispositions. I did not have to form this belief; I could have decided that this was a piece of propaganda and ignored the poster content.

In short, believing, like thinking in general, is a complex notion, where a diversity of accounts provides for a richness of understanding the phenomena. In different contexts it can be understood dispositionally (where we are not conscious of our believing or of the propositions believed) or in terms of a mental act (where we have such consciousness). The implications of this we will pursue in our final chapter.

7

Epistemic Obligations and Accountability

At the outset of our study we considered four cases in which it is appropriate to say that the individuals in question had epistemic obligations. We looked at a case where Dale and Leilani Neumann had beliefs that they and others felt were true.[1] However, acting on those beliefs led to the tragic consequence of their daughter's death. In the second case we saw that J. W. Milam had a set of beliefs that most would agree were false and that likewise led to death, in this case to the vicious murder of a boy visiting from Chicago. The third case concerned Richard Williamson, who held a set of beliefs most would deem to be false but who did not perform any actions following from those beliefs that one might consider immoral. And finally, we considered a hypothetical case of Adalet, a woman of Turkish descent about whom we might wonder whether she has epistemic obligations to have certain beliefs about events that have no particular concern or interest to her, or in which she might have an interest but about which she is uninformed. In the course of presenting these four case studies we posed nine central questions regarding epistemic obligations. By now, following upon our considerations in chapters 2 through 6, most of those questions have been answered.

First, we asked whether we have such things as epistemic obligations. Did Kara's parents have epistemic obligations regarding the beliefs they held, in their case, about God, sickness, medicine, and healing? Did Milam have epistemic obligations with regard to his racist beliefs about people of color? Does Williamson have a right to believe what he wants about the Holocaust, even in the face of papal admonition? Does Adalet have epistemic obligations to form beliefs about the Armenian genocide, regardless of whether she has any interest in or knowledge about these events? We have argued that we do not have the right to believe whatever we want, that we do in fact have epistemic obligations to hold true beliefs and avoid false beliefs. These obligations lie at the root of our philosophical endeavors to find the truth, form the basis of our educational structures to assist students in fostering critical thinking skills that we hope will enable them to arrive at contextually relevant truths, are presupposed in religious discussions about what God will hold us accountable for, and are invoked in our ordinary interpersonal discourse and daily experience. They lie at the heart of every academic discipline insofar as those exercising the discipline engage in research, writing, and persuasively defending their views about what they think is true. In all scientific and other disciplinary discourse we expect researchers to present in their reports and papers what they believe to be true, and beyond that what they have reason to believe is true. Indeed, epistemic obligations extend to our very lives as we interact with each other expecting that our discourse is permeated with truth-telling. And as we have seen, the assertion that we have epistemic obligations leads to additional questions on which our extended discussions focused.

Second, what are the epistemic obligations we have? We noted in chapter 2 that though epistemic obligations connect us to believing truth and avoiding error, this description is fraught with ambiguity. We rejected the view that epistemic obligations commit us to knowing all truths, to bringing it about that every belief we either have or have an interest in is true, or to believing only significant truths. Rather, building on the analogy between moral and epistemic obligations, we suggested that we have an epistemic *prohibition* from believing propositions that are false. We have epistemic *requirements* to believe significant truths that both are immediately contextual and that in some broader sense extend beyond our understanding of our immediate context, connecting to other possible contexts and to being human in general. To complete the analogy, in line with epistemic excellence, we argued that with epistemic *permissibility* we are not obligated to believe every truth, though there is a host of truths that an epistemically excellent person would be *praiseworthy* in knowing. While these latter truths may not be significant or even useful, they enrich our personal, intellectual, and social life and hence are part of our epistemic excellence. We might summarize the connection of epistemic obligation to truth by saying that if we are to fulfill our epistemic duties, we need to minimize, if not eliminate, our false beliefs and maximize contextually significant true beliefs, both those of our immediate context and those of contexts that might relate to our personal and social well-being.

This analysis of epistemic obligations does not provide a set of necessary and sufficient conditions for determining which true propositions any particular person should believe. Yet we realize that such a set of conditions is impossible to delineate and unnecessary for epistemic functioning, for just as we can recognize moral obligations without being able to provide a set of conditions precisely delineating those obligations, we can do the same for epistemic obligations. As moral obligations occur situationally, structured in part by the contexts in which they are invoked, so epistemic obligations occur situationally, structured in part by the contexts in which they are invoked. Yet both are recognizable respectively by persons who understand that they have moral or epistemic obligations and engage in the arts of practical and theoretical wisdom.

Third, do we have an epistemic obligation to believe what we don't have an interest in? Does Adalet have obligations with regard to believing certain things about, for example, the Armenian genocide that she currently does not believe or has no interest in? If so, what is she obligated to believe? At the very least she ought to believe her contextually significant relevant truths. But since we are members of communities and of the broader society, and participate in the larger environment that sustains human life and promotes human well-being, the truths she ought to believe extend beyond her immediate personal interests. Though we don't have an obligation to believe all truths, we at least have an obligation to seriously consider matters other than what we are currently considering or have an interest in if such beliefs are or may be significant to us or are of general significance to our society or our environment, or because we are human beings. Our humanity and connectedness commit us to arrive at true beliefs other than those in which we merely have an interest.

This, of course, is vague; it provides no prescription for what we ought to believe beyond our immediate context. Yet the discussion cannot be otherwise, for there is no canon of beliefs that we are obligated to hold, given the broad human diversity of abilities, interests, living contexts, cultural ethoi, and perspectives on the world. If our attempts to arrive at an accepted canon of literature are hopelessly mired in disputes, one can imagine what it would be like to propose any canon of true beliefs. At the same time, one can say that in many cultures the mark of educated persons is their intellectual curiosity. Wanting to extend their knowledge and understanding and to expand their intellectual horizons, and developing the requisite tools to achieve this, provide clear indications of the presence of epistemic excellence. If nothing else, this constitutes a defining feature—a hallmark—of liberal arts education and of the liberally educated person. This also probably constitutes a defining feature of a meaningful life, for the unreflective life lacks the meaning and fulfillment it could attain. Broad curiosity and attention to the skills and abilities to satisfy or realize this are epistemic virtues.

Fourth, what is the basis or ground for epistemic obligations? We rejected the view that the ground of epistemic obligations is to be found in the prudential. Only if truth is understood in a utilitarian or pragmatic sense can our epistemic obligations be satisfied prudentially without severing the relationship between belief and truth. But if the deontological grounding of the obligation is to be preserved, a different grounding for epistemic obligations is required. In the case of Milam, one might argue that the evidence of his epistemic failure is found in the moral consequences of his acts. In that his racist beliefs helped shape his morally repugnant action, his epistemic failure contributed significantly to his moral failure. Similarly, the pope might say it is good or beneficial for Williamson to believe differently. Beliefs about the relative insignificance of the Holocaust can cast suspicion on the Catholic Church, particularly in light of the alleged complicity of Pope Pius XII. We have seen how this echoes Clifford, who likewise grounds epistemic obligations in their moral consequences, so that the failure of the shipowner to fulfill his epistemic obligations led to the moral catastrophe of the loss of life at sea. In effect, epistemic obligations often connect consequentially to moral obligations, despite the possibility that at times the respective obligations may conflict.

If epistemic virtues are forms of or at least related to moral virtues, and since we have moral duties with respect to both being virtuously motivated and acting in a way that virtues have a successful outcome, we likewise have moral duties (broadly conceived) of being virtuously motivated intellectually and engaging in truth-conducive epistemic practices. The mere holding of the belief does not fulfill the duty; the belief must be held from the right motive and with the right understanding. Understood in terms of virtues, our epistemic obligation is to form the appropriate virtues, rooted in the intrinsically good motivation to know and understand, that successfully produce true beliefs. Epistemic obligations, then, are grounded in morality, not strictly in terms of particular outcomes or duties, for not every true or false belief makes a moral difference, but in terms of the excellence of agents who have and exercise the appropriate intellectual virtues characteristic of human flourishing.

These multiple accounts suggest that one can provide a moral grounding for epistemic obligations conjointly in both an act and a virtue ethic. The first emphasizes that often true and false beliefs have consequences for moral action, and although a particular false belief might not result in an immoral action, as Clifford emphasized, the practice of forming false beliefs will indeed have a negative impact, if not on others, at least on our own moral character. Conversely, the practice of forming and holding true beliefs will have positive moral consequences for our lives, society, and character. And we develop practices by meeting our obligations one at a time. The second emphasizes that we fulfill intrinsic goods when we develop the appropriate epistemic and moral virtues. Intellectual virtues, found in the motivation to know and understand the truth, lead us to true beliefs through the use of reliable belief-forming procedures. So understood, epistemic obligations involve more than having justified true beliefs and avoiding false beliefs; they also connect with having certain skills, dispositions, practices, and motivations whose implementation successfully leads to the achievement of wisdom. And these are either intrinsically good or part of a fulfilled human existence.

This raises the fifth question: since our epistemic practices and resulting judgments are fallible, how do we know which propositions are true and to be believed? The traditional response appeals to justification; we utilize the processes of justification to help us determine which beliefs are true and may be justifiably held. As we saw, however, that a belief is justified does not mean that the belief is true, so that reducing epistemic obligations to the employment of critical thinking abilities in the service of justification removes us a distance from the characterization of epistemic obligations in terms of arriving at contextually significant true beliefs and avoiding false beliefs.

Reducing epistemic obligations to holding justified beliefs encounters numerous problems. The Neumanns believed they were justified, based on their prior experiences. One might contend that they failed to do the appropriate critical investigation. But how would one decide what that investigation should be? Should it be such that it comes to a particular conclusion that recognizes that relying on faith and prayer is inappropriate to healing or that it should be supplemented by use of Western medicine? On this view, they would have failed in their epistemic duty because they held an unjustified belief about healing and God. But why is such a belief unjustified? One might respond that we know their belief was unjustified because of the outcome: Kara died from her illness because of medical neglect, which could be traced to her parents' beliefs. But we cannot decide whether beliefs are justified or not or whether appropriate investigation was conducted based simply on the results. For example, I cannot determine that my belief that since the traffic light turned green I can enter the intersection is unjustified because in this case another driver decided to run the red light and, crashing into my car, totaled it. My belief about proceeding into the intersection is justified on antecedent factors, not consequential ones. If we decide justification based on results, the Neumanns' belief would have been justified and their prior experience or investigation sufficiently justificatory if Kara had survived. But again, her demise or survival is not determinative of the justified status of the belief or adequacy of the investigation.

One might hold that it is unjustified because of the theological or philosophical assumptions the Neumanns made about God, illness, and healing. Since God does not exist or is only deistically related to the world, healing is facilitated only by skilled persons such as physicians who use a cornucopia of medicines and techniques, not by God. But why should holding this view about God determine what is justified? Christians and others might well be justified in believing that God does heal and that it is appropriate to petition him for healing. If we determine what is justified based on prior sets of beliefs, whether one thinks that the Neumanns held an unjustified belief depends in part on the evaluator's subjective worldview and whether what the Neumanns believed accords with that view. And it is not clear, without a good deal of other argument, that a naturalistic or deistic view is more justified than the theistic view.

Similarly, what research should Williamson have done, and how much? Is the answer to "how much research" or "lack of appropriate evidence" determined by the conclusion one comes to, that is, if one does not come to the "right" conclusion, one has conducted inadequate research? And what will that conclusion be? Can it be determined ahead of time, and who is it that determines it? The fact that Williamson disagrees with most educated views on the subject of the Holocaust does not show that his view is unjustified. That can only be done by a careful assessment of his arguments, and again the question arises regarding whose assessment is determinative and what criteria are to be used to assess his reasoning. It is not that we cannot conduct justification and assessment of claims to justification; but it is to realize that significant subjective elements enter into the process. Justification is not person-neutral, but is justification for someone.

At the same time, however, mere possession of truth is not sufficient for creating epistemic excellence. We may hold a true belief for the wrong reasons or for no reasons at all. We may arrive at a true belief merely by accident. In these cases, although we may hold true beliefs, we have not manifested epistemic excellence.[2] So, in considering epistemic excellence, we need to wed obligations to believe contextually significant truths and avoid false beliefs, a concern for justification on the basis of which we have some reason though no guarantee to think that the beliefs are true, and the development of an appropriate epistemic character.

Regarding the sixth question, we argued that epistemic obligations require that we have some control over our beliefs. If the pope is to legitimately demand of Williamson that he recant his Holocaust denial and genuinely acknowledge the opposite belief, Williamson must have the power to change his belief. The fact that the pope asked him to do this directly and not through a careful investigation that might leave the outcome of what he is to believe in doubt suggests that the pope believes that Williamson has control over at least some of his beliefs.

We have seen that it is commonplace today for philosophers to deny such power over our beliefs. However, we argued that several analyses of beliefs are possible, that beliefs in circumstances where we are unaware of them are dispositions, whereas believings involving conscious awareness of them are actions. In both cases, whether belief is a disposition or an action, we have some degree of control over our beliefs. At the same time, we took great pains to argue that our control occurs in the context of reasons and causes; there are no entirely unencumbered actions or beliefs. Just as the believer in human freedom is not committed to choice as random but can legitimately hold that actions have causal conditions and persons still are free so long as they are not necessitated, so the belief voluntarist can hold that we have a degree of control over our beliefs insofar as they are not necessitated by reasons or causes. We can exercise some control over their formation and maintenance. Belief voluntarists are not wedded to belief by fiat but rather hold that our beliefs are conditioned but not necessitated by reasons and ultimately held because they seem to us to be true.

Seventh, we inquired about the nature of belief. We argued that while belief at times may be considered as dispositions, a dispositional account by itself is inadequate. Rather, we contended that belief at times may also be thought of as mental acts or believings, involving the action of forming, maintaining, entertaining, adopting, or assenting to propositions. In particular, we focused on belief formation (coming to believe), maintaining a belief (having a belief), and asserting or affirming something. All three not only look like events that involve actions but can best be understood properly as actions, so that not only are there dispositional beliefs, but actions of believing (believings).

Two questions remain to be considered. We take these up in this final chapter. First, can we hold persons accountable for their beliefs? If we cannot, does this affect our assessment of the Neumanns' and Milam's responsibility for their actions, especially because we may reasonably believe that their actions followed consistently from their beliefs? If we can, what does it mean to hold people accountable? Second, how do we bring about doxastic change so that someone meets their epistemic obligations? How can we influence people to hold true beliefs? What is the most effective moral way to bring about beliefs or belief change? In particular, can we put restraints on people's beliefs? With moral obligations, we create rewards and punishments to bring about the correct moral behavior. Through laws and social pressures and constrictions we attempt to control how people act. In effect, we carefully and somewhat (but not entirely) judiciously limit the freedom that people have to do what they want. Indeed, the number of laws governing our conduct in everything from operating a motor vehicle to crossing a street, from voting to paying taxes, from garbage disposal to water usage, from what we wear to what we can say in public, from whom we can marry to how we bury the deceased, is truly astounding, enough to keep hordes of politicians and lawyers in business billing every quarter hour to their clients. Does an analogy exist with epistemic obligations, so that rewards and punishments, voluntary encouragement and compulsion, are morally appropriate with respect to inculcating the desire to fulfill one's epistemic obligation? As we restrain actions, should we likewise place restraints on people's beliefs? Should we limit what people believe, or should there be epistemic obligations without corresponding belief enforcement? Should we use information, persuasion, exposure to experience, and peer social pressure to help persons to change their minds? This in many cases would be praised. But suppose Bishop Williamson is recalcitrant and refuses to change his beliefs; would it be appropriate for the pope to use some form of indoctrination to "make sure" that Williamson held a true belief? The pope threatened to remove Williamson from his bishopric. Was this appropriate? Should the pope have taken sterner steps, recommending that Williamson receive education or be required to read certain pieces of evidence that would present him with the relevant facts? Is there a clear enough causal chain between evidence and its use in indoctrination and true belief to warrant its use? If we sanction stronger measures to bring about compliance with epistemic obligations, have we crossed some threshold of intellectual freedom and begun to create a state of thought police to complement our present action police? We will devote the remainder of this final chapter to responding to these two questions.

HOLDING PEOPLE ACCOUNTABLE FOR THEIR BELIEFS

Suppose we are correct in the conclusions we have drawn in the previous chapters about epistemic obligations and the voluntariness of belief; what implications remain with respect to our accountability for our beliefs? Traditionally philosophers have held that persons are not morally accountable when they hold mistaken beliefs about the facts of the case. Mistaken or false beliefs, if sincerely held, provide a basis for constructing excuses for immoral actions.[3] However, "mistaken" has to be carefully qualified by investigating the grounds for the mistaken beliefs. Traditionally, if persons hold beliefs where being mistaken happens through no fault of their own, then the holding of the mistaken beliefs is excusable. If, however, the mistake occurs because of their own fault, then they are accountable for their mistaken belief.

Simple as this analysis sounds, it is oversimplified. For one thing, the question of fault is often more a matter of degree than of black and white. People are often more or less at fault in their actions. In many automobile accidents, the blame can be shared among the respective parties. This is why, in some places, jurisdictions have gone to no-fault approaches to vehicle accidents, relieving to some extent the burden of litigation to determine who is how much at fault when it comes to reimbursing medical expenses. We examine a person's upbringing, the people with whom the person associated, circumstances of good and bad luck, the racial and social attitudes in the person's community, and the person's educational opportunities, to search for compelling reasons to account for his or her actions, sometimes giving the person credit for moral successes, but more often finding excuses or mitigating reasons for bad behavior. Similarly with mistaken beliefs. Although we do not have "no-fault" theories of belief, we often attempt to "share the blame" for beliefs people have. We acknowledge the influences of family, educators, peers, popular role models, culture, economic status, illness, and the like in how they form their beliefs.

For another, determining fault is much easier in theory than it is in practice. What counts as a fault that would constitute a mitigating factor in providing reasonable excuse for mistaken beliefs? Consider again the case of Bishop Williamson. Let us assume, as is most reasonable, that his beliefs about the Holocaust are mistaken. To what extent is he to be held accountable for his mistaken beliefs? He is accountable because he holds a false belief; in this regard he has failed in his epistemic duty not to hold false beliefs. That much is clear. But perhaps this accountability can be tempered by a claim that he is to be excused for his belief because he thinks that the belief is true or that it is justified. Or perhaps it is tempered because he has been strongly influenced by his peers in the Society of St. Pius X, to which he belongs, and through his confidence in them, based on their spirituality or general trustworthiness, they have persuaded him to this position. Maybe he has arrived at his view through processes like testimony that can be reliable. One might conjecture a number of extenuating circumstances that could be taken into account when determining the degree of accountability for his belief.

The fact that the belief seems true to him does not make it true. Neither will thinking it to be true relieve him of accountability. Otherwise, if we are correct that beliefs aim at truth, we are not accountable for any of our false beliefs since all the beliefs we hold, by virtue of being formed by truth-seeking mechanisms, are what we think or take or what seem to be true. If they went awry, it is not our fault; the cause of error must be traced elsewhere. This extreme subjectivist viewpoint too radically removes all personal accountability for holding false beliefs or failing to pursue true beliefs. It returns us to a view rejected in chapter 2, namely, that our epistemic obligations consist in trying to achieve the truth, regardless of the success.

Earlier we saw that for persons like Clifford being justified is more important than holding a true belief. It is good if the belief is true but far superior if the belief is justified. If the belief is not justified, persons are not legitimately entitled to hold these beliefs. If persons have done their reasonable best to find out the truth and despite this still hold a false belief, we might excuse them for that. What constitutes reasonable best? Terry Price suggests that reasonableness is not to be found in doing the very best anybody can, which is probably an unrealistic goal to be expected in every case, but rather in whether someone is doing "enough to meet our reasonable expectations of him."[4]

What are these reasonable expectations that we might have? To what extent are they person-relative or culturally conditioned? Milam might argue that he has met his own standards (no matter how low) or at least the reasonable expectations of his local society in his holding of the belief that black persons are inferior to and to be dominated by white people. If we object, he might reply, why should the views of white liberals count as reasonable but not the views of being reasonable held by his peers or his local white community? Although it is sometimes difficult in practice to parse the variety of influences affecting what a person believes, it is not totally impossible. Often at the root are personal experiences that are couched in and colored by the culture or society in which one lives. It would be unreasonable to expect Milam, who was raised in the racist culture of Mississippi in the 1940s and 1950s, to have held northern liberal views of racial relations. He shared neither northern liberal culture nor the culture of black persons who lived in his area, which would have allowed him to experience empathy with others different from himself. Black persons existed in a world apart, in shanty houses on roads where the macadam ended, educated in segregated schools, restricted in their relations with the white community to where and how they could go, eat, sleep, or travel.

But this cultural parsing is insufficient to excuse his beliefs. The murder was horrific, and none of what we said above justifies murder. As a human being, Milam should have known the truth (had true beliefs) about the evils of murder, that he was killing another person, let alone a boy, and that even in a racist society murder remains murder. And he should have known (had true beliefs) that black boys don't differ all that much from "uppity white folks," himself included. These constitute fundamental truths of which he should have been aware. Apparently he never did make the effort to understand and form true beliefs about his black neighbors. It is true that his society did not encourage such investigation or interaction. But his words betray his own character. "I like niggers—in their place—I know how to work 'em. But I just decided it was time a few people got put on notice. As long as I live and can do anything about it, niggers are gonna stay in their place. Niggers ain't gonna vote where I live. If they did, they'd control the government. They ain't gonna go to school with my kids."

It is not only Milam's moral character but his epistemic character that is at issue. His confession reveals neither motivational aspects of aiming at truth nor any of the success dimensions of actually attaining true beliefs or knowledge about other people. He does not believe or know in a virtuous manner; his beliefs fail to stem from the right motives and right understanding. Had Milam a better character, he would have possessed a more truthful system of beliefs.[5]

Clearly, to reduce reasonable expectations to what the individuals themselves accept or to what is accepted in a given community or subculture would substantially weaken any notion of accountability for one's beliefs. The norms have to be more than merely subjectively acceptable. How do we strengthen the notion of "reasonable attempt" so as to be able to excuse anyone who has made a reasonable attempt to arrive at believing the truth, even if the person winds up holding false beliefs, while at the same time not capitulating to subjectivism? In the analogous case of morals, though we often excuse persons who commit wrong who justifiably (in a subjective sense) hold those beliefs, still, if their acts are egregious enough, we say that they should have known better. Fundamental moral intuitions call into play suspicions that one's actions fail to meet basic human standards. There is widespread agreement that many kinds of actions are simply wrong and should not be done. Unless seriously corrupted, society does operate by some commonly held though not necessarily overtly agreed on rules, principles, or values. Even where group behavior might indicate that the group denies the fundamental principle that killing people is wrong, the group tacitly affirms its wrongness when they justify their acts of killing individuals who are outside the group by using "people" or "human" to denote their own group, thereby leaving others outside the pale of protected humanity. By analogy, one might argue that persons who wind up holding false beliefs that they think they are subjectively or culturally justified in holding, but that run contrary to the beliefs reasonably held by humanity at large, might be held accountable on the grounds that their beliefs are so out of line with normal human beliefs about what is true that they should have known better. It is in this regard that we might say that although Milam might argue that subjectively he was justified in holding his racist beliefs because of the standards invoked by his community, his beliefs are so egregiously false that he should have known better. The intuitive falsity of his beliefs will not be the evidence of his failure to satisfy the criterion of "reasonable expectation," but the falsity functions as least to indicate his possible failure. Our appeal is to fundamental true beliefs that people should hold, regardless of their particular social setting.

Can we, however, say more than this about reasonable expectations? Are they embedded in some set of objective standards of critical thinking and justificatory practice? There are widely accepted standards of investigation and critical thinking practices. Zagzebski's contention that a person is justified in holding a belief when it is "what a person who is motivated by intellectual virtue, and who has the understanding of his cognitive situation that a virtuous person would have, might believe in like circumstances" is a place to begin the conversation. Even given the fact that application of these criteria often is ambiguous in that it may be difficult to tell whether, or to what degree, someone has satisfied those criteria, there is no doubt that Milam did not exhibit "intellectual carefulness, perseverance, humility, vigor, flexibility, courage, and thoroughness, as well as open-mindedness, fair-mindedness, insightfulness, and the virtues opposed to wishful thinking, obtuseness, and conformity."[6] Despite the difficulties of assessing the degree to which standards are met in particular situations, standards do exist in our discourse that need to be and can be realistically contextualized to persons who have epistemic obligations.

ACCOUNTABILITY AND THE CONVERSATIONAL STANCE

Accountability for our beliefs and the obligations to hold true beliefs extend beyond individuals to the practices in which we engage. Philip Pettit and Michael Smith describe what they term the "conversational stance." We might engage in conversations for various reasons, but conversations of an intellectual kind involve at least three assumptions. First, the conversants assume that the participants form and have beliefs that bear on the topic under discussion; second, in holding these beliefs, the conversants are worth listening to; and finally, evidence is relevant to determining which beliefs are true, holding out at least the possibility for some agreement based on the examination of the relevant evidence.[7] Whether agreement is attained is another matter, but the conversation at least presupposes that it is possible.

The appeal to evidence as providing the basis for the possibility of agreement suggests that the conversants assume that there are norms that are relevant to deciding what the conversants should believe. These norms that the conversants can recognize and respond to provide the basis or lead us to say that it is right or wrong for the respective conversants to maintain these beliefs and, correspondingly, make these assertions. These norms govern what it is permissible or impermissible to believe in light of other claims made by the participants, the evidence available, experience, the rules of logic, fundamental moral principles, and so on.

Moreover, not only do such epistemic norms exist, but we presuppose that both we and the others with whom we converse hold that those norms apply to both of us. Not only are our beliefs subject to these epistemic norms; we likewise hold that the beliefs of others are subject to these epistemic norms. Beliefs that fail to comport should be rejected; those that comport we are permitted to affirm. Should any of the conversants reject these norms but continue to hold beliefs that they admit violate these norms, the intellectual conversation would no longer hold much point. As Pettit and Smith put it, we would no longer invest the conversant with the authority to speak or hold beliefs on a particular topic. The conversants have failed in their epistemic obligation.

The case where conversants reject epistemic norms must be distinguished from the case where they reason poorly. In the former case, if the conversants reject norms governing true beliefs and their justification, we are left without rules or criteria whereby we can adjudicate the respective beliefs. The basis for reasonable dialogue has been shattered and can only be left in disrepair. In the latter case, criteria or norms still apply; the conversants acknowledge the norms, but various reasons might exist for their maintaining their beliefs. For example, they might suffer from logical ineptitude or the inability to follow the argument or recognize the relevant presuppositions; they might fail to understand the evidence or its significance; they might entertain interpretations of the evidence that vary from the way the other conversants understand or interpret the evidence; they might possess a bias that differs from those held by the others; and so on. Whatever the reasons that lie behind the diversity of beliefs and the inability to reconcile them, intellectual conversation is possible only when the conversants recognize that epistemic norms hold regarding the beliefs espoused.[8]

If there are such epistemic norms, they provide the grounds for determining the beliefs for which the conversants are responsible. That is, conversants are responsible in some way or other to form, maintain, or alter their beliefs with respect to those norms. And this means that we have epistemic responsibilities with respect to our beliefs. We do not have the right to believe whatever we want but presume in intellectual conversation that norms or criteria of some epistemic sort are relevant to our holding the beliefs.

Other writers pick up on this dialogic feature, noting that having epistemic obligations or responsibilities has a social dimension. For example, scientists not only believe they have epistemic obligations or responsibilities for their beliefs; they hold each other accountable for their beliefs. Investigating the truth of others' beliefs is embedded in scientific practice. Much the same can be said for the practices of other disciplines, including and especially philosophy.

J. T. Stevenson suggests that holding each other accountable takes place within a social setting, where we mutually accept duties and responsibilities in order to succeed. "A community's survival and welfare depends in part on the stock of beliefs, hopefully knowledge, which it receives from past generations and which it transmits to future generations. . . . We all have a stake in seeing that this communal heritage is not seriously corrupted."[9] And we do this by taking responsibility for making sure that we have and transmit true beliefs.

Stevenson finds this responsibility occurring in several sectors. Scientists maintain a strict accountability regarding the beliefs they promulgate. "The practices involved in holding people responsible can and should vary from institution to institution depending upon their purposes and membership.

The practice in the case of science is a sort of perpetual game of challenge and response: scientists constantly demand of each other and themselves justification for their beliefs."[10] This is obvious when experimental conclusions arrived at by one researcher or a group of scientists are reviewed by others. Though reviewers often show enthusiasm for the process of discovery or the creativity of the new hypothesis, they often express a tentative hesitancy that the results might not fully support the hypothesis, at least until more experimentation or data gathering is done.

In all of this practice, whatever the discipline, norms or criteria exist by which the scholars, researchers, disputants, writers, and critics judge and are judged. These criteria revolve around the obligation both that the claims made be true and also that the evidence be relevant, public, properly interpreted, and carefully reasoned. The very practices of the disciplines, which hold their participants accountable, presuppose this.

Perhaps what makes epistemic obligations so appealing for me and some of my readers is that they connect in a fundamental way to the conversation that is at the root of education. Education is a conversation between peers and colleagues, teachers and their students, the academy and the public. If the former of each pair do not believe that they have an obligation to have true beliefs and are unwilling to be held accountable for what they say and believe, what they contribute to society will be the source of great suspicion. If the latter in each pair cannot assume that the former have epistemic obligations and are willing to be held accountable for what they say and believe, then we lose the trust essential to the educational and dialogic enterprise. The very practice of education rests on epistemic obligations and the willingness of the conversants to be held accountable for the beliefs that are shared.

Our educational practices evidence the substantial degree to which epistemic obligations are embedded in our educational system. We teachers recommend certain beliefs our students should hold, beliefs about what we conceive as the truths of our discipline, about truths regarding how we conduct the academic enterprise (truths about justice, integrity, tolerance, openness, and academic honesty), and about truths concerning what makes for a meaningful vocation and what really matters in life. Our lectures, discussions, tutoring, and seminars focus on what we consider to be truths we want our students to believe. And at the heart of these educational practices is the assumption that educators and students can be held accountable for what they both believe and say, implemented pedagogically. We construct and conduct assessments of diverse sorts to measure our students' beliefs, testing them against what we conceive to be the truth. We look for right answers and disvalue wrong answers, presuming all the while that these reflect the beliefs of the students.

Educators also value (or at least should value) epistemic excellence. By our pedagogical practices we seek to encourage and foster not only true beliefs but the epistemic virtues or habits that we think will tend to or successfully produce true beliefs. We stress that students should believe the truth for good reasons and in pursuit of excellence develop the skills and dispositions of critical thinking and conduct investigations with an eye toward successfully producing true beliefs. They should embrace the motivation necessary to arrive at knowledge and wisdom. Thus, as educators who are concerned about the epistemic excellence of our students, we are concerned about more than having true beliefs. We encourage the practices that we hope but cannot guarantee will be truth-conducive.

In short, education aims at both true beliefs as an epistemic obligation and at developing the epistemic virtues as lifelong ways of exploring the evidence. Both are critical and essential features of a good education. Excellent educators want students, as conversants, to have true beliefs, and they want the conversant to have the skills that successfully produce them. Both direct and indirect voluntarism are in view in the educational enterprise, but the latter serves the former. We want successful critical thinking because we value truth.

EPISTEMIC RESTRAINTS

If persons can be held accountable for their beliefs, what response should we give to individuals who fail in their epistemic obligations? Even voluntarists exhibit great discomfort with taking action to directly, let alone indirectly, occasion beliefs. For example, Chisholm suggests that although we have voluntary control over our beliefs we do not punish violators because "when a man fails to conform to the ethics of belief he is, *ipso facto*, behaving irrationally."[11] But if believing is a voluntary though conditioned act, and if one can choose with regard to forming or maintaining a belief, that is, between believing, not believing, or suspending belief, one should not so easily conclude that people who don't believe what someone else thinks is true or justified are acting irrationally. Similar assumptions often are made about people who act contrary to what we think would be the moral or prudent way to act. If they act contrary to our norms or those of society, we often quickly and mistakenly judge that they are acting irrationally. But action contrary to communal or societal norms is not necessarily irrational. Such persons might perceive the truth differently than we do, or they might have conducted their justificatory endeavors differently than we did, or even in the same manner but derived different results. But neither of these cases necessarily indicate irrationality, rather only diversity of thought.

Chisholm's second argument is that punishing persons for their beliefs runs counter to "our right to freedom of thought."[12] But this argument brings us full circle to the question of epistemic obligations. If we have epistemic obligations, as we have argued, epistemic autonomy is false. We have no absolute right to believe whatever we want. Everyone is not simply entitled to one's own opinion.

Holding people accountable for their beliefs is a bracing proposal. There are legitimate worries about subjecting people to inquisitions, gulags, indoctrination, brainwashing, and the like, where they can be punished or tortured unless they change their beliefs.[13] At the most radical end are programs such as brainwashing to bring people to hold beliefs. The term, coined by Edward Hunter,[14] evoked a fear-creating sensation during the early part of the Cold War era. It was adapted from the Chinese *xi nao* (wash brain), which referred to the attempt by Chinese revolutionaries to reform the thinking of persons to fit into the new socialist system of thought. Practically it can be questioned whether compelling belief ultimately works. Studies by Robert Lifton and Edgar Schein concluded that the success of the brainwashing practiced by the Chinese was often short-lived,[15] though in some cases—especially where people apparently had a weak sense of their own identity—the victims suffered long term physical, psychological, emotional, and epistemic effects.[16] People who felt self-confident and self-assured were better able to resist the pressures.

While those who underwent the forced-belief conditioning saw it as an evil forced on them, accompanied by unspeakable torture, physical deprivation, and gross mental theft, those who advocated brainwashing saw it as a positive step in reeducating people: "In all of this it is important to realize that *what we see as a set of coercive maneuvers, the Chinese Communists view as a morally uplifting, harmonizing, and scientifically therapeutic experience.*"[17] That people saw it differently does not justify the practice, but it is a reminder that what beliefs we should hold can be differently assessed by various individuals. In itself, this insight should give us both pause and humility about the entire project of forcefully altering beliefs. In the final analysis, "At its heart brainwashing is a malignant idea, the dream of totally controlling a human mind. . . . Brainwashing is the ultimate invasion of privacy: it seeks to control not only how people act but what they think. It arouses our deepest fears, threatening our loss of freedom and even identity."[18] Even on a less radical level, forcing people to believe something can be counterproductive in that people in a mode of resistance become more obstinately attached to their beliefs. (This lesson parents soon learn in rearing adolescents.) It also can lead to people failing to think for themselves and relying simply on others for discerning what to believe. That is, it can lead to epistemic weakness and sloth.[19] In effect, compulsory belief is often both immoral and counterproductive.

But likewise worrisome is the proposal that we should not take any steps at all to help people to form true beliefs and avoid false beliefs, on the grounds that they have the right to believe whatever they want. Milam's beliefs about Till and blacks is a case in point; surely it would have been good for someone to attempt to dissuade him from his beliefs. That we hold each other accountable for our beliefs need not lead to the extremes of inquisitions, just as holding each other morally accountable for our actions need not lead to a morally enforcing "big brother." We don't reject holding people morally accountable for their acts on the ground that accountability can be abused. So likewise we need not reject holding people epistemically accountable on the ground that epistemic accountability can be abused. What we need to guarantee in both cases is that accountability not be abused.

But to state the negative—that bringing about belief change should not engage in or sanction coercion—still leaves undetermined what steps morally can be sanctioned. Granted that we don't want to even think about creating ideological gulags, we still want to think about how we can bring about epistemic change in ways that comport with fundamental moral principles, human dignity, and human freedom. We want not only belief excellence, but the development of the requisite epistemic virtues that successfully lead to true beliefs. To put it more broadly, we want to help people develop ways to avoid mental coercion[20] while at the same time assisting people to internalize and develop epistemic virtues in their pursuit of truth. The goal, in effect, is to assist in the development of epistemic virtues understood as developing the character traits that result in the successful production of true beliefs.

CHANGING BELIEFS

Jonathan Renshon writes, "Despite its central importance, our understanding of when and why beliefs change is far from perfect. A survey of the relevant literature in the fields of social and cognitive psychology, behavior economics, and political psychology reveals a surprising lack of attention paid to the question of when and why beliefs change. Do beliefs shift imperceptibly over time? Do they change instantaneously in response to traumatic events? Must a cluster of related beliefs change at the same time? Or can specific beliefs change in isolation (implying a more fragmented belief system)?"[21] These are serious questions that must be addressed in detail elsewhere, for they require extensive experimental study. My surmise is that one will find that all these options apply at diverse times; we do not change beliefs in only one way. But what is of note is that central to the question of bringing about and changing beliefs are at least three factors. One is that not all of our beliefs are held with the same assurance or, indeed, the same centrality. It is common, following Quine, to speak about a web of beliefs. We have beliefs that lie at the outside of the web that can change without significantly affecting the entire structure of the web. We hold other beliefs that lie at the core of the web, and adding to or altering these will significantly affect the entire belief structure. So if we are going to study belief creation and belief change, we would have to take into account where the respective beliefs that we want to change lie in the complex web of beliefs. Are they peripheral or central or core beliefs? Mediate or auxiliary? The response to this determines how difficult it will be to change the belief, to what extent we endanger an entire belief system, and what emotional and epistemic trauma such an undertaking will occasion.

The second fact is the relative stability of our core beliefs over time. Though our more peripheral beliefs might change with greater frequency, though even here change is often gradual, those beliefs that are central to our worldview and even to our identity possess a fundamental cognitive consistency.[22] In part this is because when we receive new information, we link that information with our already existing beliefs. Information that agrees with, confirms, strengthens, or adds to our existing core beliefs is readily accepted and integrated into our web of beliefs. Information that conflicts with our core beliefs is rejected, ignored altogether, or minimized.[23] Although entry into the peripheral part of the web is easier in that this zone is more malleable, being accepted into the web of beliefs depends upon consistency with present beliefs. This points to the third fact, namely, that we attempt to hold a consistent set of beliefs. Beliefs are not isolated but linked in robust fashion. This does not mean that all our beliefs are consistent; beliefs might indeed be compartmentalized, so that what we believe in one area is internally consistent but might not be consistent with beliefs in other areas. Though even here, if pressed, we might argue that if people could see the whole they would realize that in fact the various areas do fit together in that there are important bridge principles that enable us to maintain consistency (at least apparent consistency to the person holding them).

The upshot is that belief change is a complex activity. It depends on the importance of the belief, the location of the belief within the entire belief structure, and the role that the belief plays vis-à-vis other beliefs. The beliefs to which we referred in chapter 1—the Neumanns' belief in faith healing, Milam's belief about racial superiority, and Williamson's belief regarding the Holocaust—would be more than mere peripheral beliefs for those holding them, and hence to change them would involve significant changes to beliefs housed elsewhere in the web. The Neumanns' belief connects with their core beliefs about God, and altering their beliefs about faith healing would probably require a significant change in their core beliefs about the nature of God, God's relation to and concern for individual human persons, and God's acts in the world, as well as changes in their beliefs about their community and its members. Milam's belief about blacks likewise is central to his worldview; his racist views colored all his social interactions, for they determined what could be said between persons, where persons could live or go in the society, how Milam was to treat others, and so on. Williamson's belief about the Holocaust is more difficult to locate, for it is unclear how close to the center of his web of beliefs it lies. On the one hand, it would seem to be quite peripheral, since holding beliefs about the Holocaust is not central to the role of being a Roman Catholic or one of its bishops; on the other hand, it may connect with his other views of the society to which he belongs or about Jews, namely, that Jews still should be held accountable for the crucifixion death of Jesus. In the latter case, the question then becomes how central his view of the Jews is insofar as it connects to the core of his beliefs. The degree to which change of belief or belief formation is possible, then, depends on a great variety of factors.

That does not mean that belief change is impossible. When change occurs, it may be through gradual altering of the web, pulling here and pushing there, or it may be because of some traumatic or painful event or some favorable or pleasurable event that encourages or urges persons to alter their beliefs. The gradual change might be occasioned by diverse experiences over time, the gentle winds of persuasion, or our gradual maturation. Change in the face of trauma might occur because of experiences so radical that a cognitive shift is required for the person to seriously address the issue. For example, people develop or alter their norms or values when they encounter turmoil or significant suffering in their own lives or the lives of others. Suddenly, the disease that strikes their child now becomes a disease that has not been adequately funded or addressed by research. They become an advocate for research on the disease and create a foundation or nonprofit organization to channel funds into addressing this significant disease. Events, then, play a substantial role in our belief formation and belief change. They are part of the causes and reasons we employ in adopting and altering our beliefs.

This suggests that perhaps belief formation or change in others need not be carried out directly, that is, by limiting or compelling beliefs. Perhaps we can avoid enforcing epistemic propriety by influencing people's actions rather than their beliefs. Since actions flow from beliefs, and since actions in turn affect beliefs, both in terms of their creation and their reinforcement or diminution, finding ways that encourage change in actions is the best tactic to develop belief change. Not only might belief change be more moral when it is done using moral actions, but it might be more pragmatically successful, for when persons consciously and freely adopt a belief change it is more likely that the new beliefs will remain since the new beliefs are more truly the person's own than any system forced on them.

Not only would we want to help people change their beliefs, but we would want to help them change their epistemic character where this is faulty, undeveloped, or simply not appropriately practiced. If connection holds between forming and then carrying out our epistemic virtues, then it would be appropriate to assist people to develop the proper epistemic character. As Aristotle noted, the development of epistemic virtues comes about by education and training, and we might add, practice. As such, as educators we need to think not only about helping students to know the truth, to enlighten them about the facts—something we are very good at doing in much of our educational structure. But just as importantly, we need to be engaged in helping students to learn what the appropriate epistemic virtues are and to engage in the appropriate practice of them until they form the respective habits. Educational research—and classroom experience—shows that individual truths and even principles are quickly forgotten; retention of data is short-lived. But if we are interested in lifelong learning, we need to assist epistemic character development. Once the proper epistemic virtues are formed, they have a greater chance of both remaining and being practiced. And as virtues, their successful practice should in general (though not infallibly) lead persons to believe the truth. Thus, though we have argued against reducing epistemic obligations to believe the truth to the practice of proper epistemic practices, helping people form the appropriate virtues and encouraging them to implement the practices is one way of effecting belief change.

Although to push further on the nature and role of persuasion and influence would lead to a different book, one thing needs to be said about finding ways to help people believe contextually significant truths by forming true beliefs or changing false beliefs. When we control the actions of others, control must be exercised morally; otherwise the very immoral actions we seek to discourage or prevent are invoked on behalf of the change. Justice plays a central role in how one controls the actions of others. Where one person restrains the actions of another, it must be done justly. The action taken must be the minimum that is necessary to bring an end to the immoral action. The action must treat the offenders as human beings, respecting as far as possible their dignity, rights, and freedoms. The restraint must not only be moral but within the limits of the law; as the saying goes, two wrongs do not make a right. When those who enforce the law respect by demonstration the very law they enforce, they show not only the power but the justice of the law.[24]

In a similar vein, in helping others to form true beliefs and develop the appropriate epistemic virtues, the actions that should be taken are actions that brim full of justice. The actions must respect the integrity of the individual in that the person needs to form and shape the beliefs and virtues for him or her own self. Actions of others must respect the dignity of the person, so that cooperatively the person can bring about the change or formation of belief and practice. The implications of this for education are significant. Education no longer is indoctrination, where the person is merely told what to believe, often under the threat of force or duress, but occurs in the nature of a dialogue where the individual, as a result of the experience, is helped to see what the truth is, to form appropriate beliefs about it, and to understand the relevant justification for it. Education does not suppress individuals and their initiative but provides the necessary information, skills, and encouragement of habits that enable persons to voluntarily fulfill their epistemic obligations.

CONCLUDING NOTE

It might be observed, after all is said and done, that in advocating epistemic obligations as part of epistemic excellence, we have not traveled far from Socrates. He too, in his own way, advocated both of these concepts and paid the ultimate price for maintaining that we have epistemic obligations. Yet his memorable phrase still rings true: "The unexamined life is not worth living."[25] Since we have epistemic obligations, we face the challenge to examine what it is that we believe so as to maximize contextually significant truths and minimize our false beliefs, preferably in light of the evidence and reasons that we think support it. Likewise, we have the obligation to develop the epistemic virtues and practices that will lead us toward achieving the goal of epistemic excellence.

Notes

Chapter 1

1 One notable exception to this concerns what are termed hate crimes. The same act may be punished differently and more or less severely depending on the beliefs held by the agent and that allegedly informed or motivated the crime.

2 "Trials Loom for Parents Who Embraced Faith over Medicine," *New York Times*, January 21, 2009, A18.

3 David Eells, "Unleavened Bread Ministries," Press Release, March 27, 2008, http://www.wsaw.com/news/misc/17059726.html.

4 Jeff Starck, "Leilani Neumann Testifies, Petition Targets Judge," Live Blog, July 28, 2009, http://www.wausaudailyherald.com/apps/pbcs.dll/article?AID=/20090728/WDH0101/90728076.

5 Jeff Starck, "Dale Neumann Trial Testimony Begins," Live Blog, July 27, 2009, http://www.wausaudailyherald.com/apps/pbcs.dll/article?AID=/20090730/WDH0101/90730033.

6 Starck, "Leilani Neumann Testifies."

7 Starck, "Dale Neumann Trial Testimony Begins."

8 One has to be careful about delineating precisely what they believed. Their belief that God can heal could still be true without Kara actually being healed. God's action would have been sufficient for healing had God chosen to act in this fashion.

9 William Bradford Huie, "The Shocking Story of Approved Killing in Mississippi," *Look*, January 24, 1956.

10 Technically, Williamson's making remarks about the Holocaust

would indicate that he took actions on his beliefs. I treat this as a case of not taking action in that his action of asserting his beliefs did not stem from the content of his beliefs, but from his having the beliefs. That is, the action of asserting his belief would follow from any belief regardless of the content; that it was about the Holocaust did not affect the asserting per se, only what was asserted.

11 Following the pope's orders, Williamson actually did say that he "regretted having made such remarks, and that if I had known beforehand the full harm and hurt to which they would give rise, especially to the church, but also to survivors and relatives of victims of injustice under the Third Reich, I would not have made them. . . . To all souls that took honest scandal from what I said, before God I apologize." However, this is not a retraction of a belief about the Holocaust, but an apology for making his beliefs public. "Bishop Offers Apology for Holocaust Remarks," *New York Times*, February 27, 2009, A6.

12 See the historical novel by Franz Werfel, *The Forty Days of Musa Dagh* (New York: Carroll & Graf, 1934).

13 Mike Degenhardt, "The Ethics of Belief and the Ethics of Teaching," *Journal of Philosophy of Education* 32 (1998): 333.

14 Degenhardt, "The Ethics of Belief," 342. This echoes Socrates in *Meno* 86, b–c. "I do not insist that my argument is right in all other respects, but I would contend at all costs both in word and deed as far as I can that we will be better persons, braver and less idle, if we believe that one must search for the things one does not know, rather than if we believe that it is not possible to find out what we do not know and that we must not look for it."

15 "True" here is understood in a nonpragmatic sense. If truth is equivalent to workability or promoting growth, then what accomplishes these tasks is thereby true, and what does not is thereby false.

16 Sharon Ryan hints at this but does not develop it. "Doxastic Compatibilism and the Ethics of Belief," *Philosophical Studies* 114 (2003): 62.

Chapter 2

1 Roderick Chisholm, "Firth and the Ethics of Belief," *Philosophy and Phenomenological Research* 1 (1991): 123–24.

2 This is not to say that we don't sometimes encourage *others* to hold false beliefs. Criminals mislead police; chess players deceive their opponents; teenagers at times might want their parents to believe something other than the facts; businesspersons do not want their competitors to know the details of their business ventures. But the beliefs of the former in each case are directed at knowing the truth for themselves—and believing the truth is a prerequisite for the deception. We will return to self-deception later.

3 Bernard Williams, "Deciding to Believe," in Williams, *Problems of*

the Self. Cambridge: Cambridge University Press (1973), 137; John Locke, *Essay Concerning Human Understanding* 4.17.24.

4 William James, "The Will to Believe," in *The Will to Believe and Other Essays in Popular Philosophy* (New York: Dover, 1956), 17.

5 James, "The Will to Believe," 18–19.

6 William Clifford, "The Ethics of Belief," in *The Ethics of Belief and Other Essays* (Amherst, N.Y.: Prometheus Books, 1999), 77.

7 Richard J. Hall and Charles R. Johnson, "The Epistemic Duty to Seek More Evidence," *American Philosophical Quarterly* 35 (1998): 135.

8 Compare with Karl Popper's fable of the man who wrote in a notebook everything he observed each day and bequeathed it to the Royal Society, which discarded it as meaningless. Jacob Bronowski, *Science and Human Values* (New York: Harper, 1956), 24–25.

9 Richard Feldman, "Epistemic Obligations," in *Epistemology*, ed. James Tomberlin, Philosophical Perspectives 2 (Arascadero, Calif.: Ridgeview, 1988): 245. Feldman notes that similar things might be said about holding a false belief. We might be epistemically obligated to hold a false belief if we really have sufficient reason to (mistakenly) believe that it is true. In short, what this shows is that epistemic obligations must be considered both subjectively and objectively and not just objectively.

10 Robert Audi, "Dispositional Beliefs and Dispositions to Believe," *Noûs* 28, no. 4 (1994): 419–34.

11 Another way of responding is to suggest that a totally dispositional account of belief is inadequate, that belief is also an active state. We will take up this discussion in chapter 6.

12 Roderick Chisholm, *Theory of Knowledge*, 2nd ed. (Englewood Cliffs, N.J.: Prentice-Hall, 1977), 14.

13 One might think of a moral parallel: trying to be good, and the trying as satisfying our moral obligations. To try to be good but never to achieve one good act or virtue would not satisfy our moral obligations.

14 Clifford, "The Ethics of Belief," 78.

15 Kevin Meeker notes that this is designed to avoid a requirement to hold beliefs about trivial matters. "Chisholming Away at Plantinga's Critique of Epistemic Deontology," *Australasian Journal of Philosophy* 76 (1998): 92.

16 Feldman, "Epistemic Obligations," 250.

17 Feldman puts this not in terms of truth but of justification, which we will take up in chapter 4.

18 Feldman, "Epistemic Obligations," 250.

19 Henry Morgenthau Sr. was the U.S. ambassador to the Ottoman Empire from 1913 until 1916. While at his diplomatic post he received reports of the events and sent them back to the U.S. government, urging that action be taken.

20 Feldman, "Epistemic Obligations," 246.

21 Roderick M. Chisholm, "Epistemic Statements and the Ethics of Belief," *Philosophy and Phenomenological Research* 16 (1956): 459.

22 But see Meiland, who interprets truth in a pragmatic sense. He argues that someone might be justified in holding a false belief because it serves a larger, pragmatic truth or good. Jack W. Meiland, "What Ought We to Believe? Or The Ethics of Belief Revisited," *American Philosophical Quarterly* 17 (1980): 15–24. We shall say more about this prudential view in the next chapter.

23 Linda Zagzebski suggests that not holding a certain belief when one should hold it is a stronger sense of epistemic duty than disbelieving when one should believe it. *Virtues of the Mind* (Cambridge: Cambridge University Press, 1996), 242. Roderick Chisholm, however, rejects the notion of obligatory or required beliefs. "Lewis' Ethics of Belief," in *The Philosophy of* C. *I. Lewis*, ed. Paul Arthur Schilpp (La Salle, Ill.: Open Court, 1968), 231.

24 Even this is contextual, for whereas giving up one's public transport seat might be supererogatory in America, in China it is required.

25 William Alston, "The Deontological Conception of Epistemic Justification," in *Epistemology*, edited by James E. Tomberlin, Philosophical Perspectives 2 (Atascadero, Calif.: Ridgeview, 1988), 257..

26 Alvin Plantinga, *Warrant: The Current Debate* (New York: Oxford University Press, 1993), 33. Plantinga objects not to epistemic deontologism, but to *classical* deontologism, where obligation is tied to justification as constituting warrant.

27 William Alston holds that we have epistemic obligations but treats them as permissive. *Epistemic Justification: Essays in the Theory of Knowledge* (Ithaca, N.Y.: Cornell University Press, 1989), 85, 116. However, in a later work, he treats them as required when he suggests that we are obliged to look for more evidence or to train ourselves to be less credulous. "Epistemic Desiderata," *Philosophy and Phenomenological Research* 53 (1993): 530.

28 Aristotle, *Nichomachean Ethics* 6.1144a.

29 This is very close to Plantinga's suggestion that "there is a duty to the truth of some kind. It may be hard to state this duty exactly; perhaps it is in the neighborhood of a requirement to do your best to believe as many important truths as possible and avoid as many important falsehoods as possible." *Warranted Christian Belief* (New York: Oxford University Press, 2000), 99–100. I am suggesting that significance should be contextualized.

30 As Alston notes, "The qualification 'in a large body of beliefs' is needed because otherwise one could best achieve the aim by restricting one's beliefs to those that are obviously true." *Epistemic Justification*, 84.

31 This describes how epistemic excellence functions in the actual world. It might look very different in a hypothetical world, such

as one governed by a deceiving Cartesian demon where truth is unavailable. In such a world the pragmatic might have to be what is believed.

32 William Alston, *Beyond "Justification"* (Ithaca, N.Y.: Cornell University Press, 2005), 75.

33 Alston, *Beyond "Justification,"* 77.

Chapter 3

1 Bas van Fraassen, *The Scientific Image* (New York: Oxford University Press, 1980), 64.

2 Jonathan L. Kvanvig, *The Value of Knowledge and the Pursuit of Understanding* (Cambridge: Cambridge University Press, 2003), 41–42.

3 Meiland, "What Ought We to Believe?," 24.

4 Jeff Jordan, "Pragmatic Arguments and Belief in God," *Stanford Encyclopedia of Philosophy*, September 29, 2009, http://plato.stanford.edu.

5 Feldman, "Epistemic Obligations," 235.

6 Louis P. Pojman, *Religious Belief and the Will* (London: Routledge & Kegan Paul, 1986), 189.

7 Meiland, "What Ought We to Believe?," 19.

8 In a section of the essay rarely noted, Clifford does allow prudential consideration to enter into epistemic obligations. He writes, "There are many cases in which it is our duty to act upon probabilities, although the evidence is not such as to justify present belief; because it is precisely by such action, and by observation of its fruits, that evidence is got which may justify future belief." He ties the prudential considerations directly back to obtaining sufficient evidence, but the considerations are prudential nonetheless. Clifford, "The Ethics of Belief," 79.

9 J. T. Stevenson, "On Doxastic Responsibility," in *Analysis and Metaphysics*, ed. Keith Lehrer (Dordrecht: D. Reidel, 1975), 237.

10 Trudy Govier, "Belief, Values, and the Will," *Dialogue* 15 (1976): 662.

11 Degenhardt, "The Ethics of Belief," 336.

12 Clifford, "The Ethics of Belief," 73.

13 James Lenman, "Belief, Desire and Motivation: An Essay in Quasi-Hydraulics," *American Philosophical Quarterly* 33 (1996): 291–301

14 Richard Swinburne, *Epistemic Justification* (Oxford: Clarendon, 2001), 85–86.

15 Chisholm, "Epistemic Statements," 447.

16 Chisholm, "Firth and the Ethics of Belief," 119.

17 Susan Haack, "'The Ethics of Belief' Reconsidered," in *The Philosophy of Roderick M. Chisholm*, ed. Lewis Edwin Hahn (Chicago: Open Court, 1997), 130–32

18 Clifford, "The Ethics of Belief," 74–75.

19 Clifford, "The Ethics of Belief," 76–77. Clifford appears to contradict himself at this point, for earlier it was not truth but justification that mattered for Clifford. Here the end is truth.
20 Clifford, "The Ethics of Belief," 73.
21 Haack, " 'The Ethics of Belief' Reconsidered," 137.
22 Haack, " 'The Ethics of Belief' Reconsidered," 132–34.
23 Feldman, "Epistemic Obligations," 236.
24 Kongzi, *Analects*, trans. by Edward Slingerland (Indianapolis: Hackett, 2003), 13.18.
25 Plato, *Euthyphro* 4.
26 Nicholas Wolterstorff, "Obligations of Belief—Two Concepts," in *The Philosophy of Roderick M. Chisholm*, ed. Lewis Edwin Hahn (Chicago: Open Court, 1997), 236.
27 Wolterstorff, "Obligations of Belief," 233.
28 Richard Feldman, "The Ethics of Belief," *Philosophy and Phenomenological Research* 60 (2000): 675.
29 Wolterstorff, "Obligations of Belief," 232.
30 Wolterstorff, "Obligations of Belief," 235.
31 A similar problem arises for those who, like Feldman, suggest that they are parallel. Feldman, "The Ethics of Belief," 667.
32 In a sense Plantinga's treatment of epistemic obligations falls into this category when he treats fulfilling epistemic obligations as an excellence, though Plantinga wants to exclude deontology from epistemology and in its place develop a theory of warranted belief. Although he rejects the view that his foundationalist warrant/proper function view falls into the virtue ethicist camp, his position might be termed "virtue reliabilism." Jason S. Baehr, "Character in Epistemology," *Philosophical Studies* 128 (2006): 479. See also James Montmarquet, *Epistemic Virtue and Doxastic Responsibility* (Lanham, Md.: Rowman & Littlefield, 1993), who treats intellectual virtues as personality traits. The central virtue, epistemic conscientiousness, in parallel with moral conscientiousness, is to be motivated to arrive at truth and avoid error.
33 Linda Zagzebski says that if there is any distinction between moral and intellectual virtues, it is to be found in that intellectual but not moral virtues are grounded in the motivation to know. *Virtues of the Mind*, 252.
34 Zagzebski, *Virtues of the Mind*, 137.
35 Zagzebski, *Virtues of the Mind*, 33.
36 Zagzebski, *Virtues of the Mind*, 243.
37 Zagzebski, *Virtues of the Mind*, 241.
38 Zagzebski, *Virtues of the Mind*, 155.
39 Zagzebski, *Virtues of the Mind*, 60.
40 Zagzebski, *Virtues of the Mind*, 203.
41 Zagzebski, *Virtues of the Mind*, 184.
42 Zagzebski, *Virtues of the Mind*, 185–86. They are not necessarily

truth-conducive individually employed. Take, for example, the virtues of being open-minded or of dogged persistence. Being open-minded is an intellectual virtue in that it allows us to see things from other perspectives, to be open to new ideas or ways of understanding that might enrich one's current point of view. However, in itself, being open-minded might result in our never arriving at a true belief, but always looking for more evidence lest we be unduly swayed by the information we already have. As Barrows Dunham wrote in another context, there is a kind of thinking where "the mind is so open that everything falls through" *Man against Myth* (Boston: Little, Brown, 1947), 134. Similarly, dogged persistence is an intellectual virtue, akin to the moral virtue of courage, in that the would-be knower continues to search for truth, even when it is not readily apparent or when paths have resulted in dead ends. At the same time, dogged persistence can lead to tunnel vision, so that in pursuing one idea we might fail to see its connection with other ideas that are strategically important and that might be essential for arriving at truth. Consequently, we have to think of exercising these intellectual virtues together, in some kind of unity. This does not entail a unity of the virtues. There might be times when being doggedly persistent and being open-minded conflict, but we have to achieve some sort of balance among them. But though the individual intellectual virtues may conflict, the motivation to achieve knowledge that underlies them is unified, so that the epistemic obligation is rooted in the motivation rather than the individual virtues.

Chapter 4

1 Jonathan Kvanvig questions the claim that holding a true belief for good reasons rather than accidentally or for bad or no reasons enhances epistemic excellence. He contends that the supporting argument that justified true beliefs are more stable and longer lasting is undermined by the fact that beliefs can be fixed or stabilized in various ways that have nothing to do with justification—for example, by providing survival value. *The Value of Knowledge,* 14–15.

2 Clifford, "The Ethics of Belief," 71.

3 Clifford, "The Ethics of Belief," 71–72.

4 Jonathan Adler, *Belief's Own Ethics* (Cambridge Mass.: MIT Press, 2002), 25.

5 Alston, *Epistemic Justification,* 83. Alston's way of putting justification seems to lead to an infinite regress. "S is cognitively justified in believing that *p* *iff* S is justified in believing that he possesses adequate evidence of *p*." But if we supply this definition of being justified to replace "justified" in the definiens, we get the claim that S is cognitively justified in believing that *p* *iff* S is justified in believing

that he has adequate evidence for believing that he has adequate evidence for *p*.

6 John Greco objects to a perspectivalist account on the grounds that we might have made epistemic commitments prior to what we recall or are aware of as part of our justification, and these epistemic commitments affect the justification of our belief, either for good or for ill. "Internalism and Epistemically Responsible Belief," *Synthese* 85 (1990): 246–47. The current justification might be sound, but the prior commitments might not. Greco cites an example of Marie, who believes that her favorite singer is Italian. Her belief is based on the fact that she clearly remembers that she has had this belief for a long time. However, suppose that her belief came from the testimony of her mother, who believes that everyone Maria likes is Italian. Here a factor in the justification, which is outside Maria's perspectival purview, militates against the contention that her belief is justified. Thus, since the justification of the belief may depend on some factor or factors outside the person's perspective, and since those factors may either contribute to the justification or detract from it, responsible belief cannot be tied to having the justification in mind. Greco, however, believes that an internalist version can be developed that satisfies a responsibility or deontological conception, not of justification, but of knowledge (269–74). In a later work, Greco moves to develop his own version of agent reliabilism. *Putting Skeptics in Their Place* (Cambridge: Cambridge University Press, 2000), chap. 7.

7 A related problem plagues Clifford's account that one should not believe unless one has sufficient evidence. He suggests two principles: "We may believe what goes beyond our experience, only when it is inferred from that experience by the assumption that what we do not know is like what we know (principle of uniformity). We may believe the statement of another person, when there is reasonable ground for supposing that he knows the matter of which he speaks, and that he is speaking the truth so far as he knows it." Clifford, "The Ethics of Belief," 96. Both, unfortunately, are circular. The circularity of the first was pointed out by David Hume, while the circularity of the second is seen in appealing to "reasonable ground" to define sufficient evidence, where sufficient evidence tells us what constitutes a reasonable ground.

8 Greco, "Internalism and Epistemically Responsible Belief," 245.

9 Laurence BonJour, *The Structure of Empirical Knowledge* (Cambridge, Mass.: Harvard University Press, 1985), 8.

10 Chisholm, "Epistemic Statements," 448.

11 Feldman, "The Ethics of Belief," 679.

12 Feldman, "The Ethics of Belief," 679.

13 Feldman, "The Ethics of Belief," 679–80.

14 John 1:12.

15 Feldman, "The Ethics of Belief," 687–88.

16 Such a position is argued by Richard J. Hall and Charles R. Johnson ("The Epistemic Duty," 133), who contend that the following principle of epistemic duty is true: "For any proposition that is less than certain on one's present evidence, one has an epistemic duty to seek more evidence about that proposition." Only in this way can we satisfy the epistemic requirement relevant to the "epistemic goal of believing all and only truths." The problem with this is that there is no reason to take this as our epistemic goal. As we saw in a previous chapter, such a goal would not only be unattainable, but a waste of our time, since most truths are not worthy of being investigated. The authors recognize this and distinguish between prima facie and actual duties. The above principle is a prima facie but not an actual duty; actual duties are contextualized and pragmaticized.

17 Feldman, "The Ethics of Belief," 689.

18 Alston, *Epistemic Justification*, 86. "Deontological" is understood in that sense of "epistemic obligations [that] owe their validity to the fact that fulfilling them would tend to lead to the realization of a desirable state of affairs, viz., a large body of beliefs with a favorable truth-falsity ratio" (85), what following Plantinga we have termed epistemic excellence.

19 Alston, *Epistemic Justification*, 98–99. With epistemic obligations "we are getting at something more 'internal' to S's 'perspective on the world.'"

20 Alston, *Epistemic Justification*, 85.

21 Feldman, "The Ethics of Belief," 685.

22 Montmarquet, *Epistemic Virtue and Doxastic Responsibility*, 53.

23 Alvin Goldman, "What Is Justified Belief?" in *Justification and Knowledge: New Studies in Epistemology*, ed. George Pappas (Boston: D. Reidel, 1979), 1.

24 Goldman, "What Is Justified Belief?" 14.

25 Alvin Goldman, "Reliabilism," *Stanford Encyclopedia of Philosophy*. April 21, 2008, http://www.plato.stanford.edu/entries/reliabilism, 7.

26 Alvin Goldman, "Strong and Weak Justification," in *Epistemology*, ed. James Tomberlin, Philosophical Perspectives 2 (Atascadero, Calif.: Ridgeview, 1988), 54–57.

27 Goldman, "Strong and Weak Justification."

28 "The men of Reserve Police Battalion 101, like the rest of German society, were immersed in a deluge of racist and anti-Semitic propaganda. Furthermore, the Order Police provided for indoctrination both in basic training and as an ongoing practice within each unit. Such incessant propagandizing must have had a considerable effect in reinforcing general notions of Germanic racial superiority and 'a certain aversion' toward the Jews. . . . One would have to be quite convinced of the manipulative powers of indoctrination to believe

that any of this material could have deprived the men of Reserve Police Battalion 101 of the capacity for independent thought. Influenced and conditioned in a general way, imbued in particular with a sense of their own superiority and racial kinship as well as Jewish inferiority and otherness, many of them undoubtedly were; explicitly prepared for the task of killing Jews they most certainly were not." Christopher R. Browning, *Ordinary Men: Reserve Police Battalion 101 and the Final Solution in Poland* (New York: Harper Perennial, 1998), 184.

29 Zagzebski, *Virtues of the Mind,* 241.

30 Zagzebski, *Virtues of the Mind,* 234.

31 Zagzebski, *Virtues of the Mind,* 308–9.

32 Greco, *Putting Skeptics in Their Place,* 190–91.

33 Montmarquet, *Epistemic Virtue and Doxastic Responsibility,* chap. 2.

Chapter 5

1 Phil Goggans, "Epistemic Obligations and Doxastic Voluntarism," *Analysis* (March 1991): 105.

2 Although we won't pursue this tack, Sharon Ryan defends belief voluntarism by denying the contention that *ought* implies *can*. "Doxastic Compatibilism," 50–59.

3 Thomas Aquinas, *Summa theologica,* pt. 2, Q4, art. 2; René Descartes, *Meditations on First Philosophy*; James, "The Will to Believe"; Chisholm, "Lewis' Ethics of Belief."

4 One can find such a criticism beginning with John Locke. "Assent is no more in our power than knowledge. When the agreement of any two ideas appears to our minds, whether immediately or by the assistance of reason, I can no more refuse to perceive, no more avoid knowing it, than I can avoid seeing those objects which I turn my eyes to, and look on in daylight; and what upon full examination I find the most probable, I cannot deny my assent to. . . . Thus, in some cases we can prevent or suspend our assent: but can a man versed in modern or ancient history doubt whether there is such a place as Rome, or whether there was such a man as Julius Caesar? . . . The greater probability, I think, in that case will determine the assent: and a man can no more avoid assenting, or taking it to be true, where he perceives the greater probability, than he can avoid knowing it to be true, where he perceives the agreement or disagreement of any two ideas." John Locke, *An Essay Concerning Human Understanding* 4.20.16.

5 Acts 16:31.

6 Eventually she was sent to prison for her participation in the robbery; later her sentence was commuted by president Jimmy Carter.

7 Robert Audi, "Doxastic Voluntarism and the Ethics of Belief," *Facta Philosophica* 1 (1999): 87. Audi goes on to reject this view, however.

8 Meiland, "What Ought We to Believe?," 16.

9 Some take this language as indicating a manifestation of the belief already formed rather than the forming of the belief. Nonetheless, this caveat does not indicate that assenting to or affirming cannot be voluntary actions associated with the formation of beliefs. Audi, "Doxastic Voluntarism," 91.

10 Ryan distinguishes between having epistemic obligations and epistemic deontologism. The latter includes the view that "we can legitimately be reproached, scorned, and blamed for not believing what we ought to believe and that we can be legitimately praised and the like for believing what we ought to believe" ("Doxastic Compatibilism," 48). We will take up the second theme in our final chapter.

11 Feldman terms it the Voluntarism Argument. But since he denies the connection between epistemic obligations and voluntarism, it seems best to refer to it as the antiobligation argument. Feldman, "The Ethics of Belief," 669.

12 In a previous article, Feldman distinguished moral and prudential obligations, where "ought" does imply "can," from cases of academic or financial obligations, where the entailment allegedly fails to hold. Feldman, "Epistemic Obligations," 240–43. In the legal and financial cases, obligations remain even when we have no control over satisfying the obligations. He suggests that epistemic obligations are like financial and legal obligations, for in epistemic obligations "ought" does not entail "can." After several articles critiqued his view, he subsequently rejected contractual financial and legal obligations as a plausible model for epistemic obligations, since epistemic obligations are not contractual, and turned to roles ("The Ethics of Belief," 674).

13 Feldman, "The Ethics of Belief," 676.

14 Feldman, "The Ethics of Belief," 676.

15 Plantinga, *Warranted Christian Belief*, 96.

16 Swinburne, *Epistemic Justification*, 24.

17 Locke, *An Essay Concerning Human Understanding* 4.20.16.

18 More recently, H. H. Price concluded that in most cases beliefs arise not by free choice. Where being voluntary comes in is in directing our attention to the proposition. "By acting as if the proposition were true on all occasions to which its truth or falsity is relevant, and by increasing the number of these occasions whenever possible, . . . you will gradually get into a state of believing the proposition. You will wake up one fine day and find that you do believe it." "Belief and Will," in *Proceedings of the Aristotelian Society*, suppl. vol. 28 (London: Harrison, 1954), 68.

19 Alston, *Beyond "Justification,"* 75.

20 Blaise Pascal, *Pensées* (Oxford: Oxford University Press, 1995), 155–56.

21 See James, "The Will to Believe," 26.

22 Alston, "Epistemic Desiderata," 530. Even this recommendation is problematic, for training oneself to be less credulous indicates that we have direct control over our beliefs, which Alston denies.

23 H. H. Price argues that we should not be praised or blamed for our beliefs, and consequently should be neither rewarded nor punished for what we believe. Beliefs are states that result from assessing the evidence. Once the evidence is assessed, we cannot help but believe. The voluntary aspect is attending to the evidence. If we assent in accord with the evidence, it is likely that we will have more true than false beliefs. *Belief* (London: George Allen & Unwin, 1969), 238.

24 Alston, *Beyond "Justification,"* 78.

25 Clifford, "The Ethics of Belief," 77.

26 Alston, *Epistemic Justification*, 95–96.

27 Alston, *Beyond "Justification,"* 79.

28 Alston notes that truth-conductivity—"the reason or content must be so related to the target belief and its content that, given the truth of the former, the latter is likely to be true"—is held by many to be a necessary condition of justification. He treats it as an epistemic desideratum. "Epistemic Desiderata," 528. See Alston, *Beyond "Justification,"* 77–78.

29 Feldman, "Epistemic Obligation," 254.

30 Alston, *Beyond "Justification,"* 62.

31 Alston, *Beyond "Justification,"* 60.

32 Pojman, *Religious Belief and the Will*, 159.

33 Pojman, *Religious Belief and the Will*, 159. Williams treats this as reflecting the central contention of empirical belief that one comes to believe something because it is so and one's perceptual apparatus is reliably functioning. But as above, he has confused the objective conditions with the subjective conditions. One comes to believe it because one perceives it to be so, not simply because it is so. "Deciding to Believe," 148–49.

34 Nicholas Wolterstorff, *John Locke and the Ethics of Belief* (Cambridge: Cambridge University Press, 1996), 111.

35 Pojman, *Religious Belief and the Will*, 161.

36 For example, Brian Grant ponders whether, in the face of overwhelming evidence, he could believe that spring has come to Alberta, Canada. "Descartes, Belief and the Will," *Philosophy* 51 (1976): 403–5. See Alston, *Beyond "Justification,"* 63.

37 Plantinga, *Warranted Christian Belief*, 96.

38 Alston contends that this inability to will belief applies not only to false beliefs but also to true beliefs as well. Since "voluntary control attaches to sets of contraries," if I don't have the power to voluntarily directly will false beliefs, I likewise do not have the power to directly will true beliefs. Even obviously true beliefs like perceptual beliefs cannot be directly willed. *Beyond "Justification,"* 63. We have already addressed the second part of this argument above.

39 Alston's argument, that "it seems clear to me that I have no such power," begs the question. *Beyond "Justification,"* 63.

40 Ryan, "Doxastic Compatibilism," 64.

41 Roderick Chisholm points out that the "can" implied by the obligation need not be exercised immediately. He introduces the following.

> "(P) If a person S has the duty to perform an act A, then it is within S's power to perform A and to refrain from performing A."

But this, he notes, is ambiguous between two possibilities.

> "(P1) For any time t, if S has the duty to at t to perform A, then it is in S's power at t to perform A and to refrain from performing A.
>
> "(P2) For any time t, if S has the duty at t to perform A, then it is within S's power at t or at some time after t to perform A and to refrain from performing A."

But the first, Chisholm points out, is false. If I lend you a certain amount of money, I assume that you can pay me back. But it does not follow that you can pay me back immediately, or even at any given time. All that follows is that, as (P2) indicates, you have the power at some time or another to pay me back. Similarly with limited control over our beliefs. The fact that I cannot believe P now does not show that I do not have limited control over my beliefs. It is possible, for example, that I might be able to bring myself to believe P over a period of time. I might be able to talk myself into believing P, believe P by constant repetition of P, or employ other Pascalian techniques that may or may not involve attending to reasons for believing P. The point, however, is that simply because I cannot believe a proposition on the spot does not entail that it is not, at least partly, within my control. As Chisholm concludes, "you could go to work on it and, with luck, you would be able to succeed" ("Firth and the Ethics of Belief," 126–27). Or maybe not luck, but perseverance, self-control, self-hypnosis, or the like. However, this reply is not fully adequate for our purposes, for the scenarios Chisholm proposes might turn out to be cases of self-deception, which is not what the belief voluntarist who advocates epistemic obligations proposes. In self-deception, we abandon the contention that beliefs aim at truth, and this is essential to the position of those who hold to epistemic obligations.

42 Alvin Plantinga, "Internalist Reformed Epistemology," St. Thomas Summer Seminar in Philosophy of Religion and Philosophical Theology, St. Paul, Minn., June 2010.

43 J. L. Evans, "Error and the Will," *Philosophy* 38 (1963): 146.

44 Evans is criticizing Descartes here, but even Descartes recognized this distinction. "We must, however, observe that there is a great deal of difference between willing to be deceived and willing to

give one's assent to opinions in which error is sometimes found. For although there is no one who expressly desires to err, there is hardly one who is not willing to give his assent to things in which unsuspected error is to be found." *Principles of Philosophy*, 1, XLII, in *The Philosophical Works of Descartes*, trans. Elizabeth Sanderson Haldane and G. R. T. Ross, vol. 1. (Cambridge: Cambridge University Press, 1967), 235–36.

45 Louis Pojman, "Believing and Willing," *Canadian Journal of Philosophy* 15, no. 1 (1985): 45.

46 Pojman, *Religious Belief and the Will*, 161–62.

47 Alston, *Beyond "Justification,"* 65.

48 Alston, *Epistemic Justification*, 92.

49 Alston, *Epistemic Justification*, 124. Similarly, Feldman argues that though we have nonbasic voluntary (indirect) control over many of our beliefs, in that we can put ourselves in a position where our beliefs are formed, this does not rescue the voluntarists' case, since "we make deontological epistemic judgments about beliefs that we can't control and these judgments are as routine and commonplace as are judgments about beliefs we can control." Feldman, "The Ethics of Belief," 672.

50 Pojman, *Religious Belief and the Will*, 171. More accurately, (5) should read, "A cannot believe both that *p* and that A's belief is presently caused by his willing to believe that *p*."

51 One might object that persons think that a proposition seems to be true because of the evidence for it, and hence this supports the account of indirect belief voluntarism. It is true that we often do hold beliefs because they seem to follow from the evidence and the evidence generates or compels the belief. But this is not inconsistent with direct belief voluntarism *if* one sees that this is a description of how some of our beliefs are formed and not a complete description. That is, indirect belief voluntarism is compatible with direct belief voluntarism insofar as the former provides but a partial account of our beliefs and allows for a significant number of cases where the cause of the belief is one's volition and the desire to believe the truth.

52 Williams, "Deciding to Believe," 148.

53 Govier, "Belief, Values, and the Will," 647.

54 Swinburne, *Epistemic Justification*, 39–40.

55 Dion Scott-Kakures, "On Belief and the Captivity of the Will," *Philosophy and Phenomenological Research* 54 (1994): 77–103.

56 Scott-Kakures, "On Belief ," 93–94.

57 Scott-Kakures, "On Belief ," 95–96.

58 Scott-Kakures, "On Belief ," 94–95.

59 Dana Radcliffe, "Scott-Kakures on Believing at Will," *Philosophy and Phenomenological Research* 57 (1997): 149.

60 Govier, "Belief, Values, and the Will," 653.

61 Barbara Winters, "Believing at Will," *Journal of Philosophy* 76 (1979): 243.

62 Winters, "Believing at Will," 244–45.

63 Pojman too takes this route. "The belief must be acquired independently of evidential considerations" ("Believing and Willing," 39). However in the very next paragraph he modifies and moderates this view, noting that the belief is "underdetermined by the evidence."

64 Winters, "Believing at Will," 249.

65 Govier, "Belief, Values, and the Will," 645. Govier does not adopt this as the view required of the belief voluntarist; indeed, she thinks such a narrow view mistaken. She goes on to consider belief that is controlled by the agent's deliberation in cases where the evidence is insufficient or ambiguous. In these cases, the agent makes decisions, not about believing, but about the evidence and its significance. She takes this as deciding what to believe. In effect, she distinguishes belief by fiat from belief by deliberation in that the former addresses believing whereas the latter addresses what to believe (in light of the evidence). Her emphasis on deliberation, however, in attending to how much evidence one has and how much is needed, where to direct one's attention, and whether it is sufficient, primarily address considerations of indirect rather than direct belief.

66 Ryan, "Doxastic Compatibilism," 64.

67 Winters, "Believing at Will," 245.

68 Ryan, "Doxastic Compatibilism," 67.

69 This is not all that different from actions. I might not want to crash my car into the light pole, but I voluntarily did not get the brakes checked when the mechanic suggested that I should, and hence in a sense the accident that occurred because of my faulty brakes is in part voluntary. Or again, the partygoers might not want to engage in certain misbehavior, but their drinking has put them into such a state of intoxication that they don't know what they are doing. But, as Aristotle noted centuries ago, the state they are in is voluntary because of the earlier voluntary decisions, despite the fact that they now are ignorant about that present state and the misbehavior itself.

70 Margery Naylor says quite the opposite: the person "regards *p* as being conclusively evident or as being self-evident." "Voluntary Belief," *Philosophy and Phenomenological Research* 45 (1985): 432. She contends that the issue is whether the person believes *p* by choice, not whether the person could have believed otherwise. But this seems mistaken because if the person has conclusive evidence for the belief, then the person believes it because of the conclusive evidence, and it is no longer a direct but an indirect belief.

71 Williams, "Deciding to Believe," 137.

72 Ryan, "Doxastic Compatibilism," 65.

73 Anthony O'Hear, "Belief and the Will," *Philosophy* 47 (1972): 108–10.

74 Robert Holyer, "Belief and Will Revisited," *Dialogue* 22 (1983): 275–78.

75 Holyer, "Belief and Will Revisited," 274.

76 John Stuart Mill, *Utilitarianism*, chap. 4.

77 Holyer, "Belief and Will Revisited," 285.

78 Plantinga, *Warranted Christian Belief*, 156. Plantinga, however, for reasons given above, holds that beliefs are formed passively, and hence does not consider basic beliefs a kind of voluntaristically held belief. We responded to that reasoning earlier in this chapter.

79 Alston, *Epistemic Justification*, 122.

80 Wolterstorff, *John Locke and the Ethics of Belief*, 112.

Chapter 6

1 "We may, therefore, conclude, that belief consists merely in a certain feeling or sentiment; in something, that depends not on the will, but must arise from certain determinate causes and principles, of which we are not masters." David Hume, *A Treatise Concerning Human Nature*, appendix.

2 Brian Grant contends that Descartes is a fiatist, holding that "whether or not I acquire a particular belief is (or can be), in a perfectly unproblematic way, a matter of choice—something that I do, or don't do, quite freely" ("Descartes, Belief and the Will," 402). However, Descartes can also be read as a compatibilist who takes into account causal conditions in willing. "This is because the will simply consists in our ability to do or not do something (that is, to affirm or deny, to pursue or avoid); or rather, it consists simply in the fact that when the intellect puts something forward for affirmation or denial or for pursuit or avoidance, our inclinations are such that we do not feel we are determined by any external force. In order to be free, there is no need for me to be inclined both ways; on the contrary, the more I incline in one direction—either because I clearly understand that reasons of truth and goodness point that way, or because of a divinely produced disposition of my inmost thoughts—the freer is my choice." René Descartes, *Meditations on First Philosophy*, translated by John Cottingham (Cambridge: Cambridge University Press, 1986), Fourth Meditation.

3 For an example of this dichotomous thinking, see H. G. Classen, "Will, Belief and Knowledge," *Dialogue* 18 (1979): 67.

4 J. T. Stevenson suggests thinking about belief as a class of what he terms "doxastic attitudes," which for him include assent, dissent, suspending belief or disbelief, opining, and being convinced, sure, certain and confident, among others. "On Doxastic Responsibility," 230–31.

5 Daniel Dennett, *The Intentional Stance* (Cambridge, Mass.: MIT

Press, 1987), and "Real Patterns," *Journal of Philosophy* 87 (1991): 27–51.

6 "An agent believes that S just in case (1) under agent-centered circumstances such as desires, need, and other psychological states including other believings and (2) external circumstances (3) the agent will act as if S obtained, i.e., will act in ways appropriate to S being the case, where S is a state of affairs, actual or non-actual." Ruth B. Marcus, "The Anti-Naturalism of Some Language-Centered Accounts of Belief," *Dialectica* 49, nos. 2–4 (1995): 126.

7 R. B. Braithwaite, "The Nature of Believing," in *Knowledge and Belief*, ed. A. Phillips Griffiths (Oxford: Oxford University Press, 1967), 28–40.

8 Price, *Belief*, 243.

9 Price, *Belief*, 244.

10 Price, *Belief*, 249.

11 Audi, "Dispositional Beliefs," 423. Braithwaite proposes that to believe *p* is to "entertain *p*" and to "have a disposition to act as if *p* were true" ("The Nature of Believing," 30).

12 Price, *Belief*, 250–55.

13 Braithwaite, "The Nature of Believing," 37.

14 D. J. O'Connor and Brian Carr, *Introduction to the Theory of Knowledge* (Minneapolis: University of Minnesota Press, 1982), 56.

15 Braithwaite, "The Nature of Believing," 31–32.

16 O'Connor and Carr, *Introduction to the Theory of Knowledge*, 52.

17 This raises a difficult problem whose discussion would take us far afield, namely, what is it to believe *p*. Do I have to believe *p* directly, or can I be said to believe *p* even though I am not believing *p* but another proposition? For example, can I be said to believe *p* when I believe *q*, and though *q* entails *p*, I don't know or believe that *q* entails *p*? It seems much too generous to say that I believe every proposition that is entailed by or presupposed by the propositions I believe.

18 Audi, "Dispositional Beliefs," 419–20.

19 Audi, "Dispositional Beliefs," 424. Audi also distinguishes between a disposition to believe and the capacity to believe. The former is "a condition in which the (causal) basis for a belief is already present in such a way that, typically, the proposition need only be thought of, in order to form the belief" (426).

20 Audi, "Dispositional Beliefs," 421.

21 Audi talks about dispositional beliefs, but since on his account all beliefs are dispositions, the term is redundant.

22 Audi, "Dispositional Beliefs," 422. However, Audi appends a note that recognizes that for some philosophers being conscious is a necessary condition of having formed a belief, although he himself does not adopt the position.

23 Audi, "Dispositional Beliefs," 423.
24 Audi, "Dispositional Beliefs," 428.
25 Audi does grant the possibility of unconscious beliefs, "in the sense of beliefs one does not know one has and cannot discover without the help of another person or at least some special self-scrutiny." How much this expands the number of beliefs he does not say. "The Concept of Believing," *Personalist* 53 (1972): 61.
26 Chisholm, "Lewis' Ethics of Belief," 224.
27 Similar things might be said regarding the rationality of our choices. See Amos Tversky and Daniel Kahneman, "The Framing of Decisions and the Psychology of Choices," *Science*, n.s., 211 (1981): 453–58.
28 "'Belief' may also refer to a psychological *act*—to the fact that a man *accepts* a proposition, or *takes* it to be true." Tversky and Kahneman, "The Framing of Decisions," 223.
29 O'Connor and Carr, *Introduction to the Theory of Knowledge*, 57.
30 Pascal Engel, "Dispositional Belief, Assent, and Acceptance," *Dialectica* 53, nos. 3–4 (1999): 219–20.
31 Engel, "Dispositional Belief, Assent, and Acceptance," 225.
32 Audi, "Doxastic Voluntarism."
33 Audi, "Doxastic Voluntarism," 90–91.
34 Audi, "Doxastic Voluntarism," 94–95.
35 Audi, "Doxastic Voluntarism," 97.
36 Audi, "Doxastic Voluntarism," 100.
37 Peter Geach, *Mental Acts: Their Content and Their Objects* (London: Routledge & Kegan Paul, 1957), 4.
38 Audi, "Doxastic Voluntarism," 100.
39 Audi, "Doxastic Voluntarism," 100–101.
40 Audi, "Doxastic Voluntarism," 101.
41 Audi, "Doxastic Voluntarism," 105.
42 Audi, "Doxastic Voluntarism," 106.
43 Audi, "Doxastic Voluntarism," 106–7.
44 Audi, "Doxastic Voluntarism," 108.

Chapter 7

1 Our interest has not been in determining whether the individual beliefs were true or justified, but rather in what epistemic obligations the respective individuals had with regard to their beliefs.
2 We have already noted in chapter 4 the opposing view that all that is needed for epistemic excellence is true belief. Kvanvig, *The Value of Knowledge*.
3 Paul Moser distinguishes between epistemic blamelessness and epistemic permissibility. A person might hold a belief that fails to meet standards of epistemic rightness and still be blameless. The person is blameless because of the believer's limitations, either mental or

situational, even though the belief is not permitted. *Knowledge and Evidence* (Cambridge: Cambridge University Press, 1989), 39–40.

4 Terry L. Price, "Character, Conscientiousness, and Conformity to Will," *Journal of Value Inquiry* 35 (2001): 151. See also Alston, *Beyond "Justification,"* 79.

5 Pojman, *Religious Belief and the Will*, 181.

6 Zagzebski, *Virtues of the Mind*, 155.

7 Philip Pettit and Michael Smith, "Freedom in Belief and Desire," *Journal of Philosophy* 93 (1996): 430–31.

8 Pettit and Smith also hold that, in practical reasoning, there are norms for the desires held by the conversants as well. "Freedom in Belief and Desire," 436–40.

9 Stevenson, "On Doxastic Responsibility," 249.

10 Stevenson, "On Doxastic Responsibility," 246.

11 Chisholm, "Lewis' Ethics of Belief," 227.

12 Chisholm, "Lewis' Ethics of Belief," 227.

13 Price, *Belief*, 225.

14 Edward Hunter, "Brain Washing in 'New' China, *New Leader*, October 7, 1950; see also Hunter, *Brain-Washing in Red China: The Calculated Destruction of Men's Minds* (New York: Vanguard Press, 1951).

15 Robert Jay Lifton, *Thought Reform and the Psychology of Totalism: A Study of "Brainwashing" in China* (Chapel Hill: University of North Carolina Press, 1961); Edgar Schein, *Coercive Persuasion: A Socio-Psychological Analysis of the "Brainwashing" of American Civilian Prisoners by the Chinese Communists* (New York: W.W. Norton, 1961).

16 Lifton, *Thought Reform*, 236–39. "It should also be noted that even for the minority who returned [from Korea] to the US as Communist converts, their strongly held opinions tended to fade with time, often accompanied by increasing confusion and in some cases mental illness." Kathleen Taylor, *Brainwashing: The Science of Thought Control* (New York: Oxford University Press, 2004), 15.

17 Lifton, *Thought Reform*, 15.

18 Taylor, *Brainwashing*, ix.

19 I owe this insight to William Hasker.

20 Taylor, *Brainwashing*, chap. 15.

21 Jonathan Renshon, "Stability and Change in Belief Systems. The Operational Code of George W. Bush," *Journal of Conflict Resolution* 52 (2008): 821.

22 Renshon, "Stability and Change," 823.

23 One can find a similar thesis, using different language, in Imre Lakatos' concept of a research program, where core ideas are at the center and more auxiliary hypotheses are found at the perimeter. These auxiliary hypotheses serve to protect the core theories, and thus show much more flexibility with regard to change as they

connect with empirical data that confirm or disconfirm the hypotheses. Imre Lakatos, "Falsification and the Methodology of Scientific Research Programmes," in *Criticism and the Growth of Knowledge*, ed. Imre Lakatos and Alan Musgrave (Cambridge: Cambridge University Press, 1970), 91–196.

24 "An unjust law is a code that a numerical or power majority group compels a minority group to obey but does not make binding on itself. This is difference made legal. By the same token, a just law is a code that a majority compels a minority to follow and that it is willing to follow itself. This is sameness made legal." Martin Luther King Jr., "Letter from Birmingham Jail," April 16, 1963.

25 Plato, *Apology* 41e.

Bibliography

Adler, Jonathan E. *Belief's Own Ethics*. Cambridge, Mass.: MIT Press, 2002.

Alston, William. *Beyond "Justification."* Ithaca, N.Y.: Cornell University Press, 2005.

———. "The Deontological Conception of Epistemic Justification." In *Epistemology*, edited by James E. Tomberlin, 257–99. Philosophical Perspectives 2. Atascadero, Calif.: Ridgeview, 1988.

———. "Epistemic Desiderata." *Philosophy and Phenomenological Research* 53 (1993): 527–51.

———. *Epistemic Justification: Essays in the Theory of Knowledge*. Ithaca, N.Y.: Cornell University Press, 1989.

———. "Epistemic Warrant as Proper Function." *Philosophy and Phenomenological Research* 55 (1995): 397–402.

Audi, Robert. "The Concept of Believing." *Personalist* 53 (1972): 43–62.

———. "Dispositional Beliefs and Dispositions to Believe." *Noûs* 28, no. 4 (1994): 419–34.

———. "Doxastic Voluntarism and the Ethics of Belief." *Facta Philosophica* 1 (1999): 87–109.

———. "The Epistemic Authority of Testimony and the Ethics of Belief." In *God and the Ethics of Belief: New Essays in Philosophy of Religion*, edited by Andrew Dole and Andrew Chignell, 175–201. Cambridge: Cambridge University Press, 2005.

Baehr, Jason S. "Character in Epistemology." *Philosophical Studies* 128 (2006): 479–514.

Bennett, Jonathan. "Why Is Belief Involuntary?" *Analysis* 50 (1990): 87–107.
BonJour, Laurence. *The Structure of Empirical Knowledge*. Cambridge, Mass.: Harvard University Press, 1985.
Braithwaite, R. B. "The Nature of Believing." In *Knowledge and Belief*, edited by A. Phillips Griffiths, 28–40. London: Oxford University Press, 1967.
Chisholm, Roderick M. "Epistemic Statements and the Ethics of Belief." *Philosophy and Phenomenological Research* 16 (1956): 447–60.
———. "Firth and the Ethics of Belief." *Philosophy and Phenomenological Research* 1 (1991): 119–28.
———. "Lewis' Ethics of Belief." In *The Philosophy of* C. *I. Lewis*, edited by Paul Arthur Schilpp, 223–42. LaSalle, Ill: Open Court, 1968.
———. *Theory of Knowledge*. 2nd ed. Englewood Cliffs, N.J.: Prentice-Hall, 1977.
Classen, H. G. "Will, Belief and Knowledge." *Dialogue* 18 (1979): 64–72.
Clifford, William K. "The Ethics of Belief." In Clifford, *The Ethics of Belief and Other Essays*, 70–96. Amherst, N.Y.: Prometheus Books, 1999.
Degenhardt, Michael. "The Ethics of Belief and the Ethics of Teaching." *Journal of Philosophy of Education* 32 (1998): 333–44.
Dennett, Daniel. *The Intentional Stance*. Cambridge, Mass.: MIT Press, 1987.
———. "Real Patterns." *Journal of Philosophy* 87 (1991): 27–51.
Descartes, René. *Meditations on First Philosophy*. Translated by John Cottingham. Cambridge: Cambridge University Press, 1986.
———. *Principles of Philosophy*. In *The Philosophical Works of Descartes*, translated by Elizabeth Sanderson Haldane and G. R. T. Ross, vol. 1. Cambridge: Cambridge University Press, 1967.
Dole, Andrew, and Andrew Chignell, eds. *God and the Ethics of Belief: New Essays in Philosophy of Religion*. Cambridge: Cambridge University Press, 2005.
Dunham, Barrows. *Man against Myth*. Boston: Little, Brown, 1947.
Elliott, Carl. "Beliefs and Responsibility." *Journal of Value Inquiry* 25 (1991): 233–48.
Engel, Pascal. "Belief as a Disposition to Act: Variations on a Pragmatist Theme." *Cognitio* 6 (2005): 167–85.
———. "Dispositional Belief, Assent, and Acceptance." *Dialectica* 53, nos. 3–4 (1999): 211–26.
Evans, J. L. "Error and the Will." *Philosophy* 38 (1963): 136–48.
Feldman, Richard. "Epistemic Obligations." In *Epistemology*, edited by James E. Tomberlin, 235–56. Philosophical Perspectives 2. Atascadero, Calif.: Ridgeview, 1988.
———. "The Ethics of Belief." *Philosophy and Phenomenological Research* 60 (2000): 667–95.
Fields, Lloyd. "Moral Beliefs and Blameworthiness." *Philosophy* 69 (1994): 397–415.

Firth, Roderick. "Chisholm and the Ethics of Belief." *Philosophical Review* 68 (1959): 493–506.

Gale, Richard. "William James and the Ethics of Belief." *American Philosophical Quarterly* 17 (1980): 1–14.

Geach, Peter. *Mental Acts: Their Content and Their Objects*. London: Routledge & Kegan Paul, 1957.

Goggans, Phil. "Epistemic Obligations and Doxastic Voluntarism." *Analysis* (March 1991): 102–5.

Goldman, Alvin. "Reliabilism." *Stanford Encyclopedia of Philosophy*. April 21, 2008. http://www.plato.stanford.edu/entries/reliabilism.

———. "Strong and Weak Justification." In *Epistemology*, edited by James E. Tomberlin, 51–69. Philosophical Perspectives 2. Atascadero, Calif.: Ridgeview, 1988.

———. "What Is Justified Belief?" In *Justification and Knowledge: New Studies in Epistemology*, edited by George Pappas, 1–23. Boston: D. Reidel, 1979.

Govier, Trudy. "Belief, Values and the Will." *Dialogue: Canadian Philosophical Review* 15 (1976): 642–63.

Grant, Brian. "Descartes, Belief and the Will." *Philosophy* 51 (1976): 401–19.

Greco, John. "Internalism and Epistemically Responsible Belief." *Synthese* 85 (1990): 245–77.

———. *Putting Skeptics in Their Place*. Cambridge: Cambridge University Press, 2000.

Haack, Susan. "'The Ethics of Belief' Reconsidered." In *The Philosophy of Roderick M. Chisholm*, edited by Lewis E. Hahn, 129–44. Chicago: Open Court, 1997.

Hall, Richard J., and Charles R. Johnson. "The Epistemic Duty to Seek More Evidence." *American Philosophical Quarterly* 35 (1998): 129–40.

Hess, Peter. "Doxastic Obligations and the Traditional Definition of Knowledge." *Dialogue: Canadian Philosophical Review* 22, no. 2 (1983): 291–98.

Holyer, Robert. "Belief and Will Revisited." *Dialogue: Canadian Philosophical Review* 22 (1983): 273–90.

Hunter, David. "Beliefs and Dispositions." *Journal of Philosophical Research* 34 (2009): 243–62.

Hunter, Edward. *Brain-Washing in Red China: The Calculated Destruction of Men's Minds*. New York: Vanguard Press, 1951.

James, William. *The Will to Believe and Other Essays in Popular Philosophy*. New York: Dover, 1956.

Jordan, Jeff. "Pragmatic Arguments and Belief in God." *Stanford Encyclopedia of Philosophy*. September 29, 2009. http://plato.stanford.edu.

Kongzi. *Analects*. Translated by Edward Slingerland. Indianapolis: Hackett, 2003.

Kvanvig, Jonathan L. *The Value of Knowledge and the Pursuit of Understanding*. Cambridge: Cambridge University Press, 2003.

Lakatos, Imre. "Falsification and the Methodology of Scientific Research Programmes." In *Criticism and the Growth of Knowledge,* edited by Imre Lakatos and Alan Musgrave, 91–196. Cambridge: Cambridge University Press, 1970.

Lee, J. Roger. "Belief as a Dispositional Property." *Philosophical Studies* 30 (1976): 207–8.

Lenman, James. "Belief, Desire and Motivation: An Essay in Quasi-Hydraulics." *American Philosophical Quarterly* 33 (1996): 291–301.

Lifton, Robert Jay. *Thought Reform and the Psychology of Totalism: A Study of "Brainwashing" in China.* Chapel Hill: University of North Carolina Press, 1961.

Marcus, Ruth B. "The Anti-Naturalism of Some Language-Centered Accounts of Belief." *Dialectica* 49, nos. 2–4 (1995): 119–30.

Meeker, Kevin. "Chisholming Away at Plantinga's Critique of Epistemic Deontology." *Australasian Journal of Philosophy* 76 (1998): 90–96.

Meiland, Jack W. "What Ought We to Believe? Or The Ethics of Belief Revisited." *American Philosophical Quarterly* 17 (1980): 15–24.

Montmarquet, James. *Epistemic Virtue and Doxastic Responsibility.* Lanham, Md.: Rowman & Littlefield, 1993.

———. "The Voluntariness of Belief." *Analysis* 46 (1986): 49–53.

Moser, Paul. *Empirical Justification.* Dordrecht: D. Reidel, 1985.

———. *Knowledge and Evidence.* Cambridge: Cambridge University Press, 1989.

Naylor, Margery Bedford. "Voluntary Belief." *Philosophy and Phenomenological Research* 45 (1985): 427–36.

O'Connor, D. J., and Brian Carr. *Introduction to the Theory of Knowledge.* Minneapolis: University of Minnesota Press, 1982.

O'Hear, Anthony. "Belief and the Will." *Philosophy* 47 (1972): 95–112.

Pascal, Blaise. *Pensées.* Oxford: Oxford University Press, 1995.

Pettit, Philip, and Michael Smith. "Freedom in Belief and Desire." *Journal of Philosophy* 93 (1996): 429–49.

Plantinga, Alvin. "Internalist Reformed Epistemology." St. Thomas Summer Seminar in Philosophy of Religion and Philosophical Theology, St. Paul, Minn., June 2010.

———. *Warranted Christian Belief.* New York: Oxford University Press, 2000.

———. *Warrant: The Current Debate.* New York: Oxford University Press, 1993.

Pojman, Louis P. "Believing and Willing." *Canadian Journal of Philosophy* 15 (1985): 37–55.

———. "A Critique of Holyer's Volitionalism." *Dialogue: Canadian Philosophical Review* 23 (1984): 695–700.

———. *Religious Belief and the Will.* London: Routledge & Kegan Paul, 1986.

Price, H. H. *Belief.* London: George Allen & Unwin, 1969.

———. "Belief and Will." In *Proceedings of the Aristotelian Society,* 1–26. Suppl. vol. 28. London: Harrison, 1954.

Price, Terry. "Character, Conscientiousness, and Conformity to Will." *Journal of Value Inquiry* 35 (2001): 151–63.

Radcliffe, Dana. "Scott-Kakures on Believing at Will." *Philosophy and Phenomenological Research* 57 (1997): 145–51.

Renshon, Jonathan. "Stability and Change in Belief Systems: The Operational Code of George W. Bush." *Journal of Conflict Resolution* 52 (2008): 820–49.

Ryan, Sharon. "Doxastic Compatibilism and the Ethics of Belief." *Philosophical Studies* 114 (2003): 47–79.

Schein, Edgar. *Coercive Persuasion: A Socio-Psychological Analysis of the "Brainwashing" of American Civilian Prisoners by the Chinese Communists.* New York: W.W. Norton, 1961.

Scott-Kakures, Dion. "On Belief and the Captivity of the Will." *Philosophy and Phenomenological Research* 54 (1994): 77–103.

Segars, Nathan. "The Will and Evidence toward Belief: A Critical Essay on Jonathan E. Adler's Belief's Own Ethics." *Social Epistemology* 20 (2006): 79–91.

Stalnaker, Robert. *Inquiry.* Cambridge, Mass.: MIT Press, 1984.

Stevenson, J. T. "On Doxastic Responsibility." In *Analysis and Metaphysics,* edited by Keith Lehrer, 229–53. Dordrecht: D. Reidel, 1975.

Swinburne, Richard. *Epistemic Justification.* Oxford: Clarendon, 2001.

Taylor, Kathleen. *Brainwashing: The Science of Thought Control.* New York: Oxford University Press, 2004.

Tversky, Amos, and Daniel Kahneman. "The Framing of Decisions and the Psychology of Choices." *Science,* n.s., 211 (1981): 453–58.

van Fraassen, Bas. "Belief and the Will." *Journal of Philosophy* 181 (1984): 235–56.

———. *The Scientific Image.* New York: Oxford University Press, 1980.

Weintraub, Ruth. "Dispositionalism and Decision." *Ratio* 2, no. 9 (1987): 148–62.

Werfel, Franz. *The Forty Days of Musa Dagh.* New York: Carroll & Graf, 1934.

Williams, Bernard. "Deciding to Believe." In Williams, *Problems of the Self.* Cambridge: Cambridge University Press, 1973.

Winters, Barbara. "Believing at Will." *Journal of Philosophy* 76 (1979): 243–56.

Wolterstorff, Nicholas. *John Locke and the Ethics of Belief.* Cambridge: Cambridge University Press, 1996.

———. "Obligations of Belief—Two Concepts." In *The Philosophy of Roderick M. Chisholm,* edited by Lewis E. Hahn, 218–38. Chicago: Open Court, 1997

Zagzebski, Linda. *Virtues of the Mind.* Cambridge: Cambridge University Press, 1996.

Zamulinski, Brian. "A Defense of the Ethics of Belief." *Philo* 7 (2004): 79–96.

Zimmerman, Michael. *The Nature of Intrinsic Value*. Lanham, Md.: Rowman & Littlefield, 2000.

Index